MW01255808

Spirit's Gift

ANTONIO LÓPEZ, F.S.C.B.

Spirit's Gift

THE METAPHYSICAL INSIGHT
OF CLAUDE BRUAIRE

THE CATHOLIC UNIVERSITY
OF AMERICA PRESS
WASHINGTON, D.C.

LIBRARY OF CONGRESS CATALOGING-IN-PUBLICATION DATA
López, Antonio, 1968–
    Spirit's gift : the metaphysical insight of Claude Bruaire / Antonio López.
      p. cm.
    Includes bibliographical references and index.
    ISBN-13: 978-0-8132-1443-6 (cloth : alk. paper)
    ISBN-10: 0-8132-1443-2 (cloth : alk. paper)
    1. Generosity.   2. Gifts.   3. Philosophical theology.
4. Christianity—Philosophy.   5. Bruaire, Claude, 1932–   6. Metaphysics.
I. Title.
BJ1533.G4L67 2005
194—dc22
                                   2005016826

Contents

Foreword

Father Antonio López has given us a comprehensive study of an original thinker whose work is too little known in English language scholarship. He has traced with firmness and clarity both the development and the final expression of his subject's thought. Claude Bruaire's originality is not impaired by the wealth of philosophical and theological sources from which he weaves his reflection on being-as-spirit-and-as-gift. As Professor López keeps before the reader's attention, the horizon within which Bruaire develops his thought is derived above all from Hegel, though not without a fundamental transformation which the present careful study continually makes clear. Central to that transposition is Hegel's understanding of the Concept *(Begriff)*, which is the master-guide to the reinterpretation of Hegel.

At the same time, however, Professor López shows that Bruaire does not simply dismiss the traditional understanding of the concept formulated by Aristotle, and to that degree the French philosopher conjoins the transformation of Hegel with the pre-speculative tradition. Indeed, though Bruaire relegates the Aristotelian understanding of the concept to a secondary and derivative status, yet he does adopt the famous Categories, while restricting them to the finite domain of the human spirit.

Whereas the Hegelian *Begriff* is the conductor of Bruaire's orchestration, he also puts into play the threefold syllogism so prominent in the Hegelian Logic. It is not inexact, then, to characterize Bruaire's own thought as proceeding within the dynamic structure of the Hegelian Speculative Project. But there are other resources in play as well that help him to modify Hegel's own thought and to expose what Bruaire takes to be its key deficiencies. In this "correction," Bruaire draws upon Schelling, Marcel, and Gaston Fessard, as well as upon Thomas Aquinas regarding the understanding of the notion of person.

More decisively still, however, the Catholic understanding of Trinitarian theology provides the detailed substantive content of Bruaire's Speculative

Sunday. For the energy that moves within the modified structure is neither the Aristotelian *energeia,* nor even the Hegelian negation of negation, but the positivity enshrined in the self-gift of the Absolute, whose formulation is found in the self-giving-of-self-to-self, expressed theologically in the donation of the Father, Son, and Holy Spirit, and recuperated philosophically by Bruaire's reflection. What emerges from Fr. López's intricate interplay of this radically modified logic of essence is the singularity of Absolute Gift, a reinterpretation that remedies Hegel's original ambiguity regarding necessity and freedom and that fully recovers the modern appreciation of freedom as *conatus* and as more than choice: that is, freedom as revelatory of the very essential character of being itself, once being is seen as spirit, gift and freedom.

Now, it is a most delicate and subtle point to indicate in what sense Bruaire's thought, as Fr. López presents it in the last portion of the present text, does not pass over simply and without remainder into theology. Without a doubt, Bruaire has secured the unassailable difference between the fullness of the Absolute and the relative indigence of the created order. What is perhaps not so clear is whether he has had equal success in rescuing the philosophical reflection from the language of Revelation. Bruaire is fully aware of the subtlety and the possibility of confusion, for he intends to bring Revelation and philosophy into closer encounter with each other. He is not ready to let Revelation merely shed a suggestive light on philosophical reflection, after the manner of Blondel and other "Christian philosophers." Indeed, he insists upon an intimate yet nonintrusive presence of theology in its encounter with philosophical reflection, so that the outcome of his reflection might legitimate its claim to be authentically philosophical. The wellspring of this close association is the experienced event of the gift.

While he insists upon the distinction between limited human reason and the Absolute, Bruaire also insists upon the overarching unity of reason, "the whole reason" that is as much the horizon for philosophical thought as it is for revealed theology. And here Bruaire echoes Hegel's key insight that the relation of faith and reason not only contains a boundary that differentiates but also a juncture that unites.

In the life of the finite human spirit, gift is experienced as both a reception already given and an expectation that cannot be fulfilled by a simple return to its indigent self. It is only in the disclosure of the Absolute self-gifting that the human spirit finds the possibility of its expectation fulfilled.

All of this Professor López makes clear in a profound exegesis, while at the same time he expresses his own appreciation of a certain incompleteness and ambiguity in Bruaire's thought. Of especial value in Fr. López's hermeneutic are the pivotal points that he makes evident in Bruaire's whole series of works as he follows Bruaire's own deepening and increasingly radical exploration of the meaning of being, spirit, gift, and the singularity of freedom.

I have already mentioned the pivotal role of the Hegelian Concept and its unfolding in the triple syllogism of the Logic of Essence. Within the unity of the concept of the Absolute Gift, Bruaire is at pains to differentiate its univocity as operative within the finite human spirit with its relative poverty, on the one hand, and, on the other, the fullness of the Absolute and Infinite Self-gift. On this point, Fr. López registers a cautionary note that some form of analogy—if not the *analogia entis*—would seem to preserve Bruaire's differentiation of finite and infinite spirit. Bruaire marks this difference by acknowledging the fullness of Absolute spirit and the relative poverty of finite human spirit.

Fr. López alerts the reader to leading "road signs" by which he traces the direction and goal of Bruaire's awakening to the full significance of the gift. He shows in what way the French thinker has engaged the notion of generosity, not simply as an outpouring to another, but as the innate fullness of being to-and-in-itself, a plenitude that overflows in freedom to the Other within the Absolute and to others in finite freedom.

Bruaire accomplishes this transformation by overcoming the "power of the negative" in Hegel, and even in Schelling, replacing it with the fullness of a positivity that is characterized as the "donative power of love." In this way the positive ontology of self-giving Being founds the negative anthropology of the finite human spirit. The original fullness rescues spirit from Kant's neglect of the noumenal order, from Hegel's reduction of the divine Logos to human language, and from Husserl's return of things *(Sache)* to the subjectivity of human consciousness. For the finite human spirit owes its being-given, not to itself or to nature or society, nor to its parents, but to its origin in Absolute spirit.

This prefatory set of road signs scarcely touches the richness which Fr. López's own reflection has brought to expression and which leads us into the depths of an original thinker's movement from the phenomenology of self-determination to the ontology of the Gift. In so doing, Fr. López shows how Bruaire engages in the effort to rescue the philosophy of being from its hiding places in modern thought. Worthy of study in itself, Fr. López's exegesis places before us the purity of a reflection that has a certain shock value in this awakening to the ontology of freedom. And he warns us that the movement of Bruaire's thought is neither an induction from finite human experience, nor a deduction *a priori* from a given idea, but rather a "trans-deductive" hermeneutic in which, within the human experience of self-giving, there is disclosed the intimate presence and outlines of Absolute self-gift. Bruaire proceeds from the indigence and passivity of finite spirit to the concept of the fullness of Absolute spirit and, only when that is secured, to creation as gift. From this vantage point, the character of being-as-spirit discloses itself in freedom.

On several important points, Fr. López introduces critical questions regarding Bruaire's thought, thus introducing the broader context that contributes to Fr. López's presentation of Bruaire's radical originality. These points include Bruaire's criticism of Thomas Aquinas regarding the unicity of act between finite and infinite being, the reduction of the natural world to its relation to finite human spirit, and a certain ambiguity between the play of univocity and analogy.

Each reader, I am convinced, will come away—whatever his or her objections on this or that point, and even regarding the whole project—with a significantly enriched understanding of the ontological depth of the generous self-giftedness of being, and of the inexhaustible surprise therein. This provides a strong antidote to the forces of technical control that shape our everyday culture. My own reading of Fr. López's study has signalled a further interiorization of causality as gift, seeing the gift not only as donation to the finite order of creation but as interior to the primordial generosity of the First Cause Itself. It discloses the absolute fullness that is characteristic of the very texture of being itself and its Source, so that Love becomes the fitting name for that Original Plenitude.

Kenneth L. Schmitz

Abbreviations

Claude Bruaire:

AD	L'affirmation de Dieu. Essai sur la logique de l'existence
As	"Absolu"
CD	"Connaître Dieu"
CEM	"Certitude, énigme ou mythe du sujet"
CF	La confession de la foi chrétienne
DD	Le droit de Dieu
D	La dialectique
EdEES	"L'être de l'esprit et L'Esprit Saint"
EdE	"L'être de l'esprit"
EE	L'être et l'esprit
EM	Une éthique pour la médecine
EnP	"L'enjeu politique d'une réflexion sur l'éternité"
FE	La force de l'esprit: Entretiens avec Emmanuel Hirsch (France-Culture)
Hg	"Hegel"
HoMD	"L'homme, miroir de Dieu"
LR	Logique et religion chrétienne dans la philosophie de Hegel
MS	La morale, sagesse et salut
PC	Philosophie du corps
PdC	"La prière du chrétien"
PdD	"Philosophie du droit et le problème de la morale"
PM	Pour la métaphysique

POnEs	"Pour une ontologie de l'esprit"
PrMC	"Problème de la métaphysique et conversion"
RP	La raison politique
SQ	Schelling ou la quête du secret de l'être

Others:

CrR	"Created Receptivity and the Philosophy of the Concrete"—Kenneth L. Schmitz
De Ver.	Quaestiones Disputatae De veritate—Aquinas
Enzyklopädie	Enzyklopädie der philosophischen Wissenschaften im Grundrisse—Hegel
KrV	Kritik der reinen Vernunft—Kant
Met.	Metaphysics—Aristotle
QDP	Quaestiones Disputatae De potentia—Aquinas
SCG	Summa Contra Gentiles—Aquinas
ST	Summa Theologiae—Aquinas
VPR	Vorlesungen über die Philosophie der Religion—Hegel
WL	Die Wissenschaft der Logik—Hegel

Spirit's Gift

Introduction

"*Has anyone promised us anything?* Why then are we still waiting?"[1] These disturbing questions that Cesare Pavese's skepticism was unable to hush set us in front of a dilemma. If we respond negatively to the first question, then we find ourselves unable to explain why it is that the resilient longing suggested by the second question is so unwilling to fade away. On the other hand, if we reply positively to the first question, then human existence finds itself thrust into an open-ended, dramatic dialogue with the giver of that assurance, that is, someone who is adamantly opposed to closing off any questions. Reality's resistance to being brought down by the evil that swamps human life, and by the nihilism this evil begets, discreetly suggests that positivity might not be, after all, a chimera that naively resists coming to terms with its own dreadful fate. Strangely enough, positivity resists being received without being welcomed—this is why it always manages to elude facile acceptance and to rouse up disengaged spirits. It is, however, fairly common to set positivity on the shelf along with other disregardable matters, or to pack it away as one among many other insights which, however alluring, do not come to grips with the real questions. Nevertheless, if one heeds positivity's persistence, then, perhaps, one might be able to perceive that it has something fundamental to say about the nature of being itself.

Any approach to the issue of being's positivity—an endeavor that is normally undertaken through the study of different categories such as gift, fullness, gratuity, and donation—cannot neglect the existence of evil. Nev-

---

1. Cesare Pavese, *Il mestiere di vivere. Diario (1935–1950)* (Turin: Einaudi, 1997), 276.

ertheless, evil should not be seen as a dialectic partner to being's positivity, for this would threaten to counterbalance gift by claiming an equiprimordial status for evil with regard to givenness. Feebleness presupposes gift. In fact, at its heart, evil is always a rejection of love.[2]

Admittedly, to approach positivity from the category of gift could very easily lead to circumscribing donation to the bestowal of goods or ills, that is, to an exchange in which what is not given or what one expects in return matters more than the gift itself.[3] In this interpretation, the reflection on gift would have to examine whether, bearing in mind the presence of evil, gratuitous giving is at all possible and whether gift's demand of an inextricable "for its own sake" is indeed able to undo any utilitarian reduction.

The coexistence of gift's demand for no return and the everyday, self-seeking search for reciprocity in the exchange of gifts may require understanding gift and the dynamics of giving and receiving in an altogether new fashion. Jacques Derrida, for instance, contends that gift should be thought of without any reference to a giver, a gift, or a receiver. It is only then, he says, that one is able to see that gift is an inevitable pathway to thinking the unthinkable and that in considering gift, one must acknowledge that gift is both possible and impossible because there is no decidable origin or destination of the gift. Gift, then, reveals something fundamental that pertains to the whole, if there is any: otherness is in such relation to

2. In this sense, as the work of Paul Ricoeur cogently shows, the presence of real evil leaves the door open to that of real gift. See Paul Ricoeur, *Temps et récit,* 3 vols. (Paris: Nabert, 1983); id., *Le mal. Un défi à la philosophie et à la théologie* (Paris: Labor et fides, 1996); id., *Philosophie de la volonté,* vol. 1: *Le volontaire et l'involontaire;* vol. 2: *Finitude et culpabilité: I) L'homme faillible. II) La symbolique du mal.* (Paris: Aubier, 1949–60); id., *Conflict des interprétations; essais d'herméneutique* (Paris: Seuil, 1969).

3. In fact, several sociological or economical approaches to the category of gift have shown that this logic of exchange tends to transform the axiom *do ut des* (I give so that you can give further) into the claim to receive (I give so that you can give back to me) which thus prompts the search for wealth for its own sake. See Alain Mattheeuws, *Les "dons" du mariage: Recherche de théologie morale et sacramentelle* (Brussels: Culture et vérité, 1996), 99. See, among others: Marcel Mauss, "Essai sur le don." This article originally appeared in *L'anné sociologique,* 1923–24, and it can now be found in Marcel Mauss, *Sociologie et anthropologie* (Paris: Quadrige/PUF, 1999), 145–279; Maurice Godelier, *L'énigme du don* (Paris: Fayard, 1996); Jacques Godbout, *L'esprit du don* (Paris: La découverte, 1992). For an understanding of economy rooted in a positive ontology of gift see David L. Schindler, "'Homelessness' and Market Liberalism: Toward an Economic Culture of Gift and Gratitude," in Doug Bandow and David L. Schindler, eds., *Wealth, Poverty, and Human Destiny* (Wilmington, Del.: ISI Books, 2003), 347–413, 509–15.

the self that identity is made possible and impossible by a multiplicity of origins—where "origins" does not mean dialectically opposed primordial identities but selfless, contrasting relations.[4] The concurrence of "gratuity" and "interested reciprocity," however, does not undercut a common presupposition that Jean-Luc Marion's phenomenology tries to bring to light. Although gift can be seen as merely one phenomenon among others, it is nonetheless a privileged phenomenon because through it, once it has been phenomenologically reduced, one can reach that which constitutes every phenomenon: givenness. Following Heidegger but also moving away from him, Marion tries to retrieve givenness' radically totalizing nature (which does not stand for "factuality," "obviousness," or self-referential "data") and contends that it is able adequately to name what appears.[5]

Both the postmodernist and the phenomenological approaches have the advantage of recognizing the breadth and depth of the matter at stake. In this sense, they move from the particular gift to that "which is not given" in the exchange of gifts and which makes possible every concrete gift, namely, positivity, givenness. Nevertheless, they tend to steer clear of an ontological reflection on givenness, either because they consider metaphysics to be nothing but an archeological inquiry that is unable to in-

---

4. Cf. Jacques Derrida, *La fausse monnaie,* vol. 1 of *Donner le temps* (Paris: Galilée, 1991); id., *La question de l'esprit* (Paris: Galilée, 1987); id., "Donner la mort," in *L'éthique du don. Jacques Derrida et la pensée du don,* ed. Jean-Michel Rabaté and Michael Wetzel (Paris: Métailié-Transition, 1992), 11–108; id., *Marges de la philosophie* (Paris: Éditions de Minuit, 1972); Marc Boss, "Jacques Derrida et l'événement du don," *Revue de théologie et de philosophie* 128 (1996): 113–26; Jeffrey L. Kosky, "The Disqualification of Intentionality: The Gift in Derrida, Levinas, and Michel Henry," *Philosophy Today* 41 (1997): 186–97. See also Rodolphe Gasché, *The Tain of the Mirror: Derrida and the Philosophy of Reflection* (Cambridge: Harvard University Press, 1986); John Milbank, "Can a Gift Be Given? Prolegomena to a Future Trinitarian Metaphysics," *Modern Theology* 11 (1995): 119–61.

5. See Martin Heidegger, *Being and Time,* trans. Joan Stambaugh (New York: State University of New York Press, 1996); id., *Über den Humanismus* (Frankfurt: M. V. Klostermann, 1949); Jean-Luc Marion, *L'idole et la distance* (Paris: Grasset, 1977); id., *Réduction et donation: Recherches sur Hegel, Heidegger et la phénoménologie* (Paris: PUF, 1989); id., *Étant donné: Essai d'une phénoménologie de la donation* (Paris: PUF, 1998); id., *De surcroît* (Paris: PUF, 2001); id., "L'événement, le phénomène et le révélé," *Transversalités* 70 (1999): 4–25; John D. Caputo and Michael J. Scanlon, eds., *God, the Gift, and Postmodernism* (Bloomington: Indiana University Press, 1999); John D. Caputo, "Apostles of the Impossible: On God and the Gift in Derrida and Marion," in *God, the Gift, and Postmodernism,* 185–222. For another interesting phenomenological approach to givenness see Michel Henry, *C'est moi la vérité* (Paris: Seuil, 1996); id., *L'essence et la manifestation* (Paris: PUF, 1990); id., *Voir l'invisible: Sur Kandinsky* (Paris: F. Bourin, 1988); id., *Phénoménologie matérielle* (Paris: PUF, 1990).

tegrate modernity's basic tenets, or because they conceive causality as a logically and ontologically unnecessary category. I propose, instead, that if positivity (or gift) does have something fundamental to offer to our understanding of what God and man are, it is because it says something about the nature of the whole, something about the nature of being itself.[6] Obviously, if an affirmation of this kind is to have any bearing, the move from anthropology and theology to ontology must be clarified. The difficulty of this radically nonabstract path toward being itself, however, should not impede our acknowledging that, without diluting metaphysics into sheer rhetorical vagueness, being should be thought of in terms of gift—understood as both verb and noun. Positivity, then, seems to indicate that being *is* gift. This strategy, of course, entails that before any other type of approach, gift should be conceived of ontologically.

To affirm being as gift is to invite metaphysics to retrieve the understanding of being in terms of pure act and to interpret it not so much as a monolithic Parmenidean totality in which everything has already come to pass but as a superabundant and uncontainable fullness (positivity) that gives itself to itself and then to what is not itself. To think of being as pure act, as absolute fullness, as gift, calls, then, for the difficult integration of being and freedom, which, if not thought out carefully, can lead one to mistake fullness for an eternal coming-to-be, after the fashion of our contemporary understanding of history. If one wants to think radically, this endeavor requires that even the ontological difference be perceived within this framework. The alternative is to think that "being" is that primordial subject that gives something (e.g., existence, essence, etc.), and in this case, we would be back to the partial logic of the exchange of goods and ills.

Claude Bruaire (1932–86) elaborates a rigorous and extremely rich ontology of gift, *ontodology* as he calls it, with an uncommon speculative depth and vigor.[7] Two insights govern his philosophical reflection. First, he

6. In this regard it is interesting to see, among others, Kenneth L. Schmitz, *The Gift: Creation* (Milwaukee: Marquette University Press, 1982); John Paul II, *Theology of the Body: Human Love in the Divine Plan* (Boston: Pauline Books and Media, 1997); David L. Schindler, *Heart of the World, Center of the Church: Communio Ecclesiology, Liberalism, and Liberation* (Grand Rapids, Mich.: Eerdmans, 1996); Ferdinand Ulrich, *Leben in der Einheit von Leben und Tod* (Frankfurt am Main: J. Knecht, 1973); Gustav Siewerth, *Das Schicksal der Metaphysik von Thomas zu Heidegger* (Düsseldorf: Patmos Verlag, 1987).

7. The neologism *ontodologie,* which combines being *(onto)* and gift *(don),* is forged by

contends that the circumincession of being and freedom, which requires thinking of pure act in terms of fullness, is sustainable only because gift is being in its spiritual way of being. "Spiritual" *(geistlich)* in this case does not stand for one quality among others but, more radically, for that which makes being be what it is, what makes being be one. As Bruaire perceives it, the coalescence of being, freedom, and spirit is what grounds the claim that being is gift. Second, being is gift only if the fullness proper to the pure act is first of all donation in itself and to itself, before being donation to another. That is to say, if metaphysics were able to integrate the claim of Christian revelation that absolute being is Triune, then it would be possible to contend that even prior to any creation, being is, in itself, gift. Once being is recognized as gift, it is possible both to understand better what being is and to undergird all the other senses of gift: social, economical, phenomenological, and anthropological. The purpose of this book is then to examine Bruaire's as yet little-known proposal and to explore the light it sheds on the apparent relation between being and positivity (gift).

To this end, the book is divided into two parts that reflect the mirror-fugue structure of Bruaire's thought, which from 1964 to 1980 elaborated a "negative" anthropology and an understanding of the absolute in terms of self-determination and from 1980 to 1986 produced a metaphysical reflection on the concept of gift. The first section, *Self-Determining Freedom,* is the negative face of Bruaire's ontodology, and the second section, *Ontology of Gift,* is its positive counterpart. In the first part, I present his understanding of the relation between theology and philosophy (chap. 1), which sets the ongoing methodological parameters that give his reflection its form. The second chapter presents Bruaire's systematic anthropology, which can be defined as "negative" in contrast to Hegel's understanding of the spirit's movement of self-determination, according to which the spirit successfully returns to itself after having become the other of itself. For Bruaire, the human being-of-spirit is unable to return to itself because it is neither its own origin, nor its own destiny.[8] Between 1964 and 1980, in addition

---

Bruaire and appears for the first time in *Pour la métaphysique* (Paris: Fayard, 1980), 262 and then in *L'être et l'esprit* (Paris: PUF, 1983), 51; "L'être de l'esprit," in *L'univers philosophique,* ed. André Jacob (Paris: PUF, 1987), 37. I have translated this neologism with *"ontodology"* to respect Bruaire's intention best. All the translations in the present book, unless otherwise stated, are mine.

8. The remarkable speculative effort undertaken by Bruaire in order to elaborate a philo-

to this "negative" anthropology, Bruaire elaborated an understanding of the absolute as self-determinate, self-determining infinite freedom. He proceeded here by correcting Hegel's view on this subject with Schelling's and then by correcting the work of both with the perception of Christian revelation learned from his two masters, Gaston Fessard and Gabriel Marcel. The third chapter gives an account of this conception of the absolute, which needs to integrate Christian positivity if it is to overcome the negative movement of self-determination that characterizes German thought.[9]

The second part of the book shows that the reverse reading of Bruaire's "negative" anthropology is a positive ontology that conceives both the human being and God in terms of gift. Without claiming to present all of Bruaire's thought, I need to indicate that each of these two parts requires the other if one wants to understand both of them fully. Since Bruaire proceeds from freedom to spirit and from spirit to being, the first issue I approach in the second part is Bruaire's concept of spirit and his argument that metaphysics must restore this concept if it wants to liberate being from the oblivion where it is relegated.[10] The analysis of the concept of

---

sophical anthropology is deployed in three consecutive steps. The first one is his doctoral dissertation, which consists of two related but independent parts. The first part, *The Affirmation of God* (*L'affirmation de Dieu: Essai sur la logique de l'existence* [Paris: Seuil, 1964] [hereafter *AD*]), presents an analysis of the logic of human existence which concludes with an ontological affirmation of God and its existential implications. This proof of God calls for the elaboration of an ontology in which the dialogue from and to God is to be studied. The second part, *Logic and Religion in the Philosophy of Hegel* (*Logique et religion chrétienne dans la philosophie de Hegel* [Paris: Seuil, 1964] [hereafter *LR*]), examines Hegel's *Logic* and its relationship to Christian revelation. The analysis of human existence requires first an analysis of corporeality, so as not to remain abstract. This is the question examined in *Philosophy of the Body* (*Philosophie du corps* [Paris: Seuil, 1968] [hereafter *PC*]). This book allows Bruaire to move further: the human being lives in a world and interacts with others. *Political Reason* (*La raison politique* [Paris: Fayard, 1974] [hereafter *RP*]) presents a study of the relationships between individuals and states, whose end is to show how the major political categories need to be conceived in order to build a society that respects both human and the divine nature.

9. In this chapter, along with some key articles, attention is paid to the main works of Claude Bruaire between 1964 and 1978, before he undertook his metaphysical work in 1980: *Schelling or the Search for the Mystery of Being* (*Schelling ou la quête du secret de l'être* [Paris: Seghers, 1970] [hereafter *SQ*]); *The Right of God* (*Le droit de Dieu* [Paris: Aubier, 1974] [hereafter *DD*]), which was originally written for a German audience under the title *Die Aufgabe: Gott zu denken* (1973), and *An Ethics for Medicine* (*Une éthique pour la médecine* [Paris: Fayard, 1978] [hereafter *EM*]).

10. This section examines Bruaire's metaphysical work written between 1980 and 1986. The first, *For Metaphysics* (*Pour la métaphysique*, 1980 [hereafter *PM*]), is a collection of a

spirit leads me to explore in chapter 5 the sense in which finite being-of-spirit is given to itself in order to become itself. As I mentioned, Bruaire rightly sees that considering the human being in terms of gift would be ultimately irrelevant unless absolute spirit can also be conceived in those terms. The last two chapters present, then, in what sense, for Bruaire, absolute spirit is the infinite pure and eternal act of donation, pure gift, which not only gives itself to itself (begets the Word) but also confirms the gift (because the absolute spirit is also Holy Spirit) and shows itself to be the bottomless gratuity that gives itself to what it is not, the finite other, and confirms it in being. It is in this way that, according to Bruaire, both finite and infinite being, and thus being as such, call for being interpreted in terms of gift.

A Biographical Intermezzo

Claude Bruaire's life was an interweaving of encounters with different personalities of the European intellectual world through whom he discovered Christianity's cultural and existential novelty. In continuous dialogue with colleagues and friends, Bruaire put the Christian truth to the test and tried to give an answer to the contemporary philosophical situation by proposing an anthropology and an ontology whose depths have already been highlighted by many.[11]

---

series of articles and papers, the earliest of which dates from 1965. Although each one of these papers, most of which were given at an annual colloquium held in Rome, responded to different topics, there is a unifying thread: the need to elaborate an ontology and the direction which this should follow. Jean-Luc Marion proposed at the time that Bruaire write a more systematic approach to metaphysics. The result was a book published in the series *Épiméthée*, which Marion edits for PUF, entitled *Being and Spirit* (*L'être et l'esprit*, 1983 [hereafter *EE*]). This book is the most refined and sophisticated presentation of Bruaire's metaphysics, and as such it will be my main reference for the second part of the book. I shall also refer to his last book, *Dialectics* (*La dialectique* [Paris: PUF, 1985] [hereafter *D*]), the posthumous work, *The Strength of the Spirit* (*La force de l'esprit: Entretiens avec Emmanuel Hirsch (France-Culture)* [Paris: Desclée de Brouwer, 1986] [hereafter *FE*])—a transcription of a series of interviews he gave to *Radio France*—and to articles: *Dictionnaire de spiritualité, ascétique et mystique, doctrine et histoire* (Paris: Beauchesne, 1984), s.v. "Philosophie et spiritualité," 1377–86; *L'univers philosophique* (Paris: 1989), s.v. "L'être de l'esprit," 34 (hereafter *EdE*).

11. Rolf Kühn, *Französische Reflexions und Geistesphilosophie. Profile und Analysen* (Frankfurt: Anton Hain, 1993); id., "Bedürfen und Vorstellungsdestruktion. Phänomenologie des Bedürfnis auf dem Hintergrund der Seinsgabe bei M. Heidegger, S. Weil und C.

Bruaire's first contact with contemporary French theology took place during his years in the seminary, where he went to discern a possible missionary vocation. He began at the seminary at Versailles and was then transferred to Paris (Seminaire des Carmes). During those years, Bruaire also frequented the Institut Catholique, where he became friends with Gaston Fessard, S.J. (1897–1978), and Dominque Dubarle, O.P. The friendship with Fessard was one of the most enduring and fruitful he ever had.[12] When Bruaire left the seminary, he began his philosophical studies at the Sorbonne. He graduated with a double dissertation under the direction of Paul Ricoeur in 1964.[13] After teaching at the high school level, he was hired at the university of Tours, where he taught from 1967 to 1972 as assistant professor and from 1972 to 1979 as professor in the department of philosophy. He left Tours in 1979 to go to the Sorbonne in Paris. It was during his years there that he met Gabriel Marcel, who was to become one of the two people Bruaire would recognize as his masters (the other was Fessard).[14] He participated in the philosophical circle at Gabriel Marcel's house. In addition to philosophers, there were also among Bruaire's interlocutors a number of medical doctors, with whom he sustained a continuous and thorough conversation regarding bioethical issues. Through his relationship with his wife, who was herself a physician, Bruaire was well acquainted with the daily problems and difficulties doctors face.[15]

Bruaire was also a man of action, very involved in politics, and a faith-

---

Bruaire," *Gregorianum* 76 (1995): 323–42; Xavier Tilliette, "In Memoriam: Claude Bruaire 1932–1986," *Giornale di Metafisica*, n.s., 9 (1987): 689–709; Nunzio Incardona, "L'Ontodologie di Claude Bruaire," *Giornale di Metafisica*, n.s., 6 (1984): 397–410; Paul Gilbert, "L'acte d'être: un don," *Science et esprit* 41 (1989): 265–86.

12. Bruaire is well known for being a very solid, vigorous, and systematic thinker. It is also known how sparing he was in quoting and giving references to the sources of his own thought. One of the few exceptions was Fr. Fessard's main work, *La dialectique des "Exercices spirituels" de Saint Ignace de Loyola* (Paris: Aubier, 1956). Bruaire, as a professor, first in Tours and then at the Sorbonne in Paris, made this book a required reading. See Denise Leduc-Fayette, "Claude Bruaire, 1932–1986," *Revue philosophique* 1 (1987): 12. For Bruaire's in-depth presentation of Fessard's dialectics see *D*, 109–22.

13. *AD* and *LR*.

14. Claude Bruaire, "Compte Rendu de Gabriel Marcel-Gaston Fessard: Correspondance," *Archives de philosophie* 49 (1986): 497.

15. As a result of these conversations and the course he taught for doctors while at Tours, he wrote *EM*. The importance of this book for Bruaire's philosophical reflection should not be overlooked.

ful participant and organizer of many conferences and congresses.[16] Notable among these is the group of French and Belgian philosophers and theologians whom he gathered at Chantilly: Xavier Tilliette, Rémi Brague, Georges Chantraine, Alain Cugno, Albert Chapelle, André Léonard, Jean-Luc Marion, and Jean Robert Armogathe, among others.[17] Bruaire directed the series *L'athéisme interroge* for the publishing house Desclée. He was also one of the founders and, from 1975, editor of the French edition of *Communio, International Catholic Review.*[18] Discussions with Marion, Jean Duchesne, and Brague, members at the time of the editorial board of *Communio,* helped Bruaire to formulate his idea of donation and to express the nuances of the task that philosophy faces in the contemporary academy.[19] Through his work in *Communio,* he met and established an intense conversation with prominent theologians such as Henri de Lubac and Hans Urs von Balthasar. A sudden pulmonary embolism brought his life to an end after the summer of 1986.[20]

16. His close friend Xavier Tilliette depicts Bruaire's political interests and activity in this fashion: "A l'Hôtel des Orangers, aux Parioli, il s'amusait de l'affolement d'un Löwith aux prises avec une panne de courant. Lui-même savait ce qu'étaient la gestion et l'administration d'une commune. Il était premier adjoint de la municipalité de Prades en Haute-Loire—pays de son père—un adjoint aussi efficace que cordial et simple; il aimait 'son village' du Gévaudan, il y retournait fréquemment, il y retrouvait ses racines, l'espace, le grand air, la chasse . . . C'était autre chose qu'un passe-temps [as Mme. Bruaire told me, he enjoyed spending the afternoons in the bar of the square talking about and discussing any given issue with those who lived there]. La province profonde et le service public font parti intégrante du portrait de Claude Bruaire, professeur de Sorbonne. C'est ce qui le rapprochait du conseiller 'occulte' de Georges Pompidou, Pierre Juilliet, auquel il était lié d'amitié" (Tilliette, "In memoriam," 238).

17. The results of these gatherings are published in two collected works which Bruaire edited: *La confession de la foi chrétienne* (Paris: Fayard, 1977) (hereafter *CF*) and *La morale, sagesse et salut* (Paris: Communio/Fayard, 1981) (hereafter *MS*).

18. As we shall have the opportunity to see, the editorials and articles he wrote for *Communio* played a significant role in the development of the idea of *donation.*

19. There is little doubt that Bruaire also benefitted from the dialogue with Marion and Brague. See Rémi Brague, "Comme quoi le bon Dieu ne se donne pas sans confession," in *CF,* 305–16.

20. See Henri de Lubac, "Préface," in *CF,* 340–41. Although Balthasar's thought was already formed when he met Bruaire, an influence of the latter on the former can be traced. Cf. Hans Urs von Balthasar, *Epilog* (Trier: Johannes Verlag, 1987); id., *Theologik,* 3 vols. (Trier: Johannes Verlag, 1947–87) (Bruaire's influence can be seen in vols. 2 and 3 of the *Theologik*); id., *Theodramatik,* 4 vols. (Trier: Johannes Verlag, 1973–83).

PART I

Self-Determining Freedom

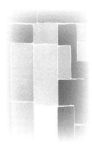

CHAPTER 1

The Encounter between Philosophy and Theology

No question is foreign to metaphysics, Bruaire contends, because metaphysics deals with that most important issue which is presupposed in all the other disciplines.[1] Philosophy addresses the decisive, eternal question: "what is being?"[2] Yet, according to Bruaire, to ask about "that which is" is to pose the question concerning the nature of the principle that sustains whatever exists, namely, the *absolute,* which in theological terms is called God.[3] This is philosophy's *inevitable prejudice:* every philosophy has as its object the absolute, as Schelling stated.[4] Bruaire considers that the question of the absolute is *the* question that must be confronted, because every philosophy stands or falls precisely in establishing its principle.[5] Nothing is more vital for philosophy than answering the questions whether the absolute can be affirmed, in what way this should be done, and how the understanding of the human self is determined by it.[6] For this reason,

1. *FE,* 80, 67.

2. Aristotle, *Metaphysics* 4.1.1003a25, Eng. trans. by William D. Ross, vol. 8 of *The Works of Aristotle* (Oxford: The Clarendon Press, 1928) (hereafter *Met.*).

3. "L'idée-force de Bruaire est qu'il y a une nécessité intrinsèque de l'autodétermination de l'Absolu, qui fait que l'Absolu métaphysique au point de départ est identique, sans rupture et sans hiatus, au Dieu révélé du christianisme. Peu de métaphysiques sont ainsi d'un seul tenant, d'une seule fibre" (Xavier Tilliette, "La théologie philosophique de Claude Bruaire," *Gregorianum* 74 [1993]: 689).

4. *PM,* 139.   5. *DD,* 82.

6. It is no mere coincidence that the opening sentences of Bruaire's doctoral dissertation and first book, *L'affirmation de Dieu* (1968)—phrased in a very Blondelian fashion—and the

the question regarding the absolute does not stop merely when its existence is recognized: as we shall see, every discourse about God comes from a dialogue within God that confers on human existence a dramatic form whose most fundamental element is dialogue with God.[7]

An adequate understanding of Christianity, says Bruaire following Hegel, reveals the indispensability of the dialogue between philosophy and theology. In fact, "Christian religion, as the others do, would only offer a particular and aleatory representation of the veiled divinity if it were not truly the revealed religion. If the absolute is *revealed* in Christian religion, one must recognize that it is the *absolute* religion; the face of God has manifested itself in full light."[8] Even though philosophy and theology approach the absolute from different angles and use different methods to study it, they each have the same object: the *absolute.* Therefore, according to Bruaire, the presumption that philosophy and theology should be indifferent to one another only reinforces the idea that the universal and the true are *a priori* incompatible—something which undermines *both* philosophy and theology.[9] If philosophy and theology claim that their respective contents of truth cannot "transgress" the boundaries of the other, that each claim for truth has nothing to say to the other, then this would result in the relativization of philosophical and theological truth. Both of them would lose their claim to universality. Of course, there is always a boundary separating them; otherwise philosophy would absorb theology into it-

---

last sentences of *L'être et l'esprit* (1983) are essentially the same. In the first, Bruaire asks: "Yes or no: does the affirmation of God, supposing that it be possible and that it impose itself, give meaning to our life? Does it have a value, does it bring joy, light, hope?" (*AD,* 9). In *L'action,* Blondel begins in the exact same way: "Oui ou non, la vie humaine a-t-elle un sens, et l'homme a-t-il une destinée?" (Maurice Blondel, *L'action* (1893) [Paris: Quadrige/PUF, 1993], vii). In *L'être et l'esprit,* Bruaire states that philosophy must return to its principle, that is to say, the Principle without principle. "For this reason even when it denies the existence of God, the absolute, philosophy remains always metaphysics. If philosophy necessarily thinks of the absolute, which religion calls God, and if the absolute is its main preoccupation and the content of its knowledge, then philosophy needs to remain in an indispensable, albeit difficult, spiritual exchange with theology" (*EE,* 204). See also *EE,* 159–94.

7. *AD,* 154–69, 219–51.

8. *LR,* 13. Bruaire's emphasis. Bruaire quotes G. W. F. Hegel, *Vorlesungen über die Philosophie der Religion,* vol. 16 of *Werke* (Frankfurt am Main: Suhrkamp, 1986) (hereafter *VPR*). Unless otherwise indicated, Hegel's German texts are taken from *Hauptwerke,* 6 vols. (Hamburg: Felix Meiner, 1999).

9. *PM,* 134.

self (Hegel), or theology would be reduced to a fideistic reflection. Bruaire takes this circularity seriously and contends that philosophy thinks of the absolute adequately only when it welcomes the suggestions of Christian revelation, and that philosophy does not lose its proper nature by doing so. Their mutual relationship is hence necessary and noninvasive. It is thus crucial to grasp from the outset this premise upon which the structure of Bruaire's philosophical system depends. Failure to understand his way of conceiving the relation between philosophy and theology will prevent any adequate comprehension of Bruaire's ontology of gift.

From Theology to Philosophy

The concern for preserving philosophy's integrity has led some to perceive any relation with theology as a threat to the pursuit of truth. In the search for autonomy, says Bruaire, the rationalist philosophy of the seventeenth to the nineteenth century claims that reason must be freed not only from historical contingency but also from every unreflected and uncriticized assumption. It needs to be liberated from *any* type of presupposition. Thus, "pure reason," says Bruaire, regards unconsidered assumptions as burdensome prejudices that, perhaps, encumber speculative knowledge more than history does. In its quest for truth, reason cannot rely upon anything whose validity has not been sufficiently tested by reason itself. If pure reason is to know something with certainty, it must first uncover and examine whatever was previously taken for granted. The concern to free philosophy from unjustified presuppositions prompted rationalist philosophy to embrace a concept of reason abstracted both from reality and from the act of knowing. Once freed from unnecessary presuppositions, reason becomes law for itself, autonomous.

Nevertheless, Bruaire denies that the ultimate ground of this understanding of pure reason lies with reason itself. Descartes's much-celebrated "methodical doubt," Bruaire contends, is nothing other than the desire for some ultimate ground that admits no dependency. What undergirds rationalist philosophy is then a very specific understanding of *freedom*. The search for "autonomy" presupposes first and foremost a conception of freedom that determines the nature ascribed to reason. The quest for reason's autonomy is ultimately the demand for independence. For Bruaire, the philosophical activity of "putting everything into question" is simply the expression of the philosopher's desire for absolute freedom. The suspension of every presupposition, undertaken in the fashion proposed by modernity, has at its origin a *negative* conception of freedom. That is to say, freedom is understood as *non*-dependence, whereas its positive meaning of auto-determination or affirmation is neglected. Following this thread to the end, Bruaire indicates that this understanding of human freedom is patterned after a precise idea of *absolute* freedom. In fact, to conceive of human freedom as essentially independent implies that finite freedom images an infinite freedom seen as *absolute freedom* and *absolute empty negativity,* that is to say, as an absolute "which posits that which it presupposes, but which is condemned by this native sterility to being effectively able to posit nothing."[10] Consequently, says Bruaire, the rejection of every presupposition as prejudice reveals the illusory nature of a philosophy without presuppositions, because methodical doubt is nothing other than the affirmation of the presupposition that absolute freedom is pure negativity, something which, as we shall see, contradicts the very nature of the absolute and of human reason.

The contention that reason should not be conceived abstractly from— and hence independently of—Christian revelation does not, on the other hand, imply that the two are simply juxtaposed. Although his work has indeed been described as "Christian philosophy," "Christian rationalism," and even "philosophical theology," Bruaire himself despised the label of "Christian philosophy."[11] It was, as he described it, a source of "daily embarrassment." To consider oneself a *Christian* philosopher, says Bruaire, may hint at a certain schizophrenia.[12] The qualification "Christian philosophy" tends to presuppose a separation between faith and reason, betraying a specific vision that is insufficiently radical, that is unable to see the ultimate nature of the question regarding the absolute, and that is incapa-

---

10. *PM,* 135.

11. Cf. Xavier Tilliette, "Le rationalisme chrétien de Claude Bruaire," *Les Études philosophiques* 3 (1988): 315–22; id., "La théologie philosophique de Claude Bruaire," 704–8; Jean-Louis Vieillard-Baron, "La notion d'esprit dans la philosophie chrétienne de Claude Bruaire," *Les Études philosophiques* 3 (1988): 301–8; Leduc-Fayette, "Claude Bruaire: 1932–86," 5–19; and my "El Ser y el espíritu o la ontología como donación," *Revista española de teología* 61 (2001): 149–71.

12. *PM,* 133.

ble of acknowledging how the absolute gives form to every single thought and reality.[13] Without an adequate perception of their circularity, attempts to work out the relation between philosophy and theology can bear no fruit. For Bruaire, Christian revelation offers a fundamental contribution to philosophy, and the fecundity of the latter depends upon the acceptance of the former's provocation and upon the way in which this is utilized.

In contrast to the sort of Christian apologetics that is so distorted by an inadequate rationalistic philosophy that it tends to circumscribe reason to a formalistic and unappealing logic whose sole reference points are a creatureless, mechanistic cosmos, an isolated transcendental ego, and an impersonal absolute, Bruaire's thought follows Fessard and walks a narrow path from theology to philosophy.[14] Following this itinerary, the relationship between philosophy and theology can be conceived not only in terms of frontier *(Grenze)* but also of encounter. In fact, the border is not only that which separates two countries; it is also precisely the line where they meet. For this reason, Bruaire replaces the highly contested ideas of "independence" and "autonomy" with the concept of a noninvasive, mutually enriching "encounter." The absolute's self-revelation sheds light upon the philosophical task of thinking the absolute, and reflection upon the absolute's being, in turn, enhances theology. Bruaire characterizes this circular, noninvasive, and indispensable encounter between philosophy and theology as "Christian intimations of free thought" and "religion's encouragement to reset philosophy in motion."[15]

13. Perhaps Bruaire's rejection of this qualification of philosophy is prompted by an overreaction to the debate which held sway among the great French philosophers in the first half of the twentieth century. See Pope Leo XIII, "Aeterni Patris. On the Restoration of Christian Philosophy," in *The Church Speaks to the Modern World: The Social Teaching of Leo XIII,* ed. Etienne Gilson (New York: Doubleday/Image 1954), 29–54; Etienne Gilson, "What Is Christian Philosophy?" in *A Gilson Reader,* ed. Anton C. Pegis (New York: Doubleday/Image, 1957), 38–73; Jacques Maritain, *De la philosophie chrétienne* (Paris: Desclée de Brouwer, 1933); Emile Bréhier, "Y-a-t-il une philosophie chrétienne?" *Revue de métaphysique et de morale* 38 (1931): 133–62; Antoine R. Motte, O.P., "Le problème de la philosophie chrétienne," *Bulletin thomiste* 4 (1934–36): 311–18; and 5 (1937–39): 230–55; Maurice Nédoncelle, *Existe-t-il une philosophie chrétienne?* (Paris: Fayard, 1956); Henri de Lubac, "On Christian Philosophy," *Communio* 19 (1992): 478–506.

14. Fessard, *Dialectique des "Exercices".* For a fine introduction to Fessard's thought see Michel Sales, *Gaston Fessard (1897–1978): Genèse d'une pensée* (Paris: Culture et vérité, 1996).

15. *EE,* 113. Bruaire uses these two expressions to describe theology's contribution to philosophy. Hegel, Blondel, SieWerth, and Fessard are just a few of the other philosophers who have tried to follow the same path from theology to philosophy.

The Whole of Reason

To understand how the encounter between theology and philosophy does not violate philosophy's integrity but, on the contrary, supports its task of reflection, Bruaire argues that the work of philosophy should proceed not according to "reason alone" but by taking into account the "whole of reason."[16] The first point here is that human rationality, or language, as he calls it, is rooted within the logic of human existence and so is always associated with the other two principles that constitute the unified human being: freedom and desire. In this sense, reflection on truth is prompted by man's *desire* to know, that is to say, by a longing for absolute knowledge that is at the heart of his own *freedom,* that is, his having to become what he is. If one considers man's concrete rationality, it is possible to discover, says Bruaire in *The Affirmation of God,* that the unity of man's existence is not just a fact that can be taken for granted. The unity of his being in its threefold dimension of desire, language, and freedom is given to him, instead, so that he may live the logic of this unity in full awareness that what is at stake is his very self. Hence, the logic of human existence not only shows that "reason" is inseparably connected to desire and freedom; it also illustrates that man's existence cannot be comprehended outside his relation with God, a relation that determines his very being. The "whole of reason," then, must take into account both the whole of the human being with his specific way of knowing and the relation with this other that prompts and makes possible his very search for truth.

Let us then look more closely at Bruaire's approach to the logic of human existence. The "logic" of human existence is the analysis of the necessary relations between freedom, desire, and language. Freedom is conceived of by Bruaire as concrete singularity, desire as undetermined universality, and language as determined universality. The relations between them, for a harmonious inclusion of all three, must pass through conflicting, self-destructing relationships in which the universal is opposed to the singular and not to the particular. The former is expressed in a syllogistic form and the latter through dialectics. The *logic of existence* consists, then, in the study of the ties between these three principles that, together, creatively represent the unity proper to the historical existence of the human being.[17]

16. *DD,* 111.

17. To a certain extent, Bruaire's understanding of logic follows Hegel's and not Aristo-

Bruaire's analysis of human existence begins by proposing a fundamental category that philosophical reflection tends to overlook: *desire*. In Bruaire's work, this term does not refer to an inclination toward a good which is not yet possessed, nor is it a psychological category. Though there is a certain apprehension of the good, without a "representation" of it—and this is why desire is what makes us perceive reality for what it is, a *gift*—desire is essentially undetermined.[18] Desire, deeply rooted in the natural order, albeit distinct from it, stands for that *universality* proper to the order of action, that is, the movement that prompts the human being to "that active search for the unlimited being." It is that silent force which puts everything in motion: it moves freedom to choose and to act, and it moves language to reason. In this respect, desire is the specific universality of the will, not far from Schelling's idea of *conatus,* in which desire is seen as freedom breaking through all form and structure.[19]

---

tle's. In fact, Aristotle understands the categories "universal," "particular," and "singular" as referring to the extension of a given subject in a proposition. For him, while dialectics is just the means used to convince those who are unwilling or unable to recognize the validity of the first principles—and thus it remains always in the realm of opinion and probability—syllogistic theory remains within the realm of propositional logic. Cf. Aristotle, *Topica* 1.2.101b, Eng. trans. *Topica and the Sophisticis Elenchis,* trans. W. A. Pickard, vol. 1 of *The Works of Aristotle* (London: Oxford University Press, 1955). For Hegel, as John Findlay clarifies, the universal refers to the *self-identical* inasmuch as it includes within itself the singular and the particular. It is the totality in an undeveloped form, which needs to become itself by gathering all the moments in its self-determination. The singular refers to a *subject,* which is but one moment in the constitution of the individual, not an actual concrete being. The particular refers to the distinct or the *determinate,* but "so taken as to be universal in itself and also singular" (John Niemeyer Findlay, *Hegel: A Reexamination* [New York: Oxford University Press, 1958], 225). In the *Greater Logic,* Hegel illustrates that the syllogism, which explains the structure both of speculative thought and of reality itself, is the clearly posited and fully realized unity of the concept's three main elements: universality, particularity, and singularity. Therefore, the syllogism is inductive rather than deductive. The syllogism is a threefold unity which expresses the circular movement of absolute spirit, and thus it also develops and progresses toward its own fullness—something that is unacceptable for Aristotle. (Cf. Aristotle, *Analytica Posteriora* 1.3.72b5–38.) In a nutshell, whereas for Aristotle the syllogism is mainly *quantitative,* for Hegel it is *qualitative.* Bruaire's way of understanding syllogistic theory draws many decisive elements from Hegel. Nevertheless, it represents a significant shift: the syllogism, for Bruaire, cannot be categorized as quantitative or qualitative; it is ontological. See *RP,* 135–40 and 243–63 and *EE,* 179–93. The following chapters provide a more detailed account of Hegel's syllogistic theory and Bruaire's use of it.

18. *AD,* 52.

19. *AD,* 13. Bruaire also mentions Ravaisson as the modern philosopher who offers the best reflection on the concept of desire. See *AD,* 18; cf. Félix Ravaisson, *De l'habitude: Métaphysique et morale* (Paris: Quadrige/PUF, 1999).

Human nature's second fundamental principle is *freedom*. Through freedom, the human being possesses himself and determines himself to action. For Bruaire, freedom is that principle which constitutes the *singularity* of the subject, its personal uniqueness, which cannot be compared to the empirical particular. Freedom represents *concrete* singularity, which, as such, is able to open up to universality because, as we shall see, it somehow includes it within its fullness.[20]

Bruaire's concept of freedom, which is of utmost importance for his work, is cast in the form of post-Kantian idealism (Hegel and Schelling), although it cannot be simply identified with it. In keeping with this form, freedom, for Bruaire, is not an attribute with which a finite being is endowed. Bruaire's conception of freedom is also not the "freedom of choice" so familiar to English and French readers. It is also different from the *liberum arbitrium* of the Latin tradition. Bruaire understands freedom *ontologically* and includes within his own all other concepts of freedom. His analysis views freedom and the human spirit as coextensive: freedom describes the whole of the human spirit. Nevertheless, Bruaire reattaches this conception of freedom to the traditional Catholic teaching, which, though not fully elaborated, can be found in the medieval tradition. With regard to the human being, freedom pertains both to the capacity for self-determination and to the basis for moral action. The ontological sense of freedom indicates then that the person is a subject whose being is always already dynamically ordered to God. Yet this orientation, given the co-implication of being and freedom, is to be seen in terms of a call first to accept this primordial orientation toward the absolute and then to determine itself in its conversion to its source.[21]

20. What is said here concerning the concrete singularity of freedom needs to be read along with the metaphysical analysis that Bruaire undertakes in *EE*. Although we will explore this issue in detail later on, it is important to anticipate here that to speak of freedom in terms of concrete singularity presupposes the representation of spirit in terms of fullness and positivity, rather than an indivisible unity. It also introduces receptivity, openness, incompleteness, and relativity in the very essence of the human being. This is another issue in which Marcel's influence can be recognized.

21. With regard to God, to say that absolute spirit is free means more than that God creates without any constraint, or that his relation with the human spirit is not determined by the latter's needs. The being-free of the absolute is self-determination—which is relative for the finite spirit. Kenneth Schmitz explains that German idealism formulates a notion of freedom that, although not as weak as the Kantian one, considers freedom under the aspect of moral autonomy. It is not strong enough to uphold the concept of creation. "In place of

The third principle is *language*. When Bruaire uses this term he refers to a "constitutive element of the human essence" and not to a historically determined and culturally changeable expression. Obviously language, or rationality, expresses itself through particular historical languages, but it cannot be identified with any of them. "Language" is most fittingly defined by the term *word (verbe)*. Because *logos* refers only to the logical, formal aspect of language and *parole* refers to the spoken word alone, the only term capable of expressing the organic unity of discourse—that is, the unity of the expression and the structure—is *verbe*. Language *(verbe)*, like desire, is universal. This time, however, it is not the undetermined universality proper to *desire* but rather the universality of the idea, the *concept*. To illustrate the necessary relationship between the three terms, Bruaire deems it indispensable to examine the factors that lead to the elimination of one of them. For this reason, *The Affirmation of God* offers first the *dialectical* relation between desire, freedom, and language. This dialectical analysis grounds the speculative reflection on the logic of human existence, following a *syllogistic* pattern. According to this syllogistic structure, the logic of human existence must show how desire, freedom, and language are able to form a coherent unity. That is to say, it must demonstrate in what sense language (determined universality) is able to mediate between freedom (singularity) and desire (undetermined universality).[22] Language, says Bruaire, can mediate between freedom and desire because desire, for its part, is able to show the necessary bond between language and freedom.[23] Finally, this mediation proper to desire is possible because, at least in principle, freedom is able to uphold the necessary association between language and desire, to which the desire for absolute knowledge attests.[24]

---

a creator God or a moral hero, a transcendental subjectivity, grown beyond the finitude to which Kant and Fichte had confined it, has taken place as *absolute Geist;* and it is this Spirit that carries this distinctive freedom within itself as a cosmic force" (Kenneth L. Schmitz, "The Idealism of the German Romantics," in *The Emergence of German Idealism,* vol. 34 of *Studies in Philosophy and History of Philosophy,* ed. Michael Baur and Daniel O. Dahlstorm [Washington, D.C.: Catholic University of America Press, 1999], 176–97, 188). As we shall see, the conjunction of the German and Catholic understanding of freedom is what allows Bruaire's concept of freedom to posit an absolute self-determining spirit whose *positivity* is such that it is able to create that which he is not, i.e., a finite spirit, and remain independent from it. Freedom, for Bruaire, then, is ontological *and,* contrary to German idealism, able to supply the basis for creation.

22. *AD*, 113–34.   23. *AD*, 134–53.
24. *AD*, 154–68.

Bruaire's dialectics involves three different, successive, and interconnected moments. Each of these three stages of the dialectics is formed by the relationship between two of the three principles, in which both try to predominate and to annihilate the other. The result is a "ruinous" logic that propels every stage into the next. In this sense, the first pair is formed by the dialectics of desire and freedom,[25] the second by the dialectics of freedom and language,[26] and the third by language and desire.[27] Bruaire begins with the dialectics of desire and freedom. He gives freedom this structural prominence because it represents what is most characteristic of the human being, while its awakening is nevertheless bound up with desire. Each step in the dialectical process explains several "existential attitudes," which together represent the logical skeleton, "the grounds and general structure of the real attitudes which are always less pure."[28] This dialectics serves as the *via negativa* that provides Bruaire the necessary grounds upon which to construct the syllogistic, speculative level of his system: it is only here that the harmonious unity of the three principles begins to develop.

As noted, the syllogism has freedom as its starting point. The human being is free, that is, he is given to himself in order to become what he is. If the human being is to determine himself, freedom needs desire. At the same time, he must detach himself from desire in order to remain himself. What is necessary is a "moment of *conversion,* a return to oneself in the memory."[29] In other words, a third principle needs to be introduced for desire and freedom to be able to be united and reconciled. Only *language,* which is "older than the man who speaks it," can bring about that reconciliation. Language adjusts itself to the "concrete singularity" of freedom and to the "totalizing extension" of desire. Language, says Bruaire, resolves the antinomy both for logic and for ontology. It is only by means of the "exercise of the word *(parole)*" that the human being becomes free and discovers himself to be free from the immediate needs that entrap him.[30] In this way, on the one hand, language renders freedom able to express a desire and to repress desire's unrestrained passion, and, on the other hand, language universalizes freedom.

25. *AD,* 22–48.
26. *AD,* 49–70.
27. *AD,* 71–91.
28. *AD,* 21.
29. *AD,* 116–17. Bruaire's emphasis.
30. *AD,* 119. Bruaire distinguishes *désir* and *besoin.* I translate the first as *desire,* the second as *need.*

The second syllogism is the syllogism of language and has as its middle term *desire,* which unites and reconciles language with freedom. It bears repeating that desire, like language, is universal, although the universality of the former is indeterminate. By means of its effort of realization, desire also relates to the *singular* freedom. In this way, desire is able to prevent freedom from absorbing language and dominating the word *(verbe)* and is able to protect language from abstraction. Only desire is able to eliminate every kind of idealism (which is the absolutization of language) or abstract way of understanding freedom (detached from meaning). The first syllogism, the syllogism of freedom, sets the basis for temporality and time, "because freedom is not factual unless it inserts its temporality within language." With the syllogism of freedom, the individual is introduced into the flux of time in which his freedom arises. In this sense, the second syllogism, the syllogism of language, is also the syllogism of history and historicity; that is, language brings a historical dimension to freedom. With this syllogism, temporality, which language introduced in the first syllogism, attains its true significance through its grounding within the historicity of desire. Yet this parallelism between the first and the second syllogism should not be construed to mean that Bruaire identifies the "memory" of humanity with the memory of the individual. Precisely because desire is the middle term, history remains essentially open. This identification between historical and personal memory would be possible if one "could substitute desire with a unique Spirit, singular and universal, [that is also] absolute freedom, and absolute language."[31] But to do so would be to do theology, as occurs in Hegel. Instead, the syllogism of freedom only hypothesizes an absolute meaning. It is in this need for a transcendental absolute that grounds the relation between freedom, desire, and language that the syllogism of language discovers its limits and gives way to the *syllogism of desire.*

As stated, desire and language find their common ground in their own universality. Yet, that which brings them together also makes their unity impossible. On the one hand, desire is at the *origin* of every human motion, including that of language. On the other hand, language relates to desire as the end to the origin. In this regard, it seems as if language, considered in terms of absolute knowledge, represents the fulfillment and thus

31. *AD,* 152.

the end (death) of desire itself.[32] Freedom comes to the aid of this ultimately ruinous dialectic and makes the relationship between language and desire possible. Freedom's singularity enables language's universality to have a content and brings desire's potency under language's universality. In this sense, freedom roots language in desire because it gives to desire its logical expression. It also grounds desire in language by giving to reason the dynamic rhythm proper to desire.

Although it might seem at this point that freedom is the necessary link uniting desire and language, a question emerges to jeopardize this conclusion. Freedom has as its goal this perfection of absolute knowledge, but it is unable to produce it *ontologically*. In fact, Bruaire reminds us that freedom is finite, that is to say, "singular and not universal, determining without being totalizing." Freedom is necessary for "desire to be singular" and for "language to be fulfilled." Yet, because of its finitude, freedom is unable to unite language's *absolute* perfection and desire's *infinite need for satisfaction*.[33] Freedom cannot formulate a perfect, absolute language; this must be *given*, along with the "*impulse* [desire] which engages freedom with language." It is only the "inevitable and indispensable"[34] presence of desire within language that, according to Bruaire, makes the situation comprehensible.

Language's universality and desire's infinite thrust, neither of which has been invented, are found tied together in the logic of human existence because limited human freedom actualizes the unity between language and desire which is *given* to it. The singular character of human freedom makes utterly impossible the claim that human freedom can be the very *origin* of that unity between language and desire. In order for the singular freedom "to produce that unity [between desire and language], it must be *given* to it."[35] This is the point at which the syllogism of *desire* becomes *the*

32. *AD*, 154–56.
33. *AD*, 163. Léonard offers a very lucid and clear account of Bruaire's *AD*. In addition, I have also found Tilliette's and Fernando Filoni's reviews very helpful. The foregoing brief account of *AD* is in debt to all three of them. See André Léonard, *Pensées des hommes et foi en Jésus-Christ: Pour un discernement intellectuel chrétien* (Paris: Lethielleux, 1980), 234–43; Xavier Tilliette, "La philosophie et l'absolue," *Revue philosophique* 1 (1990): 79–87; Fernando Filoni, "Claude Bruaire. La ricerca ontologica e l'affermazione di Dio," *Aquinas* 28 (1985): 301–69.
34. *AD*, 164.
35. *AD*, 164.

ontological argument that proves God's existence: human freedom presupposes an *absolute* freedom. Hence, the ultimate formulation of the syllogism of desire could be stated thus: "desire proposes to freedom, which thinks through language, the perfection of speech *(discours)* as the infinite being of the perfect logos."[36] Bruaire maintains, then, that if one is faithful to the way the logic of human existence unfolds itself, and thus to the way one reasons, then one is bound to acknowledge the need for *another origin,* different from one's own freedom, at the root of the unity between desire and language. Hence, human reason, man's capacity to know, and human existence as a whole do not make sense without the ontological reference to the other that constitutes the human being. It is now useful to restate Bruaire's synthetic and clear account of his version of the ontological argument:

—In the use of the word, the human being desires the absolute word.

—Neither this desire, totalitarian in its essence, nor language, which has a universal form, can be associated *by* our freedom, which is singular and relative to the association of language and desire.

—This association is, then, *given,* given to our freedom so that it can in fact engage in its discourse.

—This association, however, due to the opposite characteristics of desire and language, cannot be operated through the mediation of a [human] freedom.

—Since this freedom cannot be relative to the other two principles just mentioned, it is, in its existence and power, an absolute freedom; it is God. It is God who makes our freedom desire the perfection of knowledge.[37]

---

36. *AD,* 162.

37. *AD,* 165. As with his understanding of desire, we can see here how important the idea of *donation* is from the very beginning of Bruaire's philosophical reflection. A shorter formulation is offered: "Our desire for an absolute language presupposes a freedom able to unite it to the universal form proper to discourse. Our freedom cannot produce this union. It can only use it in the exercise of the word. The freedom presupposed, then, a freedom that mediates the original relation between desire and word, is absolute freedom" (*AD,* 166). In *DD,* Bruaire approaches the ontological argument from a different point of view. This time, God's existence is not thought out from the analysis of the logic of human existence but rather from God himself. Bruaire states that if God is properly thought of as absolute freedom, then it is not possible to treat the idea of God as a mere concept equal to any other—including Kant's 100 thalers. See *DD,* 84.

The ideal of absolute knowledge, the search for which is what moves desire, manifests an absolute freedom that is able to reconcile, through the limited freedom of the human being, language and desire. It is absolute freedom that grounds the desiring and the rational existence of relative freedom. However, Bruaire cautions, this does not mean that human freedom and desire are in God—which would absorb the human being within the sphere of the divine. It does not mean that Bruaire sees God's existence as the result of a human choice.[38] The mediation of absolute freedom can only be understood in terms of creative mediation. Unity is given through the ontological relation with the absolute.[39]

It is important not to lose sight of the decisive role that freedom plays in Bruaire's ontological argument, because it is precisely this aspect that most of the "ontological arguments" miss. The so-called ontological argument is indispensable for establishing the synthesis of desire and logos in the realm of being. Human freedom is the *real* mediation of the gift that the absolute freedom continuously bestows. The syllogism of desire, according to Bruaire, concludes in God's existence, not because the proof of God's existence moves from the essence (idea/concept) of God to his existence, but because the analysis of the logic of human existence forces human reason to do so: absolute freedom seizes human existence and, mediated by human freedom, makes human existence possible.

Bruaire does not repropose Anselm's or Descartes's argument, because the latter's movement from the idea of perfection to the existence of a perfect being obviates the mediation of freedom. For Bruaire, one cannot automatically move from the confession to the existential conviction of his existence. The idea of perfection does require the *real* perfection, but this

38. The constitutive divine mediation is the origin of the desire and the one "making it to be the desire for (absolute) knowledge" (*AD*, 168). The statement "for freedom to desire absolute knowledge" does not mean to desire to be God, but rather to desire God. For Bruaire, the desire to be God leads to the desire to annihilate one's own I. Furthermore, Bruaire clarifies that the revelation reason demands, the only one able to fulfill that desire which constitutes the human being and which is not a claim that God would be bound to answer, is not an interior revelation proper to natural religion. The true form of the desire for God is *invocation*. In fact, the conclusion of *AD* is that the desire of God is called to become love inasmuch as it waits for the absolute freedom to speak (*AD*, 283; *PM*, 176). That absolute freedom is necessary for understanding human reason implies, then, "a conversion of reason's universal sense to divine being. It is precisely God's *concrete universal* that opens reason to waiting for a historical revelation" (*PM*, 175).

39. *AD*, 167.

is not its effective position, since it is the representative and imperative language which formulates that proof.[40] Since freedom is at stake, certainty requires personal engagement. Nevertheless, Bruaire's argument still has a universal validity because, as Tilliette explains, "here the universal sense accommodates itself *(s'ajuste)* to the singular." Tilliette notes that Bruaire quotes de Lubac to show that the kernel of the proof is the idea of God within humanity, which cannot be compared to any other idea, not even the idea of the absolute, which "can be confiscated."[41] Freedom (absolute freedom) cannot but be thought of as sovereign existence. God, in order to be thought, needs to be posited and vice versa: the existence of God needs to be affirmed in order to understand the idea of God. This necessity is demanded by the fact that the living bond between desire and language (intelligence) is fastened by absolute freedom.

The analysis of the logic of human existence, here briefly sketched, is an attempt to demonstrate that rationality, considered as the "whole" of reason, exists only in its bond with desire and freedom and that the unity of human existence is a gift given by absolute freedom. Rationality thus discovers the divine absolute freedom at its own origins and acknowledges its role within the logic of human existence, which reveals itself to be relation with God.[42] The "whole of reason" requires acknowledgment of the existence of an *absolute* mediator as that *other* which makes (the logic of) human existence possible. Once rationalism is overcome by rationality, and "pure reason," by the "whole of reason," it is possible to perceive that welcoming what theology has to offer to philosophy does not violate the "integrity" of the philosophical reflection. In fact, if the human being is made in this way, then listening to a possible revelation of God turns out to be neither a supplementary option ultimately irrelevant to any "serious" philosophical reflection, nor a disruptive transgression that shatters any possibility of true knowledge.

---

40. *AD*, 163.

41. *PM*, 62. Tilliette, "La théologie philosophique," 704. See Henri de Lubac, *Sur les chemins de Dieu* (Paris: Aubier, 1956), Eng trans., *The Discovery of God*, trans. Alexander Dru (Grand Rapids, Mich.: Eerdmans, 1996).

42. *PM*, 175. As I shall show in the next chapter, this anthropology is incomplete until it addresses the relation between the self and its bodiliness and between the self and the human others.

Christian Intimations of Philosophy

If absolute freedom intervenes in this way in human existence, and if it is at the same time absolute rationality, then God must have something to say. And, to have something to say, he cannot but be capable of language—he must be able to express himself in the Word. What is known in the ontological affirmation is not a speechless absolute, eternally unable to express itself. The absolute is the greatest being that can be thought, and hence, it is pure intelligibility, the plenitude of sense, the perfect "expression of itself." Whoever claims to know the absolute without recognizing in it the absolute *plenitude* of meaning, is thinking of an idol and not of the absolute itself.[43] In fact, says Bruaire, to think that the absolute is unable to express itself and that it can remain *indifferent* to human existence is to say that it is *no different* than the human being. And to contend that God is "no-different-than" the human being is implicitly to affirm that man understands himself as "identical with" God. The logic of human existence proves this identification between absolute spirit and human being to be unsustainable.[44]

This understanding of the absolute as having something to communicate, and able to do so because God is pure *Logos*, prompts Bruaire to formulate a discourse on language and its five different but interrelated forms: language in God, of God, about God, to God, and for God. This framework enables us to comprehend the meaning of the two expressions that Bruaire uses to describe theology's contribution to philosophy: "Christian intimations of free thought" and "religion's encouragement to reset philosophy in motion."[45]

If language is to be understood as the inseparable expression of the Logos, then one could positively conceive of a language *in* God. The absolute is also Logos, Word, which expresses itself and speaks not only to itself but also to what is different from itself, that is to say, to the human being. Only the hypothesis that God establishes a dialogue with the human being clarifies the true nature of human desire for absolute knowledge: not that of being like God but rather the desire for God. Language in God is the ground for language *of* God. The first expression of this language of

43. *EE*, 108.   44. *PM*, 33.
45. *EE*, 113.

God to the human being is in God's allowing the latter to exist in the way he does, with the dynamic proper to the human being. The existence of language of God, that word which he says to the human being, can be discovered through "logical" analysis, and it urges the human being to pay attention to a possible manifestation of his Word. That God has said himself at a certain moment in history establishes the language of God as more than merely an interior, private dialogue between a man and his mysterious origin.[46]

This language of God makes it possible for the human being to elaborate a language *about* God. It is this third type of language that best characterizes *both* philosophy and theology. I mentioned at the beginning of the chapter that these two sciences had the same object, the absolute. Now it is possible to perceive that the study of this most important subject is prompted by the very logic of human existence, since it cannot be comprehended apart from God's expression of himself. Given the fact that the absolute has also revealed himself in history, the philosopher should, in full earnest, take into account what God has disclosed of himself. Language of God and about God finds its fulfillment in language *to* God, which is proper to human invocation. This language addressed to God is the explicit response to God's initiative toward the human being. Language about and to God is also completed by a more specific type of language, language *for* God, which is proper to apologetics.

Keeping philosophy and theology within this larger framework clarifies their circular and mutually enriching relation. Bruaire's philosophy proceeds by taking revelation into account, and, in a certain sense like Blondel, he moves from theology to philosophy. Bruaire tells us that for Blondel, Christian dogmas are not only "revealed"; they are above all "revelators" for philosophy. A philosopher could accept, for example, the provocation of thinking God as Triune as one suggestion among others, "with the task of testing its consistency, although he is unable to deduce it or to prove it."[47] In this way, it would be possible to preserve simultaneously the

---

46. As *Dei Verbum* (*DV*) sets forth: "The most intimate truth which this revelation [divine revelation itself] gives us about God and the salvation of man shines forth in Christ, who is himself both the mediator and the sum total of Revelation" (*DV*, 2). The conciliar texts are taken from A. Flannery, ed., *Vatican Council II: The Conciliar and Post Conciliar Documents* (Northport, N.Y.: Costello Publishing Company, 1975).

47. *PM*, 140. The changes in Blondel's position with regard to the relationship between

provocation of revelation and philosophy's autonomy. However, according to Bruaire, this way of thinking the provocations of Christianity ends up, sooner or later, in the subordination of philosophy to theology or the reduction of the content of revelation to a more or less privileged moment of philosophical discourse. "Philosophy is neither the *preambula fidei* nor the presentment of a philosophical conquest."[48]

Bruaire's philosophical speech about God does not follow the same pattern as Hegel's philosophy either. Certainly, a great number of Hegel's main philosophical insights can be found in Bruaire's reflection: the importance that Christianity as absolute religion has for the philosophical system, the dialectical system, the significance of spirit, the centrality of Christian revelation, as well as much of Hegel's logic, including his theory of the triple syllogism. The predominance of Hegelian thought in Bruaire cannot be overemphasized.[49] Nevertheless, according to Bruaire, certain equivocations led Hegel to confuse language *in* God with language about God. The absorption *(Aufhebung)* of theology into philosophy is the direct consequence of this problem. Granting that Bruaire's philosophy makes little sense without Hegel's, one does more justice to Bruaire when one recognizes along with Chapelle that Hegel "is not his inspirational source."[50] For Bruaire, the Catholic understanding of revelation has priority over Hegel's system. As a matter of fact, the bond with which Hegel unites speculative philosophy and religious revelation is the point at which one of the main discrepancies between the two philosophers arises. "Hegel sins not

---

theology and philosophy are well known. See Blondel, *L'action;* id., *La philosophie et l'esprit chrétienne,* vol. 1: *Autonomie essentielle et connexion indéclinable* (1944); vol 2: *Conditions de la symbiose seule normale et salutaire: Exigences philosophiques du christianisme* (1950); André Hayen, "La philosophie catholique de Maurice Blondel au temps de la première 'Action,'" *Revue philosophique de Louvain* 59 (1961): 249–314.

48. *PM,* 140.

49. See *LR,* 179–83. Cf. Tilliette, "La philosophie et l'absolu," 85.

50. Albert Chapelle, "L'itinéraire philosophique de Claude Bruaire: De Hegel à la métaphysique," *Revue philosophique* 1 (1990): 5–12. For the relation between Hegel and Bruaire see also id., "Présence de Hegel en France: G. Fessard et Cl. Bruaire," *Revue philosophique* 1 (1990): 13–26; Jean Brun, "La pensée de Hegel selon Claude Bruaire," *Les Études philosophiques* 3 (1988): 309–13. See also *AA,* 21; *SE,* 182–205; *D,* 107; Bruaire, "Hegel et le problème de la théologie," in *Hegel et la théologie contemporaine: L'absolu dans l'histoire?* (Neuchâtel: Delachaux and Niestlé, 1977), 94–98; id., "Hegel et l'athéisme contemporain," *Revue international de philosophie* 91 (1970): 72–80; id., "Hegel," in *Encyclopaedia Universalis,* 3rd ed. (Paris: *Encyclopaedia Universalis,* 1990–92), 276–79 (hereafter *Hg*).

by excess, but by defect. That is to say, if the divine Word and the human language that transcribes it are identifiable, if the discourse is univocal, rejecting in this way the distinction between philosophy and the theology of revelation, then an equivocation emerges: to think each of them as indistinguishable is to reduce one to the other."[51] For this reason, continues Bruaire, Hegel's philosophy could be read as a speculative reflection whose content is revealed religion. According to Bruaire, Hegel's improper identification of the human and divine logics prevents him from conferring due importance either to human freedom or to creation.[52] In this way, although there is a sense in which Bruaire could agree with Hegel's famous statement that "philosophy explains itself in thinking religion,"[53] he does not accept Hegel's model inasmuch as his philosophical system tries to supersede theology. Bruaire does indeed perceive a tight circularity between philosophy and theology, but he conceives it differently from Blondel or Hegel, both of whose works, as I noted, substantially influenced his own.[54]

Bruaire defines theology, language *about* God, with a beautiful expression: "the memory of revelation." The concept of memory, key in Bruaire's vocabulary, does not stand here for a simple souvenir of sentences extracted from the ecclesiastical tradition or deduced from Scripture. Rather, it means the "presence," with all its being, of that which is remembered, and the certainty of its truth.[55] This is precisely the reason that, according to Bruaire, theology is not just the repetition of unreflectively assumed dogmas. Bruaire always fought against the limited understanding of theology as a mere logical exercise in combining revealed propositions. He rejected a certain theological trend that limits itself to casuistics, manuals, or to a

---

51. *Hg,* 258.

52. *LR,* 145, 181–83. *EE,* 129–44.

53. As quoted in *EE,* 113.

54. Bruaire's position before Blondel's understanding of the relationship between philosophy and theology remains burdened by a certain ambiguity. Although he said that Blondel's acceptance of revealed dogma as a source of inspiration for philosophy transforms the latter as subservient to theology, in a later publication Bruaire states that "la médiation conceptuelle peut présupposer la médiation de la mémoire de la révélation, dans le sens où Blondel nous disait que ce qui est donné à la foi doit être considéré comme donné aussi à la pensée" (Bruaire, "Réminiscence du concept et mémoire de la révélation," in *Pour une philosophie chrétienne* [Namur: Lethielleux, 1983], 151). This statement, however, does not explain how this interaction should take place. For this reason, I do not recognize a major inconsistency with the above interpretation.

55. *PM,* 149. We shall return to Bruaire's understanding of memory later on.

retrieval of the tradition while remaining oblivious to the Word's contemporaneousness to the theologian and his responsibility, the elaboration of language about God. Theological reflection must be innovative, precisely because it is language *of* God that does not tolerate a mere theological repetition. If the speaker communicating a message in the historical revelation is God himself, Bruaire says, then what he gives is infinite and inexhaustible.[56] It demands continuous innovation. Bruaire specifies that theology's innovative aspect is not to be understood as a detachment from the tradition or the invention of unheard-of truths. Theology is indeed *memory* of revelation and not the formulation of "new" truths. This understanding of theology tries to avoid both *passéisme* (a backward-looking attitude) and progressivism because neither acknowledges the fact that what has expressed itself in the historical revelation is the infinite itself. *Passéisme* reduces the content of the revealed word to a kind of "mummified system." Forgetting the fact that what is revealed is the infinite, the theologian who remains attached to the past does not accept that the reality contained in the *depositum fidei* is far larger than the mere words expressed in dogmatic propositions. The progressive theologian, for his part, believes that the memory of revelation needs to make way for the innovation of his own particular system. This position, however, forgets once more the fact that it is the infinite that has spoken, and therefore that any language about God is an approximate unfolding of the inexhaustible Word. One could say, then, that the first theologian elaborates a theology of repetition shorn of memory, whereas the second elaborates a theology of innovation without innovation. For Bruaire, theology is language *about* God, a language which is "that rational exercise which ends in the *memory* of the Word of God."[57]

Theological language about God cannot be severed from a language *to* God or, stated differently, from a dialogue with God, whose origin cannot be found in the free initiative of the human being but, rather, in the language *of* God. There is no theological language apart from faith or outside the invocation to God. Furthermore, for Bruaire, a memory of revelation which separates itself from language to God falls inevitably into

---

56. Bruaire, "L'invention dans le langage religieux," in *L'analyse du langage théologique: Colloque Castelli, Rome, 5–11 janvier 1969*, ed. Enrico Castelli (Paris: Aubier, 1969), 305–12. This article was published later in *PM*, 144–54.

57. Bruaire, "Réminiscence," 150.

atheism. Bracketing language to God is the same as thinking that there can be a discourse about God in which God is not strictly necessary, where the memory of the Word as presence and certainty is not indispensable. That, says Bruaire, would transform theology into a formalistic exercise which, at its very root, is discovered to be the identical opposite of its contrary, rationalism.[58] Theology, Bruaire writes, is prone to either *passéisme* or progressivism because "the memory of revelation, privileged memory, *must be tested* by the reminiscence of the concept without limiting itself in this test."[59]

If, for Bruaire, theology is the memory of revelation, philosophy is the *reminiscence of the concept.* Both are speculative in nature—they entail a certain use of reason—and each needs the other. In fact, the testing carried out by philosophy is not imposed on theology from the outside. Bruaire does not perceive theology to be the elaboration of language about God whose validity of claim and method is to be proven, upon completion, by pure reason. To accomplish theology's own task, the faithful creativity of the theologian requires the effort of the concept to prevent language about God from turning into either rationalism (of which progressivism is a type) or fideism (of which *passéisme* is a type). The former reduces the memory of the revealed data to the anamnesis of the concept, as if everything could be contained in the philosophical reflection of any given theology. According to Bruaire, the impression one has when reading many of the idealist philosophers is that Jesus Christ said the same things as they, although a little less elegantly. Fideism commits the opposite error, namely, thinking that the effort of the concept is completely unnecessary and that the revealed data should be assumed uncritically. On the contrary, revelation needs to be "recognized by thought," and for this reason, a philosophical verification is needed in order to appropriate the richness of theology. Theology needs the anamnesis of the concept in order to acquire a "new, affirmed, and confirmed intelligibility":

58. Language *to* God cannot be conceived as juxtaposed or extrinsic to thinking. In a certain sense, Heidegger's brief essays "Building Dwelling Thinking" and "What calls for thinking?" are a remarkable example of a secularized interpretation of thinking in terms of prayer. Cf. Martin Heidegger, *Basic Writings*, ed. David Farrell Krell (San Francisco: Harper Collins, 1993).

59. Bruaire, "Réminiscence," 150. Emphasis added.

There is nothing, not even an iota, of the revelation of God in Jesus Christ which should not be tested by an unconditional rationality. And this because, from the outset, the condition of the revealed data is the recollection of thought itself. *Voilà* this shows us at least one aspect of the relationship between theology and philosophy.[60]

The perception of philosophy as the reminiscence of the concept of the absolute and thus as subsisting in a close relationship with theology does not alter philosophy's nature or deprive it of its integrity. In fact, the risk that theology must take is that of allowing a certain part of the speculative reflection to be done by philosophy itself. As will be seen later, there is a valid philosophical reflection on the Trinity and on creation, which does not follow the methods of the theological treatise on the Trinity and which is not confronted with certain problems and questions that are proper to theology alone. What theology does not need is the rationalistic translation of the memory of revelation into conceptualistic reflection.

For Bruaire, the philosopher who is even minimally attentive to a possible revelation will respond to this call of theology and, in so doing, will discover that the memory of revelation frees philosophical questioning, actually rendering it unlimited. At that point, theology yields before conceptual necessity. In respecting this speculative need, "the theologian is a pure philosopher," and philosophy becomes the philosophy of religion whose task is also "the critical test of the metaphysical implications of that religious data."[61]

It is true that independence from theology means that philosophy does not need to respond to and to follow the same type of authority and tradition as does theology, that philosophy is deprived of the language *to*

60. *EE*, 111. John Paul II's encyclical letter *Fides et ratio* calls attention to the fundamental importance of philosophy in the practice of theology in these terms: "philosophy presents another stand worth noting *when theology itself calls upon it.* Theology in fact has always needed and still needs philosophy's contribution. As a work of critical reason in the light of faith, theology presupposes and requires in all its researches a reason formed and educated to concept and argument. Moreover, theology needs philosophy as a partner in dialogue in order to confirm the intelligibility and universal truth of its claims. It was not by accident that the Fathers of the Church and the medieval theologians adopted non-Christian philosophy. This historical fact confirms the value of philosophy's *autonomy*, which remains unimpaired when theology calls upon it; but it shows as well the profound transformation which philosophy itself must undergo" (John Paul II, *Fides et ratio* [Rome, 1998], no. 77). See also nos. 64–79.

61. *EE*, 110.

God which is of a piece with the language about God of theology, and that philosophy possesses different tools for its reflection. Yet, philosophy is to be thought in relation to theology because the latter contributes to the determination of philosophy's main task. The challenge of philosophy, to think the absolute spirit with all the rigor that the anamnesis of the concept is able to provide, implies maintaining a difficult balance that both welcomes the Christian intimations and, at the same time, preserves their undeniable autonomy.

While thinking the absolute with conceptual rigor, philosophy encounters the provocation of Christianity, which challenges its presuppositions and invites it to elaborate an *ontology* capable of rendering an adequate account both of the human being and of absolute spirit. Christian revelation provokes philosophical reflection, broadening its questions and introducing themes previously unknown to it. Pre-Christian metaphysics conceives of the absolute as undetermined, beyond language, and incompatible with history; the limited, in fact, was perceived as a sign of perfection, which the infinite or unlimited lacked. The historical revelation in Christ, on the contrary, shows that the essence of the *determinate* absolute is that of being *"absolute gift of itself* as incarnation, redemption and Trinitarian exchange." Thus, without abandoning the rigor proper to the anamnesis of the concept, philosophy is called to think the absolute under the light of a new ontology. The encounter between theology and philosophy, then, advances the conception of an absolute which is absolute gift. God gives himself to himself and to the human being. For this reason, philosophical reflection is called to conceive an ontology which will be able to undergird such an understanding of the absolute as gift.[62]

Undoubtedly, much of what Bruaire proposes could not have been accomplished without the intimations of Christian theology. Does this mean

---

62. To this end, says Bruaire, one of the main tasks that the metaphysics of gift must undertake is precisely that of converting the Aristotelian neutral categories into the categories of spirit, "particularly that of substance and identity—as the categories of being-gift (*être-de-don)*" (Bruaire, "Réminiscence," 152). There is a clear evolution here in Bruaire's thought. His metaphysical reflection grows out of his systematic anthropology. For this reason, although the essential understanding of the relationship between philosophy and theology remains unvaried from the first articles written in 1964 and collected in *PM,* there is a change in the explanation of how religion resets philosophy in motion. First it is to conceive substance as subject, and system as freedom; later on it is the renewal of ontology in the light of gift.

that, despite his continuous insistence that he is not doing an "embarrassed theology," Bruaire is an unconfessed theologian? The present study does not assert this. Nevertheless, the question remains whether the adoption of key issues taken from Christian revelation calls for a description of the encounter between philosophy and theology more adequate than "Christian intimations of free thought," and, more fundamentally, whether to take those intimations seriously does not require a more thorough reconsideration of the speculative structure Bruaire borrowed from Hegel. A fair evaluation of Bruaire's system, however, requires following this captivating speculative effort of thinking being in terms of gift to its end.

CHAPTER 2

Anthropology Beckons

During the first decade of his reflection (1964–74), Bruaire elaborated a systematic anthropology whose outcome is the recognition that man's very existence is indicative of a constitutive givenness. The interesting aspect of Bruaire's remarkable speculative effort in search of what is distinctly human, however, is that his anthropology is forged within and apart from Hegel's system. Hegel's influence can be perceived at every step of Bruaire's reflection: the circular movement of self-determination, the structure and patterns of speculative thought, the search for a unity between the finite and the absolute spirit that does not obliterate the differences, the role of freedom and the spirit, and so on.[1] Nevertheless, Bruaire's reflection offers a vision of the human being that differs radically from Hegel's basic tenets because it tries to defend the integrity of the human being's limited, but nonetheless real freedom. Given that Bruaire's anthropology is the negative obverse of his metaphysics, it finds its completion only with the latter, and, for this very reason, his ontodology cannot be conceived apart from the negative anthropology. It is this that we now need to examine. Since Bruaire's trilogy is thought with and away from Hegel, I first need to present his reading of the Hegelian system in order to see what he absorbs from Hegel and where he differs from him. Once Bruaire's work is put in perspective, it will be possible to elucidate in what sense, for him, givenness is the adequate form of human existence.[2]

1. *EE,* 6. See also *PC,* 254–56; *RP,* 9, 135–40; *EE,* 20–29, 80–83.
2. For an in-depth understanding of Hegel's system, the following works cannot go unmentioned: Findlay, *Hegel: A Re-examination;* Jean Hyppolite, *Logique et existence* (Paris:

A Theological Reading of Hegel

Opposing a common reading of Hegel, Bruaire rejects the inaccuracy of those who depict Hegel as either the epitome of atheism or as a bold idealist. The imprecision in these judgments proceeds from two main factors. The first is reading Hegel through the eyes of his opponents—Feuerbach, Marx, Lenin, and the like; the second is an unjustified identification of Hegel with that type of rationalism which he so emphatically criticized.[3] Instead, for Bruaire, the key to understanding Hegel's complex system lies in a proper emphasis on his philosophy of religion. Bruaire argues that it is not possible to ignore that "the 'Aristotle of modern times' placed philosophy of religion, especially 'absolute religion' or Christianity, at the very center of his work."[4] Understanding the precise relationship between the *Science of Logic* and the Hegelian philosophy of Christian religion is thus the hermeneutical key that allows Bruaire to take advantage of Hegel's system to elaborate an adequate anthropology without, on the one hand, flagrantly distorting Hegel's philosophical system or, on the other, falling victim to its intrinsic problems.[5]

PUF, 1953); id., *Genèse et structure de la phénoménologie de l'Esprit de Hegel* (Paris: Aubier, 1946); Albert Chapelle, *Hegel et la religion*, 3 vols. (Paris: Éditions Universitaires, 1965–71); André Léonard, *Commentaire litteral de la Logique de Hegel* (Paris: J. Vrin, 1974); Alexandre Kojève, *Introduction à la lecture de Hegel* (Paris: Gallimard, 1947); Karl Rosenkranz, *Georg Wilhelm Friedrich Hegels Leben* (Darmstadt: Wissenschaftliche Buchgesellschaft, 1971); Emil L. Fackenheim, *The Religious Dimension in Hegel's Thought* (Bloomington: Indiana University Press, 1967); Cyril O'Regan, *The Heterodox Hegel* (Albany: State University of New York Press, 1994).

3. Bruaire, "L'homme, miroir de Dieu," *Revue internationale de philosophie* 26 (1972): 345–54; id., "Hegel et le problème de la théologie," 94–98.

4. Bruaire, "Hegel et l'athéisme contemporain," *Revue internationale de philosophie* 24, no. 91 (1970): 72. Bruaire always remained faithful to this approach. In *D*, the last book he wrote, Bruaire presents the work of Fessard, who influenced his understanding of Hegel, praising him for being one of the first philosophers—at least in the French world—to approach Hegel's work within its proper milieu: Christian theological thought. See *D*, 106. See also Bruaire, "Pour une ontologie de l'esprit," in *Savoir, faire, espérer: Les limites de la raison* (Brussels: Facultés Universitaires Saint-Louis, 1976), 68–70 (hereafter *POnEs*). Bruaire has a concordant voice with Chapelle: see Chapelle, *Hegel et la religion*, vol. 3, p. 135 n. 1.

5. *LR*, 9. The most comprehensive presentation of Hegel's work is found in his *Encyclopedia of the Philosophical Sciences*. See Georg W. F. Hegel, *Enzyklopädie der philosophischen Wissenschaften im Grundrisse* (1830), vol. 6 of *Hauptwerke*, Eng. trans. *Encyclopedia of the Philosophical Sciences in Outline and Critical Writings*, trans. Stephen Taubenek (New York: Continuum, 1990) (hereafter *Enzyklopädie*). This, however, must always be read in conjunction with the *Phenomenology of Spirit* and the *Berlin Courses*. See Georg W. F. Hegel,

According to Bruaire's theological approach, Hegel's logic *(WL)* can only be understood when one realizes that the subject matter is, ultimately, the Triune God.[6] Bruaire contends that for Hegel, revelation is not simply a divine act interesting only for theologians and believers. Revelation is an "act of God for us, which, at the same time, could not be the manifestation of his very nature if it were not conformed to the eternal act by means of which God is for himself." When this revelation is expressed in human language, then, it takes the form of a logic of the absolute being. For this reason, Bruaire writes that "*absolute religion and absolute logic are, in themselves, identical;* one manifests God, and the other formulates this manifestation in a philosophical discourse which is, indistinguishably, the foundation of theological discourse."[7]

Bruaire contends that the identification of logic and religion comes from the fact that, for Hegel, the revealed God manifests his own essence in its exact determinations.[8] In fact, Christianity's novelty, in comparison

---

Phänomenologie des Geistes, vol. 2 of *Hauptwerke,* Eng. trans. *Phenomenology of Spirit,* trans. A. V. Miller (Oxford: Oxford University Press, 1977). Only a unified reading of the three works is sufficient to grasp the complex structure of the Hegelian system. The last edition of the *Enzyklopädie* (1830) is the result of fifteen years of work and, for that reason, deserves a place of prominence vis-à-vis the other works, not diminishing their significance, but rather, presupposing it. Along with the *Enzyklopädie,* however, the *Logic* deserves special attention. It is well known that Hegel's metaphysics and its main themes are both presented there and treated in depth. For this reason, the first part of the *Enzyklopädie* must be read with the Greater Logic, *Die Wissenschaft der Logik,* in *Hauptwerke,* vols. 3 and 4 (hereafter *WL*), Eng. trans. *Hegel's Science of Logic,* trans. A. V. Miller (Atlantic Highlands, N.J.: Humanities Press International, Inc., 1969). For an English translation of the *Minor Logic,* see *Hegel's Logic,* 3rd ed., trans. William Wallace (Oxford: Oxford University Press, 1975).

6. As Chapelle explains, Bruaire was not the first to emphasize the range of Hegel's theological dialectic and the importance of the philosophy of religion for Hegel's speculative thought (Janet, Wahl, Kojève, Weil, Hyppolite, and Peperzak, among others, preceded him). Yet, says Chapelle, his originality can be synthesized in three points: (1) Bruaire was the first to establish the proper place of the philosophy of religion within the whole of the Hegelian system. (2) He took seriously the contents of Hegel's philosophy of religion [in this double sense: (*a*) Hegel's philosophy of religion is a religion of Christianity, and (*b*) Bruaire re-elaborates all of Hegel's representation of Christianity]. (3) Bruaire took into account the whole of the Hegelian system and explained his own position as a Catholic thinker with reference to Hegel's philosophy. Cf. Chapelle, "Présence de Hegel en France," 16–18. Bruaire's most significant works in this regard are: *LR* (this will be our guiding text in the following pages); *EE; PM,* 270–86; "Hegel et l'athéisme contemporain"; "Hegel et le problème de la théologie"; "L'odyssée psychologique de la liberté."

7. *LR,* 17. Bruaire's emphasis.

8. "Accordingly, logic," says Hegel, "is to be understood as the system of pure reason, as the realm of pure thought. This realm is truth as it is without veil, and it is its own absolute

with other religions, lies in the fact that in it, the absolute has truly revealed itself;[9] God presents himself as a *determined* absolute being (and not as an indetermined, ineffable reality) whose nature is able to be expressed through language.[10] To say that God is the absolute and, at the same time, is determined, is to say that God, in some sense, must be in relationship, not so much with something outside himself, namely, creation, but, first of all, within himself. God, as Hegel's absolute subject, freely posits within himself the difference in himself and, at the same time, denies it; in this way, absolute spirit knows itself as absolute freedom.

If God had not manifested his own essence in its exact determinations, then one would have to acknowledge a possible difference between the God we come to know in revelation and God *in himself.* In this sense, God would have revealed something about himself, but in himself he could be different from what he appears to be. Hegel disagrees with this reading of revelation because, as Bruaire explains, it is biased by anthropomorphism; that is to say, it projects onto God the unsurpassable difference between freedom and the exercise of it which is proper to the human being. God manifests himself as he is, and he reveals to us that he is not an ineffable and undetermined absolute but rather the determinate absolute that gives his own nature to himself.[11]

If absolute religion and absolute logic can be identified, then revealed religion has a "permanent" value in Hegel's philosophical system. In fact, revealed religion is more than just a transitional "stage" for human knowledge, precisely because it is *a revealed* religion and God is truly expressed in the onto-logical discourse as he speaks himself. In this sense, absolute religion's *sublation* into philosophy, which the last section of the *Encyclopedia* suggests, does not eliminate this knowledge of the absolute acquired in revelation but unfolds it fully.[12]

---

nature. It can therefore be said that this content is the exposition of God as he is in his eternal essence before the creation of nature and a finite mind" (*WL*, 50).

9. Hegel, *VPR*, vol. 2, 188–205.

10. *Enzyklopädie*, §564.

11. *LR*, 25.

12. See *Enzyklopädie* §§574–77. For Hegel, understanding and salvation cannot be considered disjointedly, rather, "reason and salvation are of one piece" (*Hg*, 255). Exploring the depths of absolute spirit is, then, intimately connected with the understanding and the destiny of human existence. In this regard, the lack of a middle term between the finite human being and the infinite absolute caused the unhappy consciousness to be at the center of all

Bruaire points out that if one looks closely at the structure and content of the *Greater Logic*, its middle section, the doctrine of essence with its theory of *reflection*, turns out to be nothing other than a description of the process of the absolute's self-determination. Bruaire reminds us that Hegel refers to this movement of reflection whenever he tries to explain the absolute's process of self-determination and whenever he seeks to give an account of "the differences in this Christian God who relativizes himself, becomes flesh, and becomes Spirit within the community of believers." This doctrine of reflection would only be *delirium*, says Bruaire, unless it translates "God himself in his omnipotence of self-creation." This does not mean that the logic of essence describes the conditions for God's self-revelation. Rather, it is the verbalization, so to speak, of the content that revelation itself offers. The logic of essence, then, both portrays the absolute's movement from "nothingness to nothingness," that is to say, from the appearance of the phenomenon—which is being—to its truth, its essence, by means of an absolute negativity, and gives reason not only to the determination of absolute spirit but also to the "cause of its own being."[13]

The complete form of the absolute, in which this original act is finally perceived as determined and real, is the concept of the absolute, which is the manifestation of the truth of the essence. The process from being to concept through essence represents the full development of the concept toward its fullness, "from substance to subject," and translates the "divine auto-logy by means of which the absolute eternally determines itself." Although this act of autology, whereby the absolute posits itself, is so decisive for the understanding of the (divine) logic, Hegel does not begin his *Logic* with it. This is because, Bruaire tells us, the order of the movement from being to essence, and from essence to concept, is required by a cri-

---

religions (human efforts to reach the infinite) preceding Christianity (*LR*, 16). This is why for Hegel, as Bruaire writes, "incarnation fulfills rationality: all human efforts to reach the absolute, to penetrate into the infinite, remain sterile unless God comes to the human being" (*Hg*, 255).

13. *LR*, 24–26. It is useful here to remind the reader that Hegel dedicates the second and third sections of the *Logic of Essence* to this point. In the first one, *Die Erscheinung*, Hegel presents the ontological argument and talks about existence (*Die Existenz*) in terms of actuality, which is not yet posed by the reflection. In the second, *Die Wirklichkeit* (reality), the unity between the essence and its manifestation is made explicit and existence (in terms of *Wirklichkeit*) refers to the actuality posed by the reflection.

tique motif which, nevertheless, is only comprehended once the process is completed. One must begin with the simplest reality, the one closest *(vorhanden)* to nothingness, in order to be able to seize the appearance in its ultimate truth, the concept. Nevertheless, according to Bruaire, since in this process it is easy to overlook the creative source of the phenomenon, the deepest reason for this order is *theological:* "the logical discourse follows our recognition of the manifested God, whose being would appear as immediate, Christ as a man in his body, in order to reveal his divine personality. And this recognition is conformed to the constitution of the Son, Word of God, divinized nature and saturated of meaning thanks to the work of the Holy Spirit."[14]

Hegel's Logic Revisited

Bruaire, however, has no interest in pursuing a generic reading of Hegel's *Logic*. His concern, rather, is to show how its different elements may be comprehended through the same hermeneutical key. In this sense, the three stages in the pursuit of absolute knowledge (reason, dialectics, and speculative knowledge) reveal their ultimate usefulness when this theological content is made clear.[15] One cannot think of the concept of finite spirit unilaterally, sticking to its distinctive characteristics, because this would

---

14. *LR*, 28–29. This is the act of the intimate life of the absolute, which is the very content of divine revelation and without which revelation would be impossible.

15. Hegel's thought revolves around the concept of Idea, whose "full-blooded realization" is the notion of Spirit. This Idea, or Spirit, is nothing other than sheer intelligibility, the Aristotelian "noesis noeseōs" (Aristotle, *Met.* 12.7.1072b18–30), and it stands for the "whole" rather than for something pertinent to intellectual activity. All that there is, is spirit, which can have some material features—material features which are within thought itself. For Hegel, questions arise in thought and can only be resolved in thought (Hegel, *Phenomenology of Spirit*, 22). Thus one should not conceive of this Idea as something to be acquired by the human mind or something which is somehow "out there" for the human intelligence to grasp. For Hegel, there is no gap to bridge between the knower and the knowable. As he polemically phrased it, "the rational is the real and the real is the rational" (Hegel, *Phenomenology of Spirit*, 133; id., *Grundlinien der Philosophie des Rechts* [1821], vol. 5 of *Hauptwerke*, §6. See also *Enzyklopädie* §95). For Hegel, everything that speculative reason *(Vernunft)* can account for is within the realm of intelligibility already from the beginning. Thus, knowledge is not primarily referential or relational. That which must be understood is either already from the beginning within the realm of intelligibility, or it is not possible to grasp. Therefore, thinking must justify itself in terms of itself—although not in a solipsistic sense. See also Kenneth L. Schmitz, "Hegel's Philosophy of Religion," *Review of Metaphysics* 23 (1970): 717–36.

make the relationship between the finite and the infinite impossible. To supersede the finite characterizations and pass into their opposites, one must move from the level of understanding *(Verstand)* to that of dialectics. The latter shows that there is an inseparable relationship between the two terms at stake, in this case, God and the human being. Nevertheless, should human reasoning stop at the dialectical level—which should not be understood as "thesis, antithesis, synthesis"—it would remain imprisoned by oppositions or contradictions.[16] Thought would remain anchored in its negative moment, in which the finite moves into the infinite and from there back to the finite. Dialectics is thus unable to portray the necessary difference-within-unity that is proper to absolute spirit. This unity that unifies the opposites without identifying them can only be acquired at the level of speculative knowledge *(Vernunft)*.[17] At this level, one discovers that, for Hegel, the finite is within the infinite, that is to say, it is posited and, at the same time, denied. This positing of the difference within itself is valid not only for the relationship between the infinite and the finite but also within the absolute itself. Absolute spirit is thus both *determined* and *infinite* and therefore includes within itself its own difference.[18]

Hegelian logic portrays absolute spirit as *the* concept, that is to say, as

16. Understanding dialectics as thesis, antithesis, and synthesis is proper to Fichte. Hegel prefers terms such as negation, negation of the negation, and affirmation. The difference in terminology implies a difference in the understanding of the role that dialectic plays within the philosophical system and how it conceives "that which is." See *D*, 46–88. See also Emilio Brito, *Hegel et la tâche actuelle de la christologie*, trans. Théodore Dejond, S.J. (Paris: Lethielleux, 1978), with good bibliographical information regarding the theological aspect of the Hegelian dialectic; Fessard, *Dialectique des "Exercices"*. A fine presentation and judgment of Bruaire's *La Dialectique* can be found in Kühn, *Französische Reflexions*.

17. *Enzyklopädie* §§80–82.

18. *LR*, 47. The brilliant synthesis by Chapelle could clarify the issue here at stake: "La pensée spéculative, sans les séparer, distingue absolument l'acte éternel de la génération divine et le phénomène temporel du monde crée, lors même qu'elle les comprend sans les confondre, dans l'unité du mouvement de l'Esprit. La philosophie spéculative ne pense en effet la création comme position de l'autre que soi, comme différence différente de l'identité, comme particularité particularisée, que dans et par le mouvement de l'Idée qui est en soi l'Autre de soi, sa Différence non différente de soi, sa Partition immanente de soi par soi. L'identité de ce mouvement est celle de la Division absolue de l'Esprit: elle instaure la distance absolue de l'Absolu divin, conçu en soi comme totalité qui se détermine à sa position de soi dans la détermination d'une altérité sans Dieu" (Chapelle, *Hegel et la religion*, vol. 2, 161–62). For a more elaborate rendition of this important point in Hegel, see Manuel Cabada Castro, "Del 'indeterminado' griego al 'verdadero infinito hegeliano,'" *Pensamiento* 28 (1972): 321–45, 331–42.

that self-identical reality which bears within itself the particular and the singular. For Hegel, the concept is not the result of the process of abstraction. Rather, it is seen as something essentially universal (self-identical), whose nature is to determine itself in specific ways (particular) and to be expressed in a number of dialectically opposed individuals (singular).[19] The process of self-determination begins with the positing of the difference, with the partition (judgment) between the universal and the singular. The diremption (judgment) distinguishes that which belongs together; it separates that which the copula revealed as originally belonging to the same unity. Hegel believed that the different types of judgments gradually, and in an orderly manner, try to reach the unity of the elements which the judgment itself *(Ur-teil)* has separated. The classification of the different judgments (existence or inherence, reflection, necessity and notion) reveals an increasing progression toward the concrete universal. As with the level of concept, so also the level of judgment is read in a theological light, both in itself and in its relation to the level of the concept. This occurs because in the former case "judgment" describes the differentiation, deriving from an original unity, which seeks a more complete unity in which differences can be included. The latter case, the movement from concept to judgment, bespeaks even more clearly the process of the subject's own determination. This is why "the logic of judgment, like the logic of the concept, *translates the divine autology itself, the act by means of which the absolute determines itself.*"[20]

Although Hegel's apodeictic judgment is the only one that approaches that desired unity, it does not obtain it. In order for this unity to be fulfilled, a middle term able to bind the two given terms is needed. To move from abstract universality to concrete universality, the universal (which, by being the predicate of the judgment, represents its most important part) needs both the singular *and* the particular. For this process to come to completion, three elements, not two, are required: universal, singular, and particular. The process of self-determination reaches its goal, then, not at the level of judgment, but at that of the syllogism. Absolute spirit, which was only virtually present in the concept *(Begriff)*, and was present but

19. My presentation of the nature of the concept is indebted to Findlay, *Hegel: A Re-Examination,* 221–27.

20. *LR,* 52. Bruaire's emphasis.

still without perfect difference-in-unity in the judgment *(Urteil)*, is both present and united—posited and denied—in the syllogism *(Schluß)*.[21]

At the end of the *Encyclopedia*, Hegel presents philosophy as the supreme realization of the Idea, explaining with a threefold syllogism the way in which the relation among the moments of the spirit's circular process should be conceived. The syllogism—whose three terms are Logic, Nature, and Spirit—presents that movement of negation, negation of the negation, and affirmation.[22] The triplicity proper to this single speculative syllogism derives from the fact that each one, at its own term, will be the middle term of the other two, the major and the minor. Thus, the whole system can be read under the light of this "triple" syllogism: Logic-Nature-Spirit (§ 575); Nature-Spirit-Logic (§ 576); Spirit-Logic-Nature (§ 577).

The first syllogism, L-N-S, shows how absolute spirit passed over *(übergegangen)* from its beginning as a void concept (L) to the Spirit (S) through its own externalization (N).[23] This first syllogism reproposes, synthetically, the entire movement of the *Encyclopedia* itself. The exterior moment of the first syllogism is overcome by the second one, N-S-L. This, which Hegel calls the syllogism of reflection *(Reflexion)*, has the subjective and objective spirit as its center. It is the Spirit that here is seen as the means linking Nature—on which it rests—and Logic, because it gives the subjective knowledge *(subjektive Erkennen)* that characterizes philosophy. The third syllogism, S-L-N, has self-knowing Reason *(sich wissende Vernunft)*, the absolute universal, as its center. This syllogism presupposes the subjective activity of the idea, which is the characteristic of the second one, and it unifies the two previous moments, bringing forward *(fortbewegt und entwickelt)* the absolute idea to the perfect knowledge of itself. In this

21. Findlay, *Hegel: A Re-Examination*, 237–43; Hegel, "Der Schluß," *WL*, vol. 2, 90–92.

22. *Enzyklopädie* §§574–77. This triplicity can be found also in the first part of the *Enzyklopädie*. See, for example, §198, the syllogism of the State, in which Hegel brings together the three syllogisms he presented in §§181–92.

23. "The passage from the *Logik* to the *Naturphilosophie* has occasioned much difficulty, mainly on account of Hegel's riddling, anthropomorphic choice of expression. [At the end of his *Logik*,] Hegel suggests that the Idea is capable of further development: we must think of the Idea as 'freely letting itself go' *(dass die Idee sich selbst frei entlässt)*, while remaining 'certain of itself and tranquil within itself.' This complete freedom of self-determination leads to a result as completely free: the mutual 'outsideness' of Space and Time, 'existing absolutely to itself without subjectivity (cf. *Science of Logic*, II, p. 353, M. 843)" (Findlay, *Hegel: A Re-Examination*, 268). See Hegel, *Phenomenology*, 491.

syllogism, the subject and the object of knowing is the absolute idea itself, an absolute which divided itself *(sich ur-teilen)* into Nature and Spirit. The absolute idea, in this third syllogism, presupposes knowledge of itself (the second syllogism) and unites it to the actual objective knowing of itself (N).[24] This completed circle of the absolute spirit is what Hegel would call *the* true infinity.[25] True infinity is not simply a different type of negation; it is *becoming,* "it is reality in a higher sense than the former reality which was simply determinate; for there it has acquired a concrete content. It is not the finite which is the real, but the infinite."[26]

For Bruaire, Hegel's syllogistic theory, like his theory of the concept and of the judgment, affects not only the Hegelian onto-logic but also the constitution of the absolute itself *and,* because this is also connected to the coming to be and existence of finitude, the concept of Christianity as well. The syllogism is the "eternal work of divine conciliation," in which Christ unites the absolute with the finite *and,* in God, the Father with the Spirit. If this interpretation of Hegel is correct, then both the Christian religion and the concept of the absolute which Christianity discloses, the Triune God, can be illustrated syllogistically.[27]

Bruaire's ingenious theological reading of Hegel's system sheds a very

24. This trilogy can be also expressed thus: mechanicism, criticism, and absolute system. For a further clarification of the Hegelian syllogism's triple unity, see the enlightening examples in André Léonard's article "La structure du système hégélien," *Revue philosophique de Louvain* 69 (1971): 511–14. At this point it becomes comprehensible why Hegel decides to conclude the *Enzyklopädie* with a quote from *the* philosopher, Aristotle (*Met.* 12.7.1072b18-30).

25. "In Hegel's estimation, *this* circularity is true infinity—not the specious type of infinity which results from successively setting finite boundaries and then negating them, as happens in mathematical operations" (Howard P. Kainz, *G. W. F. Hegel: The Philosophical System* [New York: Twayne Publishers, 1996], 8).

26. Hegel, *Logic,* 149. See *Enzyklopädie* §65 n. 213. In his little book *Dialectics,* Bruaire describes the Hegelian movement of reflection as constituted by these four consecutive moments: (a) the beginning is an indeterminate void which, endowed with the promise of fulfillment, denies itself in order to become itself. (b) By denying itself, it becomes its other, the finite. Yet, (c) once it has become its other, it necessarily has to sublate itself by negating the first negation. The final outcome of this process (d) is absolute spirit, the concrete, singular universal. See *D,* 69–70. See also *Enzyklopädie* §94; Hegel, *Logic,* 153, remark 2, Infinity; Hegel, *Logic,* 137–57.

27. *LR,* 54. We shall return to Bruaire's treatment of Hegel's syllogistic theory when we address the issue of God's personhood and the presence of the Holy Spirit within the absolute spirit. In this chapter, the comparison between the two systems is limited to the elucidation of the specificity of Bruaire's anthropology.

helpful light on the imposing, complex work of the German philosopher and, at the same time, grounds the emblematic disagreement that separates Bruaire from him. Hegel's logic, Bruaire says, is proper to the absolute alone, but it is not applicable to the human being. To identify human with divine logic is, in Bruaire's judgment, unjustifiable. Hegel conceives divine logic univocally because divine logic is that "absolute and unique logic of the *revealed* divine life."[28] Even though the claim could be made that God's self-manifestation in history can be somehow adequately grasped by the human being, it does not follow that divine Logos and human language should be identified. Had the divine self-determination been spoken not by God but by a human being, one could then agree with Hegel's thesis equating human language about God with the divine Word.[29] Reflection on the hypostatic union of the Incarnate Word always needs to take into account Chalcedon's demarcation of the mode of the union: without confusion, alteration, change, division, or separation. That the divine Logos mysteriously speaks in the person of Jesus of Nazareth and that he does so in such a way that he can be understood by human beings does not mean that divine language has been absorbed by human language. The Christological dogma prevents us from confusing language about God with language of God (uttered by the Incarnate Word). *Deus semper maior.*

To explain his criticism of Hegel, Bruaire remarks that the syllogistic movement of the *Encyclopedia* (Logos, Nature, Spirit) shows that what is posited is also presupposed. The Spirit manifested at the end of the *Encyclopedia* is also the realized unity of Logic and History, which means, then, that the Spirit has achieved its fullness—a conclusion that confirms Bruaire's contention regarding the theological presuppositions of Hegel's philosophical system.[30] The outcome of the *Encyclopedia* thus indicates that Hegel "believes in the presence of the Spirit in him. . . . In fact, Hegel considers himself to be the absolute Word because he places himself at the end of History as the awareness of the last stage which reconciles ev-

28. Bruaire, "Hegel et l'athéisme contemporain," 80. Bruaire's emphasis.

29. *PM*, 78.

30. This is so because the Spirit is "au commencement dans le troisième syllogisme, au milieu dans le second, s'extériorisant en Nature et récupérant son Verbe à partir d'elle, créant et supportant le monde, réalisant et intégrant l'Histoire systématique et unitaire. Ainsi, la volonté de système se satisfait dans cette unification parfaite du langage absolue et de l'Histoire universelle" (*AD*, 109).

erything."[31] If this were not the case, it would not have been possible for him to appropriate absolute spirit in his reflection and to pronounce the "language of perfect Logic." The identification of the absolute spirit with human language, then, is prompted by the erroneous perception of the "presence of the Spirit" in human language. According to Bruaire, this confusion holds sway over Hegel's system because Hegel disregarded the importance of the human body for human language. In fact, it is precisely because Hegel "suppressed the role that the individual body plays, its contingency, and its *irreducible lack of conceptual meaning*," that he was "unable to explain the presence of the absolute logic of the absolute in human existence." Consequently, his neglect of the body is also one of the reasons why Hegel was unable adequately to differentiate between "the human finitude which implies the infinite, and the divine infinitude which eternally suppresses its own finitude."[32] As the analysis undertaken in the first two parts of *Philosophy of the Body* shows, there is no language if the human self is separated from the body because this is not simply a precious but disposable tool. For Bruaire, the link that unifies language, self, and body is far too profound to admit the mere use of the body as an instrument. Language, understood as rationality itself and thus as more than a set of grammatical and semantic rules, is not possible if the self is severed from the body. The separation of language from the body implies a divorce between words and ideas, a divorce that reduces language to a mere set of physical signs void of meaning.[33] If language is reduced to the multiplicity of languages, to a system of interconnected and arbitrarily chosen signs, then the *de facto* existing link with the body is lost and, with it, any acquisition of meaning is necessarily reduced to divine inspiration.[34]

Along with the importance of the body, Bruaire contends that his examination of the logic of human existence cogently illustrates the impossibility of equating human language with absolute spirit because, contrary

31. *AD*, 110.

32. *PC*, 133 (Bruaire's emphasis). It would not be exaggerated to state that Marcel's emphasis on the importance of the body to secure the distinction between the finite and the infinite prompts Bruaire's critique of Hegel here.

33. Cf. Bruaire, "Certitude, énigme ou mythe du sujet," *Revue philosophique de Louvain* 65 (1967): 226–38 (hereafter *CEM*). This article was published later in *PM*, 86–100.

34. According to Bruaire, when, as a result of modernity, the existence of God is put into question or simply denied as unreasonable, then the self, consciousness, is identified with his own body. See *CEM*.

to what occurs in the absolute, freedom and language are not identical in the human being. On the one hand, although the human being tends to complete self-determination and fulfillment, he is unable to accomplish it. The very existence of the "unhappy consciousness" witnesses to the insurmountability of human finitude. On the other hand, even though human language also expresses what God and man are, it is necessary to recognize that the human word, which in itself has a universal validity, cannot express the complete, mysterious, particular singularity of the person who uses that language.[35] Hegel's difficulty resides in the fact that his metaphysics includes a conception of the absolute which, although deriving from Christian revelation, is nonetheless "burdened by a philosophy of language which forbids its perfectly coherent exploitation." Bruaire notes that Hegel's intention in making use of Christian revelation is to overcome the otherwise unresolvable philosophical contradictions. The conjunction of scientific discourse on the absolute and Christian revelation, that is, Hegel's identification of absolute logic with absolute religion, yields a transformation of human knowledge into a system. Nevertheless, to defend this understanding of philosophy requires, according to Bruaire, the unjustifiable subsumption of divine language into human language. This is why Bruaire proposes the retrieval of a conception of language which is able to reestablish at the same time man's finitude and "the transcendence of a God who is absolutely free, and who speaks of himself, *en vérité* [truly]."[36]

Although Bruaire makes extensive use of Hegelian models of reflection (the dialectical scheme, the triple syllogism), he wants the freedom proper to the absolute spirit to be, indeed, *absolute* freedom.[37] It is in the name of freedom, understood ontologically, that Bruaire seeks to liberate God from the realm of necessity and to make his revelation in history not an inevitable consequence of his inner logic but rather a possibility with which the absolute can answer man's need for redemption. Understanding divine freedom as absolute self-determination does not, according to Bruaire,

35. Bruaire, "Réflexions d'un philosophe sur l'avenir de la religion," *Bulletin Saint Jean-Baptiste* 7 (1968): 239.

36. Bruaire, "Démythisation et conscience malheureuse (Colloque Castelli)," in *Archivio di filosofia* (1966): 383–93. The text was later published in *PM*, 71–85. See *PM*, 81. This conception of language is parallel to the distinction between finite and infinite freedom. See *Hg*, 285.

37. Bruaire, "Absolu," in *Encyclopaedia Universalis*, vol. 1 (1968), 51–54 (hereafter *As*).

bind God's essence to Hegel's tight relationship between divine and human logic. If the circular movement of reflection learned from Hegel is corrected by the insuppressible alterity between God and finite being—a difference which is secured by the existence of the human body and the specificity of human language—then Bruaire believes that it is possible to take advantage of it in order to formulate an anthropology that can preserve man's distinctive, limited, but nonetheless real freedom.

Anthropology's Seeming Negativity

Bruaire's anthropology proceeds in three consecutive and interrelated stages. The first part of the trilogy, as we already know, is his doctoral dissertation, which consists of two related, although independent parts: *The Affirmation of God* (1964) and *Logic and Religion in the Philosophy of Hegel* (1964). The analysis of human existence also requires an analysis of corporeality—the relationship between the body and the soul, to borrow more traditional terms—in order not to remain abstract. This is the question examined in *Philosophy of the Body* (1968). This book allows Bruaire to move further: the human being lives in a world and interacts with others. *Political Reason* (1974) presents a study of the polarity individual-state whose end is to show how the main political categories need to be conceived in order to build a society that respects both human and divine nature. I do not need now to give a full account of Bruaire's anthropology but should instead illustrate how at each of these three levels, the human being resists being identified with the logic proper to the absolute who, unlike the human being, exists in the perfect circle of reflection delineated in the previous pages. Bruaire adopts the form of Hegel's logic in order to plumb the dynamic of human existence, aware that the content of his logic is significantly different from Hegel's and thus requires that finite freedom and human history replace the necessity which Hegel originally conferred upon the science of logic.

The previous chapter presented the main elements of Bruaire's analysis of the logic of human existence. I should now indicate that, although following Hegel's dialectic and syllogistic speculative structure, the elements of Bruaire's dialectic and syllogistic theory are "desire, freedom, and language" and not the Hegelian "Logic, Nature, and Spirit." In Bruaire's anthropology, *desire* has taken the place of the Hegelian *Spirit,* and *freedom* replaces *Nature.* Bruaire's anthropological starting point is not that absolute spirit which needs, through its proper movement, to fulfill the promise of its own plenitude. The point of departure, instead, is desire itself, which, through language, seeks absolute spirit. Bruaire replaces Spirit with desire because he wants to safeguard both the totalizing nature of the absolute's freedom and the limited, but nonetheless real nature of human freedom. To replace "absolute spirit with desire" implies acknowledging that desire, or the human person for that matter, is not "a real and given absolute." It is freedom that brings the analysis of man's existence to "the *real* human condition" and shows itself to be, specifically, a concrete and particular freedom. Demanded by the analysis of human existence, the affirmation of absolute freedom, along with its negative sense of independence and its total self-determination, requires allowing the absolute the possibility of expressing itself (or not) in history. Giving to God what is proper to him, and thus defending the possibility over the necessity of his manifestation in history, implies that human language is not the mirror of divine logic but rather "the attempt to reveal, to represent that absolute truth we always need to have."[38]

In contrast to Hegel's understanding of the movement of the absolute spirit, Bruaire's syllogism of the logic of human existence does not result in a "complete" conversion into itself. A harmonious agreement between desire, language, and freedom would be impossible unless there were something else besides these three elements upholding the logic of human existence. In fact, at the same time that the syllogism of desire proves God's existence, it also demonstrates that human freedom is unable to sustain the unity with language and desire. Freedom's character of singularity does not allow it to prevent human disintegration. Moreover, the fact that freedom is an imperfect freedom in *reference* to the other two faculties makes it impossible for it to become the middle term able to balance and resolve the dialectical conflict between desire and language. If the logical development cannot but lead to the third syllogism, this same necessity brings us to acknowledge that, although desire proposes to freedom (which thinks speaking) the perfection of discourse as the infinite being of the perfect

38. *AD,* 110.

word, human freedom cannot ontologically produce the perfection of language that desire seeks.

Since, for Bruaire, there is a radical and real *difference* between finite spirit and absolute spirit, man's existence cannot be thought in exactly the same terms as those of the absolute's circle of reflection (i.e., reason, dialectics, syllogism). It is true indeed that for Bruaire, the logic of human existence is characterized by that circular movement in which the human being is called to become himself in his entrusting of himself to others and in returning back to himself. Thus, the human being has to live the unity proper to his existence through the difficult interaction between freedom, spirit, and language. Nevertheless, contrary to what would result from a unilateral transposition of Hegel's system of absolute reflection onto an anthropological reflection, Bruaire's understanding of the logic of human existence contends that the rhythm proper to the human being points out that the unity that constitutes the human being is constantly *given* to him.[39] Hence, the human spirit can*not* be explained from itself alone; the human spirit is radically and freely open to another in order to receive itself. The "openness" that characterizes the human spirit is a permanent dimension: it is given to itself in order to become itself in the circular movement of going outside of itself and returning to its own origin without having lost itself in the process. In order to return to its origin, the speculative conversion of the human spirit must recognize that it cannot fulfill this task without the mediation of absolute freedom. The circle of human reflection, by force of the ontological difference between finite and infinite freedom, cannot close itself *by itself*; that is to say, it cannot overcome its own finitude in a proper unity with the infinite without obliterating the difference between them. This is where one rediscovers the radical significance that desire has for Bruaire. Because of the ontologically decisive mediation of absolute spirit for the unity of the three faculties that constitutes the human being, the desire for absolute knowledge (an unhappy rationalistic expression) must be understood as the desire for God, and

---

39. Ten years after he published *AD,* Bruaire explained once more that, "En effet, où ma liberté infirme est trop petite pour inventer une alliance dont elle use, il faut une Liberté *absolue* qui en réponde, qui soit au fondement, au principe de sa réalité. Réalité d'une alliance que je peux détruire ou assumer, mais que je ne puis construire ni inventer par ma liberté qui lui est *relative*. Il y faut, en d'autres termes, le don de Dieu. Il le faut pour que soit assurée la logique de mon existence, et par elle, la logique de ma liberté même" (*DD,* 132).

not as the desire to be God—which could be another way of phrasing the problem behind Hegel's philosophy of language. This reduction would be understandable if one were to admit, with Hegel, that human language is the perfect transposition of the divine Word. Since, for the reasons given, this is not the case, the only true expression of human desire is the longing for God freely to fulfill human desire—something which is sought in the "language to God" and which the "language of God" makes possible.[40]

Bruaire's approach, while admittedly less abstract than Hegel's, could be more concrete. Undoubtedly, the human being is endowed with desire, freedom, and language. Nevertheless, he is also a historical being whose existence is not properly thought outside his *bodily* condition, a condition whose necessity must not be thought in dualistic or positivistic terms. The elucidation of this issue is the task undertaken in the second book of the trilogy, *Philosophy of the Body* (1968).[41]

Interest in the issue regarding the body derives from the fact that the human body is perceived simultaneously as necessary for and different from the human being. Although the self does not exist without a body, its essence cannot be identified with bodiliness. One cannot say "I have a body" or "I am a body" because both of these positions betray a dualism that is unable to explain the unity and the difference that constitute the human self. For this reason, Bruaire says, the search for the essence of the human self reveals a radical difference (within unity) between what I say, feel, or do, and my own self. To ask what the self is, is to ask for its own

40. The analysis of the different languages regarding God is presented as a metaphysical reflection aimed at the necessity of the affirmation of God's existence. Obviously, this "metaphysics" can only be considered such if metaphysics is conceived as the study of what is beyond the realm of physics, including man as that being in which being becomes aware of itself and looks for the meaning of its existence. If this is the case, then a case could be made that Bruaire's is a solid metaphysics. Cf. Chapelle, "L'itinéraire philosophique de Claude Bruaire," 7.

41. Besides *PC,* Bruaire studies the meaning of human corporeality in "Sens de la peine et non-sens du corps," in *Le Mythe de la Peine,* ed. Enrico Castelli (Paris: Aubier, 1967), 323–39. See Tilliette, "In memoriam," 237–48; Jean-François Marquet, "Corps et subjectivité chez Claude Bruaire," *Revue philosophique* 1 (1990): 71–78; Francis Kaplan, "Le problème de la mort dans la philosophie de Claude Bruaire," *Les Études philosophiques* 3 (1988): 329–38; id., "Philosophie du corps, par Claude Bruaire," *Revue de métaphysique et de morale* (1969): 118–22; Alain Cugno, "Bible et philosophie contemporaines du corps," in *Enjeux philosophiques de la Bible,* 145–62; Michel Renaud, "La 'Philosophie du corps' selon M. Claude Bruaire," *Revue philosophique de Louvain* 67 (1969): 104–42.

substance. "It is quite remarkable that it is the *body which brings us back to the ontology of the subject.*"[42] In order to think what the substance is, according to Bruaire, one must explain in what sense the human subject can be in itself without being, at the same time, in-and-for itself. The human self is in itself (substantial determination), and at the same time it is called to become what it is through the determination of its own freedom. Yet, the *bodily* condition *makes it impossible* for the human being to obtain, by his own means, that total self-determination which he seeks. The corporeality of the self makes of the human being a particular singularity and not a universal singularity. It is, then, corporeal existence that shows that the human being is given to itself in order to become itself. For this reason, the most concordant way of thinking the relationship between the existent determined particular subjects and the determined absolute is that of creation.[43] To know how to exist and how to live, being bound to a body in order to be someone, implies once more that at the very heart of the subject's existence there is an inexplicable source from which the human being is given and which makes his concrete existence possible. The philosophy of the body supplies, then, what the logic of existence requires in order to give to human existence its historical concreteness.[44]

Bruaire claims that in order to avoid the dualistic conclusion proposed by various negative theologies throughout the history of human thought, it must be demonstrated that only a positive understanding of the absolute as free, total self-determination can provide the reason for the corporeal human self. To affirm that there is discontinuity, a non-absolute-identity, between the subject and its corporeal system (linguistic and expressive) poses the question of the absolute which is to be thought as subject and system.[45] In other words, the conception of the absolute that is required by an understanding of the human being as singular and particular cannot but be "that of an absolute freedom, a God capable of giving to the freedom he created an ontological determination, because in this creation as in himself, God is the absolute act of determination, the institution of determined singularity."[46] By contrast, a negative theology, according to

42. *PC,* 236. Bruaire's emphasis.
43. *PC,* 253. See also *DD,* 139.
44. *PC,* 258–59.
45. Tilliette, "In memoriam," 243.
46. *PC,* 254.

Bruaire, leads to the dissolution of the absolute and of the human subject in its own corporeality.[47]

Just as there is no human freedom outside the dialogue with the absolute, so too there is no freedom apart from the relationship with nature (the most important being that of each person with his or her own corporeality) and no true exercise of freedom outside the interaction with other human beings. For Bruaire, the relation with the other entails concurrently the relation with others. Thus, *Political Reason* (1974), the book which completes the trilogy, concentrates on the study of the historical exercise of human freedom. Freedom's "social nature" prompts and requires the interaction with others and for that very reason exposes itself to the other's freedom; in doing so, it runs the inevitable risk entailed in the task of having to become itself in relationship with others.[48]

The book clarifies that the limitedness of human freedom (which in politics, among other places, can be seen in the transgressive uses of power and the inability of the weak to withstand any type of coercion) destroys any dream of a political system that is capable of giving meaning to that human freedom from which it sprang. Politics (or the politician) "ties the

47. Let me note, although *en passant*, that if the reduction of the body to the soul is properly denied, and if the substantial independence of the body and the soul is not tenable either, then *a* body is necessary in order to subsist (*PC*, 235–36). There is no salvation of the human being if it is not also a resurrection of the body. Bruaire is not stating the philosophical demonstration of the resurrection of the flesh. He is simply formulating its possibility (*PC*, 268). Kaplan disagrees with Bruaire's understanding of the relation between the body and the resurrection. Kaplan affirms that if the body with which one enters into that possible new eternal life is not the same body, but just a body, then it is difficult to see in what sense the dualism of body and soul is really overcome. Kaplan, "Le problème de la mort," 120. It seems to me that Kaplan has detected a real weakness in Bruaire's anthropology.

48. *RP*, 7–8. Other writings of Bruaire on politics worth noticing are: "L'enjeu politique d'une réflexion sur l'éternité," *Revue philosophique de Louvain* 68 (1970): 473–82 (hereafter *EnP*); "Politique et métaphysique," *Science et esprit* 22 (1970): 139–47; "Justice et eschatologie," in *Herméneutique et eschatologie. Colloque Castelli, 5–11 janvier 1971*, ed. Enrico Castelli (Paris: Aubier, 1971), 247–54; "Les ordres de justice," *Les Études philosophiques* 2 (1973): 141–44; "Politique et miséricorde," *Communio* 6 (1976): 18–22; "La justice et le droit," *Communio* 3 (1978): 2–4; *DD*, 142–51; "La philosophie du droit et le problème de la morale," in *Hegels Philosophie des Rechts. Die Theorie der Rechtsformen und ihre Logik* (Stuttgart: Klett-Cotta, 1978), 94–102 (hereafter *PdD*). Bruaire's discussion of ethical issues can be seen in *EM* and in "Réflexions d'un philosophe," in *Des motifs d'espérer?* ed. Emmanuel Hirsch (Paris: Cerf, 1986), 71–82. See also Hubert Grenier, "La pensée politique de Claude Bruaire," *Les Études philosophiques* 3 (1988): 339–45; Pascal Kyungu Ilunga, "La liberté comme sens du politique: Reflexion critique sur la pensée politique de Claude Bruaire" (Ph.D. diss., PUG, 1996).

[social] connections, but it [or he] does not give meaning to them; it constitutes societies, but it does not know the destiny of social existence."[49] Thus, in order to have a political system in which limited human freedoms are able to coexist, the difference between human history and its truth, eternity, must be affirmed. In fact, Bruaire does say that any given political theory is always sustained by a metaphysics in which the relationship between eternity and history must be thought out. The last, perhaps the most interesting part of *RP* is dedicated to the delineation of the nonantagonistic connection between eternity and history, patterned after the model of the intra-Trinitarian movement. Bruaire, following Schelling's interpretation, states that eternity should be translated as victory. Eternity is then the truth of history; it is metahistorical. Hence, it is only the power of the Spirit that is able to unite human beings, "giving them back to the Father, to the freedom of the children of God."[50] The unity that politics seeks can only be given.

Here as well it is possible to see that Bruaire claims the need to respect the *difference* between absolute and human freedom in order adequately to deal with the coexistence of human freedoms. Only in this way can a political philosophy be proposed that is able to take into consideration all the elements involved. Human beings' social interactions confirm that the architectonic of the categories involved in the analysis is not able to close the circle of reflection, as it was in Hegel.[51] *Political Reason, Philosophy of the Body,* and *The Affirmation of God* have the same outcome: an anthropology that cannot complete the circle of reflection by itself is not self-explanatory; it requires, therefore, an understanding of absolute freedom in positive terms, that is to say, an absolute freedom able to determine itself and to "create" another spirit which, although it is not absolute spirit, is "given" the task of determining itself in its relation to others.

It is precisely the recognition of that nondeducible and irreducible foundation of human existence that emerges as decisive for the structure of Bruaire's systematic anthropology. This cornerstone, as it were, is the constitutive character of "being given," which is proper to man's existence.

49. *LR*, 263.

50. *LR*, 263. Bruaire continues, "D'où le saurions-nous si le Fils lui-même ne l'atteste? Telle est la question, toute en rigueur, que le philosophe est en droit de poser. Droit pour la liberté, droit pour la raison, de capter une Bonne Nouvelle" (ibid.).

51. Bruaire, "Politique et métaphyisque," 140.

Bruaire describes the outcome of his anthropology as "negative." That is to say, the human subject does not posit itself, it does not possess itself fully, and hence it cannot complete the circle of its own self-determination. This is why, according to Bruaire, an adequate anthropology needs the other which is absolute self-determination in order to find the full reason for its own existence. The human being receives himself, in freedom, from another. Bruaire's anthropology, governed by an implicit concept of gift, is undergirded by a metaphysics that can be described as "positive," in contrast to the inner principle of negativity that characterizes the development of the absolute spirit in Hegel's *Logic*.

An Open Question

Although Bruaire contends that his systematic anthropology follows the Hegelian rhythm of Logos-Nature-Spirit—and undoubtedly his anthropology would not exist in its final form outside its tight relation with Hegel—an attentive examination of Bruaire's system precludes a too simplistic reading of the bond between the two.

Bruaire's anthropology concludes that, because divine logic cannot be absorbed into human logic, the rhythm of the Hegelian absolute spirit can only be rightly applied to the divine movement and only transgressively to human logic.[52] Bruaire thinks that the circle of reflection is an adequate approach to the *absolute,* provided that this is understood in terms of self-determining and determinate *freedom.* The Bruairean understanding of the human being's movement as "going out of himself," in order to come back to himself, so that he can be in and for himself, is different from that of the Hegelian Spirit. The Hegelian circularity of Logic-Nature-Spirit cannot, then, be simply equated with *AD-PC-RP.*

Although Bruaire's anthropology is indeed patterned after a syllogistic structure that has a Hegelian form, it is essentially determined by an understanding of alterity that has very little resemblance to Hegel's difference-within-unity. The other, as origin and destiny, as wholly Other and familiar other, with which one risks one's own existence, reveals the very anthropological incompleteness that prompts Bruaire's reflection to elaborate the positive ontology, the metaphysics of gift that upholds

52. Bruaire, "Primat de l'économie et chances de la philosophie," *Les Études philosophiques* 3 (1977): 264.

his anthropology.[53] Bruaire thus submits Hegel's system to a *radical* revision.

Bruaire nevertheless believes that it is still possible to use Hegel's logic to structure the logic of the human being. Bruaire contends that once Hegel's *Science of Logic* is understood theologically, its inner principle corrected as I have described, and the difference between the human and the divine preserved, then the elaboration of a systematic anthropology whose ultimate goal is to reanimate human freedom and to render divine freedom its due is made possible.[54] Bruaire thinks that once those corrections have been made, it is possible to use the *form* of the Hegelian system while pouring into it a different *content*. For him, the best way to understand the logic of human existence and man's endeavors in history is via a "logic" whose principle of movement is not the Hegelian negation of the negation but a *positive* donation that creates *(PC)* and sustains the finite being *(AD)*, which has to become itself *(RP)* in its relations to others. A question nevertheless remains open: is the enterprise of appropriating Hegel's speculative construction without adopting his main negative principle at all feasible? Since Bruaire's anthropology presupposes an understanding of the absolute, and given the fact that the fundamental change that Bruaire introduces inevitably affects the conception of the absolute, we must first explore his conception of the absolute and then his understanding of positivity to answer the question just raised.

53. Ibid., 266.
54. Cf. *LR*, 182–83; *DD*, 151.

CHAPTER 3

Absolute's Freedom

To enter into the question of man's existence is to immerse one-self in the mystery of the absolute itself. Every step of Bruaire's systematic anthropology reveals the impossibility of giving a satisfactory account of who man is if one's understanding of the absolute is inadequate.[1] Although from his very first works Bruaire contends that only a determinate absolute is able to make reason out of man's existence, his explication of what it means for God to be both "absolute" and "determinate" undergoes a remarkable evolution. Up until the publication of *For Metaphysics* in 1980, Bruaire's concept of God as determinate absolute advances following this pattern: first, that God is a self-determinate/self-determining freedom; then, that this self-determination is portrayed as self-donating freedom; lastly, that donation in God is best conceived as self-expressing freedom. Hence, the absolute determines itself, that is to say, it gives itself to itself; it expresses itself. During these years, the concept of gift, which at first is only an intuition prompted by Christian revelation and anthropology, acquires a grounded philosophical expression thanks to the coming together of three decisive concepts in an unconfused but nonetheless inseparable unity: freedom, spirit, and being. Bruaire's endeavor to articulate these three concepts provides us with some explicit descriptions of God in terms of

1. Xavier Tilliette reminds us that Bruaire himself said, before writing *EE*, that his anthropology could be considered finished without the metaphysics (Tilliette, "In memoriam," 240). Nevertheless, my contention is that there are crucial parts of the systematic anthropology and of his concept of the absolute that cannot be fully comprehended without his metaphysics of gift, and vice versa.

gift. At first, it seems that this attempt consists of two irreconcilable tracks: the first, absolute as self-determination, seems to be strictly philosophical, whereas the second, the absolute as revealed in Jesus Christ, could give the impression merely of being random incursions into the realm of theology. Nevertheless, the discovery that the logic of spirit should be perceived in terms of a logic of mercy breaks down this dichotomy and makes it possible to grasp absolute spirit in the light of gift.

Self-Disclosing Gift

One of the first references to the category of donation can be found in Bruaire's paper "To Know God" (1965).[2] Its overall intention is to present the terms in which the idea of God must be thought, while avoiding at all times the Scylla of anthropomorphism and the Charybdis of negative theology. Whereas the former says too little about God, because what is affirmed of him is too close to human nature, the latter, in trying to respect God's unfathomable mystery, reduces speculative reflection to silence because it posits too large a gulf between God and man. According to Bruaire, what takes place in Christian revelation is distorted in the terms of either of these two positions. In Christian revelation it is God who manifests himself in the person of Jesus Christ; it is a human announcement endowed with universal content. It should, then, be possible to say something meaningful about God without being deceived into thinking that one can completely probe the depths of God's mystery.

This interpretation is rejected by the atheistic claim of the impossibility of God's intervention in history. This judgment, says Bruaire, arises from an understanding of the absolute that is limited to its etymological sense: *ab-solvere,* that is to say, "free from something," understood here as free from any type of relationship, determination, or opposition. Thus, it is impossible to conceptualize the absolute because it is infinitely the complete other, *tout Autre.* "Accordingly, our words cannot find it": they are unable to give even a minimally acceptable rendition of it. If this is so, then the opposite is also true: God "cannot encounter us, come to this world, love

2. Bruaire, "Connaître Dieu," in *Dieu aujourd'hui: Semaine des intellectuels catholiques (10–16 mars 1965)* (Paris: Desclée de Brouwer, 1965), 157–65 (hereafter *CD*). See also Bruaire, "Démythisation et conscience malheureuse," *Archivio di filosofia* 2–3 (1966): 383–93.

us, save us."[3] In the end, any type of relationship would shatter this concept of an absolute devoid of meaning.

Instead, according to Bruaire, if God is perceived as the absolute, he should be thought in terms of "subject and freedom." The absolute is understood correctly when it is seen as an absolutely free subject. Now, if freedom in the absolute is to be perceived in this radical way, then the human being may not set limits to God's freedom by determining what he is able to do or, even more radically, be. If God is totally free, he can, if he so decides, establish a relationship with human beings and come to us without any loss of his divine nature.

> It seems to me that a Christian cannot know God if he does not recognize that whatever he offers of himself is a pure and simple gift, and that every relationship which he establishes with us is constituted by pure freedom in action, by the whole actual freedom which is his living person.[4]

Bruaire clarifies that if God is the absolute, then he is not only absolute freedom, he is also absolute intelligibility. If one avoids the error of thinking that the ontological distance between the human being and his language is also found in God, it is reasonable to affirm that God's Word expresses him completely. Since there is no difference between the Word and God, when God speaks himself he does so completely and truly. At the same time, the transparency of God's Word does not imply man's total comprehension of it. This incapacity derives from the fact that God is not a particular individual, as is the human being; rather, really and ontologically he is purely and simply, *singular.* Therefore, it is possible to elaborate a rational discourse about God without the illusion of either conceptualizing him or saying everything about him.

Philosophical discourse, however, cannot go any farther than either affirming the need for God's revelation in order to have an adequate understanding of God or recognizing the reasonableness of the possibility of God's revelation. Philosophy ends in the *waiting* that recognizes the need for God's revelation in order to know who he is and to elaborate a fuller—but never exhaustive—discourse about him.[5] When this historical

3. *CD*, 158.

4. *CD*, 160.

5. For Bruaire, philosophy brings us to the threshold of the mystery, where we must wait for a possible revelation. The same idea can be found in Plato's *Phaedo*; see *Phaedo*, trans.

manifestation of God takes place, all human expectations are frustrated *par excès*. God, in Christ, communicates that his being is pure act. God is "the initiative of the absolute gift of himself, in God and to ourselves."[6] Precisely because God is *gift* in himself, he can give himself, "come to us," without losing himself in the process.

In 1968, a number of philosophers were invited to a week-long conference for Catholic intellectuals in Paris. Its main theme was "A God-Man? Who is Jesus Christ?" Bruaire was the moderator of one of the roundtables whose participants were Levinas, François Varillon, and André Dumas. The subject for discussion was that of rigorously thinking the possibility of a God who could become flesh without loss of his divinity.[7] Besides the required conferences, the participants were asked to write a brief text in which they stated their own understanding of the revealed Word. Bruaire wrote the following:

> The Word *(Verbe)* of God became flesh. The Word offered itself to the intellect of men, which the Word secretly kept vivifying within the shadows where sin diverted man.
>
> But in this *gift*, the Word sacrificed his glory, veiling—for our sake—the light which he is, a light which perfectly expresses the whole of the *Father's freedom*. Revelation is the dispossession, the poverty, of the Son of man.
>
> The coming of Christ, origin and promise of our glory, is the abandoned splendor of the Son of God; it is the exile outside the plenitude of Joy and of Science which eternally rhythms the *play of love* of the divine Spirit.
>
> The commencement of Jesus Christ's history draws its invincible force of universal regeneration from the commencement without commencement which is the generation of the Son, first and last Fruit of the absolute Power; he is the unique Word *(mot)* of God in which everything is *created*, from which every meaning comes.
>
> What is impossible to man is the gift of God. Yet, what is possible to God is real in God: *absolute gift of himself*, complete diffusion of the divine being in the eternal Son.
>
> Jesus comes to communicate God to us, because he comes to announce the *absolute gift of God* which he *is*, exhausting the inexhaustible, the unique Fountain of Life eternally fecundated by the Spirit of Light.[8]

George M. A. Grube (Indianapolis: Hackett Publishing Co., 1977), 36. See also *AD*, 282–83; *D*, 151.

6. *CD*, 165.

7. Bruaire, "Un Dieu Homme?" *Qui est Jésus-Christ? Semaine des intellectuels catholiques: "Recherches et Débats"* (Paris: Desclée de Brouwer, 1968), 62: 185–86.

8. Bruaire, "Profession de foi," in *Qui est Jésus-Christ?* 246. Emphasis added.

If this dense response to the question "who is Jesus Christ?" is read carefully, it reveals in a synthetic fashion vital elements of Bruaire's understanding of donation. God is the absolute *gift* of himself to himself; God *is* gift. The absolute beginning without beginning generates its own Word in which he says himself completely. The very close relation between freedom and gift shows that God's dynamic of self-determination, whose moving energy is called *love,* unveils what is proper to God and beyond human capacities: total self-donation. In this gift of himself, the Son reveals that the Father is light, a light which is freedom and gift. God is free to give himself to himself, to create another being that can be in relationship with Him, to "come to us," and to bring history to its truth: eternity.[9]

Although Bruaire agrees with Schelling's saying that "the absolute is the only philosophical problem,"[10] from the outset of his reflection, and due to the intimations of Christian revelation, he perceives God not only as the absolute but as *gift.* This God, who can give himself without loss of his absoluteness, is at the same time the God of the philosophers and the God of Christian revelation. It is the same God, the same determinate absolute, studied by philosophical reflection and discovered in historical revelation, who gives Christianity its origin. Bruaire believes that *the* unavoidable provocation for any philosopher is the incarnation of God in Jesus Christ. For this reason, his interest in the idea of gift cannot be limited to a theological context. Thus, Bruaire thinks that considering the true enigma of both the human and the divine subject demands the coalescence of the categories of substance and being in terms of gift—an idea which he merely proposes at this point, to be developed further later on.

In "Certainty, Enigma, or Myth of the Subject," Bruaire writes that preserving the distinction between human and divine logic allows

9. Implicitly, this understanding of God in terms of gift means that the human being is also donation, although differently from God. The identification between donation and love is also explicit in two other important articles published shortly after this one: "Le problème de Dieu dans l'explication de l'erreur," in *L'infaillibilité. Son aspect philosophique et théologique. Colloque Castelli, Rome. 5–12 Janvier 1970,* ed. Enrico Castelli (Paris: Aubier, 1970), 73–90 and *EnP.* These two texts are published in *PM,* respectively, 156–65 and 216–27. If love is at the origin of donation, or, more precisely, if love is to be identified with gift itself, then it is necessary to elaborate this category of love—which is another way of saying positivity or infinity (*EnP,* 223)—so that it can render service to a proper metaphysics. The elaboration of this metaphysics, Bruaire tells us, has to explain God's inner movement and God's own time, eternity, in terms of an "ontological meditation of the free act" (*EnP,* 222).

10. Also in 1968, Bruaire published the article on the Absolute. See *As.*

one to recognize the Logos as "the perfect actuality of its absolute self-determination."[11] If the Logos is seen in terms of plenitude, then God's nature shows itself to be the gift of itself, and man's nature reveals itself to be a created freedom "endowed with substantial reality by the gift of existence. This gift of existence causes the human subject to be donated to itself, provided that it is true that gift, as act, contains and manifests the essence of the divine life."[12] The comprehension of the absolute as *pure act* or sheer gift makes possible an adequate comprehension of the truth of the (human) subject. Bruaire, then, is not only advocating an understanding of the absolute as gift; he is also suggesting that the truth of (divine and human) substance depends upon the category of gift. If it is true that the absolute is the absolute gift of itself to itself ("absolute self-determination," a term which still needs clarification), then the human subject *is* given to himself so that he can be. It should not pass unnoticed that if the essence of the divine life is gift, then the fact that the human subject is given does not refer only to the reason of his position in existence. That is to say, the givenness of the human subject does not refer only to the absolute, that is, to the goodness by which the absolute not only gives itself to itself but also gives itself outside of itself or *creates* what it is not. *Being-given* refers also to the truth of the substance of the human subject. In fact, the human being is not simply given, he is given "to himself," something which seems to suggest that gift is the ontological truth of the human being.[13]

Another decisive element for the development of the metaphysics of gift is to acknowledge that gift comes into play because God is thought of as the absolute, and, according to Bruaire, to think of God in these terms is to think of him as pure freedom. Indeed, God both possesses himself in the fact that he gives himself to himself (Trinitarian procession) and also gives himself outside of himself (creation). The human being, in his similarity to divine freedom, is free, not only because he is given to himself and hence possesses himself, but also in order to give himself to others.[14]

11. *CEM*, 226–38.   12. *CEM*, 100.

13. See also Bruaire, "Leibniz. L'articulation de la logique et de la théologie," in *Leibniz (1646–1716): Aspects de l'homme et de l'oeuvre. Journées Leibniz organisées au centre international de synthèse, 28–29–30 mai 1966* (Paris: Aubier, 1968), 233.

14. "Négation et dépassement de l'humanisme," in *Homo homini homo. Festschrift für Joseph Drexel zum 70. Geburtstag* (Munich: C. H. Beck'sche Verlagsbuchhandlung, 1966), 271–83.

The actual development of the category of gift, which is yet to be accomplished, must then bring together these three elements: substance (being), (absolute) freedom, and donation.

Absolute Freedom and Spirit

Between 1968 and 1974, Bruaire deepened his understanding of the nature of absolute freedom and indicated that its determination is not extrinsic, or ultimately foreign to the very essence of the absolute; rather, it is self-determination. The coalescence of the concept of freedom with that of spirit allowed Bruaire to show that self-determination is both the donation of itself to itself and the perfect expression of itself. Along with the systematic anthropology, Bruaire published three major texts in which he offers a sophisticated answer to the question concerning the nature of divine freedom. In the first, Bruaire explains what it means that the absolute is determinate. The second text is a book on Schelling (1970), in which he clarifies that the absolute's determination is to be perceived as self-determination, and this, as the donation of itself to itself. The third, the *Right of God* (1974), clarifies that the absolute's donation of itself to itself must be comprehended in terms of the perfect expression of itself, which, thanks to the mediation of spirit, is neither lost nor external to the source.

Determinate Absolute

In the article published in the *Encyclopedia Universalis* on the Absolute (1968), Bruaire acknowledges from the outset the ambiguity that characterizes this concept. Due to the influence of Fessard, as well as to his extensive study of Hegel and Schelling, the first connotation underscored by Bruaire in the concept of the absolute is the negative one: absolute means lacking relationship with what is not itself. The second meaning of this concept denotes a positive quality: "absolute" also means a completed and perfected reality.

A consideration of the absolute from its negative angle easily points us toward a misleading and fallacious understanding of the essence of the absolute. From the negative perspective, the absolute cannot have any type of determination because this would relativize and limit its very essence. Consequently, the most adequate way to describe the absolute within this outlook would be simply to say what it is not. It is not-finite, not-conditioned, form-less, change-less, and so forth. To remain in this perspective, and furthermore to avoid anthropomorphism, one must recognize that this "in-determination" places the absolute beyond the grasp of the human mind. God is said to be undetermined and thus—carrying this epistemological position to its ultimate conclusion—completely unknowable, although his existence must be postulated. Bruaire notes that once the absolute is located in that sphere of absolute otherness, it is difficult to disagree with Hegel, who stated the limiting our knowledge of the absolute to what it is *not* is practically the same as stating that the absolute *is* nothing.

This understanding of the absolute proper to negative theology, says Bruaire, presupposes conceiving the absolute as an "object" whose main characteristics are to be adequately perceived and exhaustively exposed. Nevertheless, since God's essence lies beyond the reach of the human soul, it may be concluded that it is impossible for man to know anything about God. Paradoxically, Bruaire sees that behind the irrationalism of negative theology's undetermined absolute there lurks a defective rationalism, which "refuses to understand the absolute as subject and freedom while clinging to an objective model of knowledge."[15] At this point, to be without God (the atheistic claim) and to be with a God totally beyond oneself are one and the same thing.

According to Bruaire, the negative conception of the absolute must be overcome by a positive one. Hegel's criticism of Leibniz allows Bruaire to show that only when the absolute is thought as subject and system, and not as object, can the negative conceptualization of the absolute be overcome.[16] This system cannot be represented as a perfect and independent set of rules and syntactic laws, independent of the reflective act itself. The system is the "act of the auto-determination of absolute freedom which eternally constitutes itself as the divine Word." If the absolute is thought

15. *As*, 51. In his continuous attack upon negative theology and mysticism, Bruaire is not rejecting mystical experience *in toto*. Rather, Bruaire directs himself against a contemporary understanding of negative theology wherein the affirmation of the limitedness of human reason as the measure of being results both in an utterly negative conception of the absolute and in the confusion of analogy and metaphor.

16. Bruaire's presentation of Hegel's criticism of Leibniz can be found in: *As;* "Formalisme et matérialisme," *Revue philosophique de Louvain* 65 (1967): 53–65 [also published in *PM*, 101–15]; "Leibniz. L'articulation"; "Leibniz et la critique hégélienne," in *Akten des internationalen Leibniz-Kongresses* (Wiesbaden: Franz Steiner Verlag, 1971), 5:247–54.

as subject and system, then it is possible to see that the real meaning of the absolute is not that negative perception of its "lack of relations" but rather its capacity to determine itself. "To think the absolute as a thing, as that which cannot be some*one*, is to think contradictorily and to dry up speculative thought."[17] Hence, the absolute cannot be prevented either from determining itself, or from entering into relation with itself, or with what is not itself. Given Bruaire's relationship with Hegel, in order to seek an explanation of the absolute's self-determination, one could refer without hesitation to Hegel's circle of reflection of absolute spirit. Nevertheless, for Bruaire, reference to Hegel suffices only if the intimations of Christian revelation and, no less importantly, the ingenious work of Schelling, especially his *Ages of the World,* are taken into account.[18]

Being's Mystery: Self-Determination

The opening remarks in Bruaire's book on Schelling explain that Schelling revives the search for the knowledge of the mystery of being as irreducible to what exists and that he does so in a more powerful way than Heidegger himself. This quest, spurred on by the need for truth, pursues the acquisition of the one philosophical system that alone can correspond to and adequately express the identical, simple, and irreducible idea of truth which always inhabits the human being. When the philosopher initiates his task, he discovers that the pursuit of the truth of being places him in the realm of absolute freedom. Trying to grasp what being is requires acknowledging that one must deal with eternal freedom, because freedom alone can "accomplish the identity between being and knowing."[19] For

17. *As,* 53.

18. Schelling's influence on Bruaire can be traced not only to the regard the latter had for Hegel, but also—and perhaps more importantly—to the influence of Bruaire's master, Gabriel Marcel. The influence of Schelling on Marcel's thought and the study of the former realized by the latter could not have passed unnoticed by Bruaire. Cf. Gabriel Marcel, *Coleridge et Schelling* (Paris: Aubier, 1971); id., "Schelling, fut-il un précurseur de la philosophie de l'existence?" *Revue de métaphysique et de morale* (1957): 72–78; Xavier Tilliette, "Schelling et Gabriel Marcel: Un 'compagno esaltante'," *Annuario filosofico* 3 (1987): 243–45. F. W. J. Schelling, *Urfassung der Philosophie der Offenbarung* (Hamburg: Felix Meiner Verlag, 1992); id., *System des transzendentalen Idealismus* (Hamburg: Felix Meiner Verlag, 1992); id., *Die Weltalter: Fragmente. In den Urfassungen von 1811–1813 herausgegeben von Manfred Schröter,* vol. 13 of *Sämtliche Werke,* ed. K. F. A. Schelling (Stuttgart: Cotta, 1856–61); id., *Philosophische Untersuchungen über das Wesen der menschlichen Freiheit und die damit zusammenhängenden Gegenstände* (1809), in *Sämtliche Werke,* vol. 14, 223–308.

19. *SQ,* 11.

Schelling, says Bruaire, the idea of truth carries the philosopher to that infinite freedom which escapes full conceptualization.

The infinite, contends Schelling, *is* freedom; it is not a shapeless undetermined reality but the unlimited power to give itself its own form. "The infinite rejects any boundary, even the impossibility of giving itself to itself."[20] While the human being's capacity to know the truth does not imply the power to act or to create that which is known, the absolute creative power is a real power which follows from absolute knowledge; absolute power and absolute knowledge are indivisible. The infinite's constitutive and inseparable unity of will and knowledge, says Bruaire, makes freedom itself the pivotal axis of Schelling's ontology.

The importance for Bruaire of Schelling's understanding of the absolute as freedom cannot be exaggerated. Its significance, however does not lie only in the emphasis Bruaire places on freedom but resides above all *in the way* in which freedom must be understood. In Schelling, as in Hegel, freedom is to be conceived as the movement of internal self-determination. Yet, whereas for Hegel the movement of self-determination is constituted by three moments, Schelling, the inventor of the formula later used by Hegel, remains faithful to an act which has only the *double* inverse motion of contraction followed by expansion.

For Schelling, the first movement of absolute freedom is the "self-contraction, the attraction of itself which objectivizes the subject for itself."[21] The denial of the unlimited extension of itself, which transforms the divine subject into an object for itself, is counterbalanced by the negation of the first contraction in the loving expansion of itself, which allows the absolute to recover its proper subjectivity. Despite the fact that the preponderance of the negative movement makes Schelling's rhythm of infinite freedom akin to Hegel's, a major difference separates them. Whereas Hegel considered his system to be successfully achieved, Schelling's dual movement remains deficient.

In his never finished *Weltalter,* Schelling presents his understanding of the divine essence, which begins with thinking the very possibility of God himself not from something outside of himself but from himself. Any other approach to being, to absolute freedom, including the ontological

20. *SQ,* 12.
21. *SQ,* 13.

argument, is an a posteriori examination and thus already presupposes an understanding of what God is. This task requires exploring in depth the mysterious and unfathomable absolute self-determining freedom. If one wants to grant divine freedom all that is proper to it, one must concede its right of self-determination; that is to say, one has to recognize that the divine nature does not answer to anything except itself. Contrary to what happens with other (created) beings, the nature of the divine being cannot be imposed upon itself from outside itself; it is not answerable to another greater design—regardless of whether this is conceived as blind necessity or sheer chance. To say that the divine essence has the right to determine what it wants to be does not mean that there is an entity already formed that can determine what to be or change its own being according to different possibilities. It simply means that the absolute only owes to itself what it actually is. When the human being attempts to know who he himself is, he sets out toward the *discovery* of himself because he has not made himself. In this adventure, he is forced to recognize that he cannot remove that layer of mystery which constitutes his own being. But, for the absolute to think of itself does not mean to discover itself, but rather, bearing in mind the indissociability of truth and will, it means to "make" itself. For Schelling, then, according to Bruaire, to think who God is, as from himself, means to explore the autogenesis of absolute freedom. And, as Bruaire clarifies, because Schelling is dealing with the "origin" of absolute freedom, thinking this autogenesis must be done in terms of "an eternal history which reflects itself in our history and which takes, by means of this reflection, the detour through Christian revelation." This search for God's nature, which starts from its absolute freedom, involves seeking the ontological structure of that life which God "chooses, decides upon, and gives rise to from the bosom of his freedom."[22]

Bruaire recalls that Schelling's discourse must move to the grounds of the pre-ontological in order to find an evocative discourse that is able to avoid the illusion of thinking that the ground for the ontological discourse is already there. When the human mind tries to reach the "origin itself" of absolute freedom (which is called *Ur-Grund, Ur-Wesen, Ur-Zeit, Ur-Kraft*), the most adequate symbol is that of a *father*. But here, once more, "father" must be understood in the absolute terms of a father who has not been the

22. *SQ*, 55.

son of a previous father. Bruaire points out that in his evocative language, Schelling proposes the image of a "subtle breath" in order to present what this generation is like. As the image demands, the first movement of the breath is that of inspiration. The primitive inspiration is what gives origin to the initial will that makes being possible. Yet, this force of bending into itself, this first contraction into itself, "releases the diffusive force of the expansion." The force of inspiration, the aspiration to itself, grounds the *"exclusive singularity"* of the absolute freedom by giving origin to the inexhaustible expansive force of love, which counterbalances the force of the divine seclusion within itself. Expressing the divine rhythm at the very center of this contractive energy in theological terms, Bruaire affirms that from the Father springs the Son, who reveals the entire divine essence: absolute freedom. This "divine pulse" of contraction and expansion, of systole and diastole, cannot preserve its unity without the Spirit, by which it can be perceived that these two movements, although opposed, can never exist in separation. "The Person of the Son makes present the Past of the Father only through the free will of the Spirit."[23]

It seems that conceiving self-determination as decision jeopardizes God's eternity. In fact, if God is "eternal," why speak of "origin" in God? To linger on the temporal aspect of the image proposed by Schelling is to risk depicting this beginning anthropomorphically. In fact, Bruaire says that just as the divine origin is a Father who has never been a Son, so too the beginning or the "eternal Past" which he is cannot be thought of as a beginning which follows the end of something previous to it. To think the beginning in absolute terms with Schelling implies abandoning the linear understanding of time, by which the beginning presupposes an antecedent end. In the realm of divinity, the beginning cannot be thought of separately from that which begins. In this way, this origin is a commencement without commencement, a beginning without beginning: "God does not have a nature constituted by the identity of all the qualities. His freedom gives himself to himself, but it does so by choosing to begin *the gift of himself to himself* in absolute terms."[24] And this peculiar origin is the only necessity that can be ascribed to absolute freedom.

Bruaire cautions against understanding the movement of donation

23. *SQ*, 59.
24. *SQ*, 60. Emphasis added.

inaccurately. According to Schelling, in order for the divine movement to begin, the "first step" must be negative: "a *negation* which, completely active, is *desire of itself (Sehnsucht)*." As the image of respiration shows, where the inspiration gives origin to and makes possible the expiration, in the same way, the affirmation buds forth from the negation. The divine "Yes" arises from the "No." This preponderance of negativity over positivity comes from the fact that the "No" of the retraction, of the inspiration, of the interiority, makes the beginning of its contrary possible, and neither of them can be without the other. Bruaire clarifies that to give precedence to the "inspiration" or the "systole" underlines the absoluteness of divine freedom—an absoluteness which is formed by those two moments of inspiration and expiration. There is no divine wrath without infinite love, and vice versa. The fact that the "No" underscores that absolute freedom does not respond to any prior principle in order to be itself must be seen together with the fact that divine freedom is itself only when the "No" and "Yes" are kept together. While it is true that one tends to prevail over and against the other, nevertheless, in their tension they are brought together in unity by the "third power" of the existence which is the "potential end, in the same way that the first negation is the potential beginning of eternal life." In order for these three potencies to leave the realm of potentiality and enter into that of actuality, only one thing is necessary, "the immemorial decision to exist."[25]

Bruaire sees in Schelling's philosophy the concept of an absolute freedom that determines itself by *giving* itself to itself. It is crucial, however, to acknowledge that at the heart of the absolute's "donating" movement there lies for Schelling the presence of a negativity which radically determines the nature of this "donation." The primacy of the negative in Schelling prevents us from understanding this absolute donation in terms of *gratuity,* although this does not necessarily mean that the explanation of the spirit's movement itself should be discarded altogether.

Living Spirit

Marking an advancement from his earlier writings, Bruaire's *The Right of God (DD)* approaches the reflection on man's and God's nature and their mutual relation through the concepts of *being* and (absolute)

25. *SQ,* 62.

spirit. "It is indeed necessary to reflect at the same time on our aspiration to be and on our search for the spirit."[26] Looking at the human spirit, one discovers that it is impossible to separate its desire to be from the search for the *other* spirit.

In his search for what corresponds to him, what is able to quench his thirst for being, man discovers that nature is opaque to that desire *(désir)*. Nature can only respond to some of man's needs *(besoins)*.[27] It remains silent when it comes to that other, far more decisive need *(désir)* which, although *rooted* in nature, is not "natural," but "spiritual." In this sense, "nature" cannot constitute the most proper "other" of the human being. Man's ontological lack causes him to be a "demand of spirit."[28] That sought-after spirit is not just another human spirit or even the unity of all of the human spirits. The only adequate alterity that can respond to a human being is the absolute other, which not only is never seen in opposition to the human self but is grasped as the one which alone could fulfill the promise of eternity that motivates every human endeavor.

To explain his concept of absolute spirit, Bruaire makes use of the contributions, on the one hand, of German idealism and, on the other hand, of the intimations of Christian revelation. For this reason, he is able to say that self-determination, a beginning without beginning, is the eternal decision of positing oneself—an act whereby the positing and what is posited are identical. The reflection of the absolute freedom "*gives* to itself that nature" which is the presupposition of the reflection.[29] In describing what is intended by "positing oneself," and without neglecting his analysis of Schelling, Bruaire welcomes the intimation of Christian revelation which suggests that the most adequate way of articulating the divine

26. *DD*, 70.

27. I need to alert the reader to a terminological difficulty with the term "nature" in Bruaire's system. In Bruaire's French, "la nature" means "the subhuman world." It does not stand for essence. If this were the case, "nature" would be applicable both to the finite and the infinite, and one could talk about a "human" and a "divine" nature—as is found, for example, in Aquinas. The concept of "nature" has undergone a systematic transformation: with Descartes, *natura* acquires the meaning of "*res extensa*"; with Spinoza, the meaning of "substance"; and with Hegel, a moment of the Spirit's development toward subject. In Bruaire, one can find a nonexpanded concept of nature in which "nature" and the "spirit" are thought as opposite terms.

28. *DD*, 70–71.

29. *DD*, 72. Emphasis added.

eternal movement is that of the divine processions. The absolute origin, the Father, generates the Son, and the Spirit proceeds from both. Bearing in mind that the model of this reflection is the Trinity itself, it may then be seen that the movement of self-donation implies two things: donation is unlimited and comes to full circle. To say that donation has no limits means that it is the *whole* of itself which is given. If what is given were only partially given, then the philosophical reflection surreptitiously presupposes that there is a "more original" principle which creates that absolute which is here under discussion. To avoid begging the question, it is necessary to realize that the donation of the absolute does not admit of parts. The absolute freedom, the absolute origin, must be able to give all of itself. "What Freedom gives itself to be is then freedom itself, and that infinitely, totally: what is given is *the gift* of itself."[30] In order for the self-donation of the absolute to be true and not to lose itself, in addition to its complete giving of itself, what is given must return to the origin. If the "nature of the origin" is that of giving itself completely, what is given would become "something" foreign to the origin itself unless it were able to return to the origin; in this case, absolute freedom would remain an unsurpassable indetermination. As Hegel suggested, "the rigorous conception of the absolute requires us to think as the same act" the donation of itself and "the return to itself, the return to the Origin, to the source of being, of the Fruit of the whole of freedom. This return, which closes the reflection (and which Hegel called the 'counter-thrust' of the Spirit), constitutes in the bosom of God the being-for-itself, its own being, Itself."[31]

For Bruaire, the intimation of Christian revelation indicates that the donating movement of the Father to the Son, and of the Son to the Father, can be described as the *expression of himself in himself.* God should not be thought of as a silent entity. Yet, this Word, which God pronounces and with which he remains united by the act of the Holy Spirit, is not a random expression of himself. The immemorial decision to express himself is the determination or constitution of himself. Absolute freedom is itself only in the donation of itself, in the expression of itself—a donation and an expression of itself that is not lost as is the human word but that

30. *DD*, 75. Emphasis added.
31. *DD*, 74. "Counter-thrust" attempts to translate both the German *"Gegenstoss"* and the French *"contrecoup."*

expresses the origin completely and does so by returning, in the Spirit, to it. Bruaire establishes in this way that God, the absolute freedom, is this eternal movement in which the origin expresses (gives) itself in its Word which, at the same time, in the very same movement, returns to the source thanks to the force of the Holy Spirit. Thus, the threefold movement of donation is the structure which, according to Bruaire, constitutes the eternal act of self-determination.

That absolute freedom is to be understood as a "movement" of self-determination is nothing other than the affirmation that the absolute is *spirit*. In this regard, if absolute freedom is conceived of as "spirit," then the "full but lifeless" idea of the self-determination becomes endowed with a living *rhythm* of contraction and expansion, of folding over itself and of opening, of possession and gift. Bruaire uses the Hegelian scheme of the circular reflection of absolute spirit to portray the movement of self-determination, and he uses the "ingenious meditation of Schelling" to escape from the rigid idea of a self-determining movement that lacks both rhythm and life.

> Unity, the balance of No and Yes, of the contraction which singularizes, personalizes and of the expansion in and through which infinite love is expressed, that is, God, lives countercurrently to his two Powers which neutralize themselves at the central point of their mutual flux only in order to gush forth the Word, in which they unite themselves and find their common wish (vow).[32]

Bruaire thus maintains that the movement of self-affirmation, whereby absolute freedom gives itself to itself, must be simultaneously perceived as the movement of absolute spirit which "makes God's heart beat in the rhythmic Expression of his Word."[33] Our knowledge of God as *absolute spirit*, which is the gift of himself to himself, is not complete unless philosophy proposes a thorough reflection on the concept of *spirit*. In fact, although Bruaire has dealt with the issue of the nature of freedom, the link between freedom and being and the positivity of the donating act still need to be thoroughly treated. Only in this way does it become possible to elaborate a metaphysical reflection capable of giving consistency to the interpretation of being as gift. According to Bruaire, the concept of spirit

32. *DD,* 95.
33. *DD,* 96.

is the path through which one can come into the possession of being with all its depth. In this sense, one could say that the reflection on absolute freedom brings Bruaire to the concept of spirit, and the concept of spirit brings him to that of being. Once one understands the reasons why spirit has been dismissed from the understanding of reality, it is possible to see that philosophy of spirit and ontology always go hand in hand.[34] The "urgent task," the undertaking of which is of utmost importance, is then a renewed *ontology of spirit.*[35]

The Logic of Mercy

The elaboration of an ontology of spirit is possible because during the six years between the completion of his systematic anthropology and the publication of *For Metaphysics* (1980), Bruaire's philosophy takes a major step: the affirmation of spirit's positivity. In the two previous sections, I showed that Bruaire's reflection on absolute freedom yields the concept of gift as its most adequate expression. Bruaire arrives at the concept of donation by appropriating what he considers to be the key to Christian revelation: the absolute is freedom (understood ontologically and not as an attribute); hence, it determines itself, it expresses itself, it gives itself to itself. Absolute freedom, "by its pure initiative, decides to be the gift of itself in the Son, a gift which takes place in the uniting effusion of the Spirit."[36] I have also indicated how decisive this perception of God as gift is for Bruaire's understanding of the structure of human existence—which, however, is still seen through the lenses of a "negative" anthropology—and

34. Bruaire, "Conversion et communion dans la foi aujourd'hui," in *Cahiers "Lumen Gentium"* (Paris: Association Sacerdotale "Lumen Gentium," 1978), 8. In addition to in *DD*, between 1974 and 1980 Bruaire presented his understanding of spirit in the following essays: "Le sacré et l'apparence," in *Le sacré: Études et recherches. Colloque Castelli, 4–9 janvier 1974,* ed. Enrico Castelli (Paris: Aubier, 1974), 113–20 (also in *PM*, 233–42); "Sécularisation et demandes de l'esprit," in *Herméneutique de la sécularisation. Colloqui Castelli, 3–8 janvier 1976,* ed. Enrico Castelli (Paris: Aubier, 1976), 249–55 (also in *PM*, 243–52).

35. Bruaire, "La foi chrétienne et la science d'aujourd'hui," *Revue des sciences morales et politiques* (1979): 575. For the consequences of the neglect of the Spirit see *PM*, 250; "Le nouveau défi du paganisme," *Communio* 1 (1975): 28–33; "La philosophie du droit et le problème de la morale"; and *POnEs*. See also *PM*, 245, and *EM*, 145. In *DD*, Bruaire proposes an initial explanation of the concept of spirit, which he develops in *EE*. The following chapter is dedicated to the study of this concept of spirit.

36. Bruaire, "Le Dieu de l'histoire," *Communio* 4 (1979): 5.

that the concept of "donation" in the French philosopher cannot simply be equated with Schelling's because of the primacy that the latter gives to negativity. This discrepancy between Schelling and Bruaire can also be found between Hegel and Bruaire since for Hegel too (according to Bruaire), the positive act of freedom is secondary to its principal negativity.

I mentioned that Bruaire appropriates the Hegelian reflection on the absolute and corrects it with that of Schelling, to present in the end his own understanding of absolute freedom. Yet, whereas in *DD* Bruaire seems not to distance himself from the negative aspect of the rhythm of absolute freedom (inspiration precedes the expiration movement of the loving expansion), he reaches a point of no return when he corrects the negativity of German idealism with the spirit's positivity as learned from Christian revelation (not understood in a Hegelian way). In fact, the Hegelian system, according to Bruaire, lacks the superabundance, grace, and glory that are constitutive of Christian pneumatology. Bruaire holds that attributing primacy to the negative over the positive is a very subtle anthropomorphism. "Without a doubt," he tells us, "in ourselves, only the negative connotation of independence is the sign of the absolute freedom." Nevertheless, this is not what takes place in the sphere of absolute spirit:

> If, on the contrary, absolute freedom is the *generous initiative which disarms in advance every rejection of itself, the negative [element] is not at all the first one,* and the privation of being in act is not at all original. It is rather the rejection of a negation, but as a force which repudiates the jealousy of its own sovereignty.[37]

Bruaire believes, then, that for Hegel, absolute spirit cannot but manifest itself and do so completely and in a kenotic fashion. For Bruaire, however, since the absolute is not a sheer emptiness bound to manifest itself in order to become itself, the manifestation of the Spirit does not follow a blind necessity. The manifestation of absolute spirit reveals the eternal decision of determining itself in that perfect expression of itself which is not lost because of the uniting power of the spirit. There can be no "silent absolute," not because absolute spirit must express itself in order to become itself, but rather, because in its *fullness* it cannot but say itself totally and perfectly.

---

37. *POnEs*, 70. Emphasis added.

Bruaire agrees with Hegel that there is no spirit without its manifestation. Nevertheless, it is also true that every manifestation of spirit veils at the same time that it unveils. Even though within Christian revelation we learn something decisive about God's nature, what is not seen is far greater than what one actually perceives. Historically speaking, *quoad nos,* divine revelation appears always as a mysterious kenotic love. Bruaire says that Hegel explains that this manifestation is both necessary and that it takes place not as a paradox but rather as a manifestation *sub contrario.* Yet, says Bruaire, if one wants to comprehend in what sense God's love is willing to embrace suffering in order to save mankind, this manifestation-in-hiddenness must be understood as being historically conditioned. For Bruaire, the kenotic manifestation is proper only to God's historical appearance and not to his internal movement, because God in himself is that absolute spirit which is the "superabundance of creative energy to the point that, so to speak, its manifestation infinitely exceeds its nature, and forces being to appear in full light."[38] Bruaire is able to associate the idea of spirit with that of being, without ending up at the impasse at which Hegel's system arrives, because Christian revelation teaches that the ontology of spirit must be thought within the logic proper to the spirit, the *"logic of mercy."*[39]

To speak about mercy when setting the basis for an ontology of spirit could seem a rather outrageous and unjustified transgression. What is a theological term, presumably suitable only for soteriological discourses, doing in the realm of metaphysics? Should not the concept of mercy be limited to the discussion of sin, redemption, and the Christian's social interaction? Furthermore, does not the concept of mercy, with regard to

38. *POnEs,* 69.

39. From 1974–1980, Bruaire has to come to grips with several issues which prompted him to explore the meaning of charity, both for ethics and for his philosophical reflection. Let me point out to the reader that, before the publication of *EM* (1978), there are three main publications between 1975 and 1976 that reflect upon this issue: "Le nouveau défi du paganisme" (1975); "Politique et miséricorde" (1976); and "Sécularisation et demandes d'esprit" (1976). The first use of the idea of mercy appears in 1971. Within this context, Bruaire begins to discover the significance of the "logic of mercy" for his own reflection. At first he uses this concept to explain that "mercy" is the true Christian justice. It is not until 1975 that Bruaire will approach the concept of the absolute in terms of freedom, a perspective that prompts him to elaborate a renewed ontology. See "Justice et eschatologie," 247–54 (this article is also published in *PM,* 204–15). I am indebted to Chapelle, whose article on Bruaire's thought helped me to acknowledge the importance of the concept of mercy for the formation of his *ontodology.* Cf. Chapelle, "L'itinéraire philosophique de Claude Bruaire."

the ontology of spirit, constitute a flagrant theomorphization? Although it could be said that God is merciful with the human being, in what sense can mercy be applied to the spiritual *divine* movement? Is not Bruaire absorbing philosophy into theology and thus committing the very same error as Hegel, albeit in the opposite direction? An additional complicating factor is that, according to Bruaire, in the modern perception of Christian morality, mercy has been equated with a certain kind of unwarranted and sometimes unreasonable equanimity before adverse or harmful situations. In this sense, "mercy" would be identified with a type of Christian justice which, in light of the current structure and actions of the so-called "Christian works of charity," seems not very different from the pursuit of social justice common to contemporary democratic societies.[40]

It is true that mercy is a term that humankind has learned from revelation and that it describes God's attitude before man's response to the divine decision to create an intelligent and free creature who is able to recognize absolute spirit as the master of being and, thus, his most adequate other. For this reason, it would appear to be correct to affirm that the concept of mercy is a theological intrusion into metaphysical reflection. Nevertheless, for Bruaire, in addition to its theological value—not to be confused with the contemporary watered-down understanding—the concept of mercy has an "ontological" meaning. Bruaire believes that it can be used within philosophical reflection without committing that type of transgression which reduces philosophy to an "embarrassed theology."

Mercy, Bruaire tells us, describes first and foremost the nature of the absolute beginning: it is an absolute, unexpected, and completely gratuitous beginning. In this sense, the absolute is ever-greater, ever-surprising in and for itself before being so for us. Of course, "gratuitous" does not mean that the beginning could have not taken place but rather that it is sheer positivity.[41] If divine freedom is the actuality of the spirit, mercy represents, on the one hand, the free decision to determine itself as the total gift of itself, and, on the other hand, the resolution discreetly to give itself outside itself. In this sense, Bruaire finds in the term "mercy" the same predicates as he does in the concept of "spirit."[42] When applied, then, to

40. Bruaire, "Le nouveau défi du paganisme," 28–31.

41. Bruaire, "Sciences humaines et anthropologie philosophique," *Les Études philosophiques* 2 (1978): 151.

42. Bruaire, "Politique et miséricorde," 22.

absolute spirit, mercy does not mean the forgiveness of a transgression but the superabundance of the gift which absolute spirit *is.*

Bruaire's association of the concept of absolute freedom with that of mercy brings him to the threshold of a renewed ontology in which the absolute is conceived of as pure self-determined positivity which, in its superabundance, decides to create another spirit, albeit not an absolute.[43] The conception of absolute freedom as spirit whose nature *is* mercy allows Bruaire to counterbalance Hegel's understanding of absolute spirit and to set the basis for an ontology that respects the nature of God as pure gift, while not identifying the historical manifestation with the divine movement of self-donation.[44]

43. With reference to the human spirit, the term mercy reveals an important characteristic: mercy regenerates "the gift of existence . . . and its promise binds the unity of being under the sign of the living link between nature and spirit" (*PM,* 251). With regard to the human being, mercy entails two decisive facts. Absolute spirit's first act of mercy on behalf of the human spirit is the creative act. Once the human being has come into existence, mercy takes the form of a gift which is given again (for-given), and also the form of the promise of a possible confirmation in existence in which any disunity between the human being and its own spirit would be eternally impossible. In this second sense, "mercy" represents a final and definitive confirmation in existence, i.e., the absolute's mercy gives the finite the possibility of eternally remaining in being. Undoubtedly, the issue that still needs to be studied is the problem of evil. From Bruaire's understanding of the logic of mercy, it is possible to see that evil is conceived of as rejection of one's own being and way of being. This is why mercy can be explained in terms of the reoffering of the possibility of being.

44. Bruaire's ontology never makes use of the term "mercy" to describe the absolute's positivity after 1979. This concept is replaced by another which plays a decisive role (if not *the* decisive one) in Bruaire's ontology of gift: "confirmation." As we shall see, confirmation means to reaffirm in existence, to make the spirit be, and thus it comprises mercy, whose Latin root, *misericordia,* implies "graciousness, gratuity, no claim." Confirmation is thus linked to the original (ontological) freedom, and it means that superabundance or excess of love which alone characterizes the nature of absolute spirit.

PART II

The Ontology of Gift

CHAPTER 4

Retrieving the Spirit

Bruaire's approach to metaphysics takes place within the wonder of the encounter with the *other,* which presents itself as that which *is, as* it is. Regrettably, as Bruaire illustrates, this wonder has been lost in our modern world because the reality of the spirit is no longer seen; more so, spirit has become an incomprehensible concept. To eliminate this deficiency, Bruaire proposes to restore the concept of spirit, a task which involves facing three different issues: explaining its importance and the way metaphysics should approach it; accounting for and tracing the main consequences of the disappearance of spirit; and providing a phenomenological analysis of the being-of-spirit that is able to recognize its presence and to describe its most fundamental elements. The elucidation of the last of these enables Bruaire to approach absolute spirit and to examine in what sense it can be understood in terms of gift. The pure concept of spirit, or absolute spirit, will be explained in the last two chapters, while this chapter addresses, in three parts, the concept of the human spirit. The first part presents Bruaire's understanding of the relationship between being and spirit. The second attends to the causes and consequences of the loss of the concept of spirit. The last part discusses Bruaire's concept of spirit, its semantics, and its phenomenological analysis.

Otherness and Surprise as the Beginning of Metaphysics

Bruaire's philosophical itinerary has brought him from (finite and absolute) freedom to spirit. The integral relation of these two concepts demands that both enter into the realm of being in its constitutive character of being given. What provokes Bruaire to enter into a still-despised metaphysical reflection, however, is not merely the conceptual necessity proper to a coherent logical system. Nor is it the urgency to complete the first philosophical phase of his system, his anthropology. Bruaire is indeed a systematician of outstanding quality, and so it is just to highlight the inner logic uniting the first anthropological reflection and his metaphysics. Still, for Bruaire, metaphysics is primarily the adequate response to the *surprise* in the encounter with the *other,* that is to say, with "what one traditionally used to call by this old word: *spirit.*"[1] "Surprise" is a permanent dimension of man's quest for the truth of being, a continuous beginning, so to say, and not merely the initial reaction to being's alterity. In fact, "astonishment is the awakening of a consciousness *(pensée)* which is overtaken *(surprise)* by the unexpected, the other, which imposes itself and poses the issue of its own alterity."[2] Every "surprise" involves three inseparable elements: the appearing other, the one who is surprised, and the "frustration" of a perhaps not yet fully formulated expectation.

A fundamental characteristic of the human subject discovered in the encounter with the other is that it is always in expectation, waiting for something that it cannot give to itself. This "waiting," which Bruaire on several occasions calls "man's search for his own destiny," reveals the ontological incompleteness that constitutes the human being. Calling to mind the final outcome of Bruaire's anthropology—that is, the inability of the human being to return to its origin as in the circle of divine reflection—it is easy to grasp in what sense ontological passivity characterizes the nature of the finite spirit and prompts the desire to discover its own source, or to wait for that source to manifest itself. Thus, this longing that comes always from the very beginning of the encounter with the other is not an "inactivity" in which the human subject's creativity is reduced to an idle waiting.

1. *FE,* 18.
2. *PM,* 1. To place "wonder" at the origin of philosophical reflection distances Bruaire from the negative Heideggerian question, "why are there essents rather than nothingness?" (Martin Heidegger, *An Introduction to Metaphysics,* trans. Ralph Manheim [New Haven: Yale University Press, 1975], 1). The surprise originates because the other *is,* and not because that which is could *not* be. Cf. *PM,* 1–9; *EE,* 34–43; Hansjürgen Verweyen, *Ontologische Voraussetzungen des Glaubensaktes. Zur transzendentalen Frage nach der Möglichkeit von Offenbarung* (Patmos: Verlag Düsseldorf, 1969); Joseph Pieper, *"Divine Madness": Plato's Case Against Secular Humanism,* trans. Lothar Kraut (San Francisco: Ignatius Press, 1995).

Rather, ontological passivity needs to be understood as an active receptivity, as welcoming, not as a primordial inactivity. Accepting both the other and one's own otherness translates into the intellectual inquisitiveness set in motion by the encounter with the other and the humble receptivity of the other as what it is, in its insuppressible otherness.[3] For Bruaire, the human being lives and thinks metaphysically when he discovers himself as a waiting for the other. There is no true "longing," and thus no true philosophical research, if it is not continuously regenerated in the encounter with the *other*.

The encounter with what appears, surprises and breaks every habit, expectation, or preconceived idea. The irruption of the other must then pierce through consciousness' habit of looking only for what is similar to itself, in order for the other to be seen precisely *as* other. The human being, in order to be truly philosophical, needs to accept the *other* without incorporating it into a utilitarian or positivistic mentality. He can neither absorb the other into his own self, nor reduce it to a mere phenomenon so as to make it more readily manipulable. The other surprises precisely because it is not the *same*; it is *other*. The "similar" can at most corroborate a preconceived idea, but it never surprises. In this sense, wonder's capacity to frustrate any preformulated answer is not to be seen as an occasion of bitter disappointment but rather as an unexpected richness.

Searching exclusively for what is identical to a preconceived idea of what things are, or of what they should be, is called "ideology." An ideological search, and thus an ideological philosophy, is able to see only what corresponds to its already formed system. Hence, instead of expressing *(logos)* what one sees *(eidos)*, ideology renders the human subject unable to look and to recognize the *other* for what it is. An ideological philosophy, because it deceives itself into thinking that the human mind is the origin of its ideas, is unable to see that "the ideas we form are always the conceptual memory" of the truth of being, "that Principle" to which they belong.[4] Any philosophy unwilling to become ideological needs to be opened to the other as it manifests itself, to accept that this *other* pierces through the already-acquired habits. The richness of any philosophical inquiry, then,

---

3. Bruaire, "Philosophie et spiritualité," 1379.

4. Bruaire, "Idéologie et spiritualité," *Giornale di Metafisica*, n.s., 9 (1987): 227–28. See also Leduc-Fayette, "Claude Bruaire, 1932–1986," 5–19.

lies in the fact that the difference of the *other* generates that continuous astonishment which is always willing to know further.

Although being appears as "other," otherness cannot be understood univocally. Whatever presents itself to us shows itself first and foremost as "that which is" and calls to be seen *as* it is.[5] Hence, the otherness proper to the human being is one thing and the otherness of the world is another. This is why alterity brings philosophical reflection to the heart of what is: the encounter with the *other* demands an *ontology*. Bruaire is very laconic in his treatment of the natural world's being. He always perceives it in its relationship to the human being and addresses it only in order to clarify further what the human spirit is. In fact, according to Bruaire, there is no real perception of the otherness of the world if, at the same time, one does not acknowledge its difference within man's own being. In the encounter with the natural *other,* the human being discovers that he is not "at home" among the other beings, that he is different from them.[6] In this discovery, man realizes that "in his being and in his way of being, [he is] other than any natural phenomenon; he is not reducible to the whole of the things of this world."[7] Thus, the human being, although corporeal, is more than just a "package of flesh and bones"; he has a bodily and a spiritual existence.

This apparent difference between the human spirit and the natural world also reveals "the astonishing privilege that constitutes our human condition: being spiritual without being God."[8] The surprise of the discovery of one's own *otherness* bears within it an ontological fragility. Man's contingency causes him to realize that he is given to himself in order to be himself, that is, to be free while at the same time facing the task of discovering where he comes from. This incompleteness and the inadequacy of every natural "other" in responding to man's "spiritual demands" forces him to be always "in exile, . . . always looking for his own dwelling place."[9] Although man is always haunted by the anguish of dying, his ontological precariousness is unable to cast out completely the "gladness of the gift"

5. *PM*, 2.

6. Bruaire, "Rembourser l'avortement? Non!" *Communio* 8 (1983): 93. See also id., "Problème de la métaphysique et conversion," *Archivio di filosofia* 51 (1983): 122 (hereafter *PrMC*).

7. Bruaire, "Philosophie et spiritualité," 1379.

8. Bruaire, "L'être de l'esprit et l'Esprit Saint," *Communio* 11 (1986): 73 (hereafter *EdEES*). This article also appears in the English edition of *Communio* 13 (1986): 118–24.

9. *PM*, 3.

of being.[10] When the discovery of his own contingency leads man to lose the dimension of wonder, it is because the human spirit is governed by an understanding of the absolute in terms of undetermined freedom. This conception of the absolute betrays a longing on the part of the human spirit for the absolute independence which it does not have, a longing that also is a rejection of its own bodily condition.

The *otherness* of the human being, unlike that of the natural world, is most fittingly seen as that of a *spiritual* being. Being's indissociability from spirit is what necessarily makes metaphysics the "reflection of the spirit on itself," of the human spirit in the first place and then of the absolute spirit.[11] Bruaire does not approach the question of being from the point of view of "classical" metaphysics. Aristotle dealt with the question of being within a particular cosmological framework. After presenting his reading of the physical world, Aristotle discusses that aspect common to the entire realm of nature, which therefore transcends it. This is why he calls metaphysics the science of being. Beginning in the Renaissance, the understanding of the place of the human being within the cosmos began to make a departure from Aristotelian cosmology and metaphysics. In Pico della Mirandola's *Oratio,* for instance, man is no longer perceived as a being among other beings: when God, after the creation of the whole universe, wanted to create the human being, he looked for a nature suitable for him and did not find any.[12] The cosmos is seen as having its apex in the human being; man is the synthesis of the cosmos. Thus, the question of being finds in the human being, in his essence and in the structure of his existence, its adequate entry to the realm of being.

Consistent with the modern emphasis on the centrality of man for the inquiry into the meaning of being, Bruaire strongly believes that metaphysics needs to be approached anthropologically. To ask for the meaning of being is, in the first place, to ask for the truth of the human being.[13]

10. Bruaire, "L'esprit n'est pas l'ennemi de la chair," *Communio* 7, no. 2 (1982): 3; id., *MS*, 11.

11. *PrMC,* 125.

12. Pico della Mirandola, *On the Dignity of Man,* trans. Charles Glenn Wallis (Indianapolis: Hackett Publication Co., 1998). It is interesting to note that Pico della Mirandola envisions freedom as that which most properly describes man's being.

13. Bruaire is not the first to point out this type of link between being and the self. Many other authors have indicated the pertinence of considering anthropology within ontology. See Heidegger, *Being and Time;* Hans Urs von Balthasar, *Mein Werk. Durchblicke* (Freiburg:

In this sense, his "systematic anthropology" is not only propaedeutic to metaphysics; it also determines how the question of being is posed and answered. In fact, since in the human being, one is brought to acknowledge that being and spirit are two necessarily connected realities, then, to avoid adopting a formal and abstract point of view, Bruaire has no choice but to enter the vast realm of being through the door of the being of the *human-spirit.* This particular outlook ensures that, without diminishing their own significance, all (sub-human) beings are seen in their relationship to the human being. For this reason, for Bruaire, the *other* refers first to human being and then to other beings.[14]

Other human beings, however, are equally unable to answer spiritual demands because they are also limited spiritual beings. This incapacity to respond to his own "spiritual demands" is what, according to Bruaire, moves the human being to look for the most proper other—absolute spirit. In this sense, for Bruaire, metaphysics is "always joined with onto-theology," which requires the study of the question of being and of the spirit up to its very source, absolute spirit, the most proper other of the human spirit, which religions call God.[15]

Bruaire, while insisting that metaphysical reflection must be attempted without compunction, remains aware that his perception of the need

---

Johannes Verlag, 1990), 89–96. In theology, it is worth mentioning Karl Rahner's attempt in *Hearers of the Word* (New York: Herder and Herder, 1969); id., *Foundations of Christian Faith: An Introduction to the Idea of Christianity* (New York: Crossroad, 1982).

14. Bruaire, with the reservations already mentioned, considers that idealism has correctly seen that the role of (divine and human) consciousness is not extrinsic to the constitution of any given being. The tether between being and the human self does not necessarily transform Bruaire's understanding of philosophy into subjective idealism. It would be self-contradictory for Bruaire's anthropology to hold that the human being, in thinking, not only discovers being, but creates it. In fact, if the human being does not come from himself, as Bruaire insists he does not, then affirming that the rest of reality does would not make sense. To perceive "beings" as "other" for the human being is not an ontological transgression but, on the contrary, the recognition of a situation *de facto.* The encounter with alterity is not perceived, at least from the ontological and anthropological point of view, as imposing a foreign measure on the essence of the object—as if in the definition of the object one would be able to deduce the (human) knowing subject. Yet, in order for the *other* to be intelligible, it needs to be known. In the same sense that there is no *cogito* if there is not first a *cogitor,* there is no object if it is not for a subject (first the divine subject, and, as participating in this knowledge, the human subject). See Hans Urs von Balthasar, *Wahrheit der Welt,* vol. 1 of *Theologik,* 35–48.

15. *PM,* 6. The understanding of divine transcendence that governs Bruaire's "onto-theology" prevents us from identifying it with Heidegger's.

for metaphysics and particularly for an onto-theological reflection on the (human and divine) spirit is not shared by most contemporary philosophers.[16] Heidegger is one of the few thinkers who in recent decades tried to recover the pertinence and the urgency of the study of being. His keen perception of the question of being as the main philosophical problem has brought ontology the attention it deserves. Nevertheless, Bruaire has little fondness for Heidegger's ultimate intention, or, more precisely, for his presentation of the renowned "ontological difference" as the definitive overcoming of metaphysics. According to Heidegger and his followers, there was no real understanding of being during all the centuries between Plato and Hegel. Unfortunately, says Bruaire, "after all the annoying repetition of the 'ontological difference,' which announced a new philosophical era after the blockage of 'classical metaphysics,' not even a word of ontology has emerged."[17]

The most pertinent response to the forgetfulness of being, according to Bruaire, is to perceive metaphysics as the *memory* of being-of-the-spirit.[18] "Remembering" *(faire mémoire)* is neither "to look back" nor to stop contemplating what is before oneself in order to bring to the present what now pertains only to the past.[19] Memory is the capacity to see what is before one's eyes without denying its depth. It is the perception of being's presence in whatever appears, a presence that is at hand both for theo-

16. It is not by chance that Bruaire rallies with enthusiasm the few philosophers who still consider metaphysical reflection an unavoidable enterprise: "For Metaphysics" is the title he gave to his first book devoted to metaphysics (*PM*, 1980). Cf. Incardona, "*L'ontodologie* di Claude Bruaire," 397–400; Kühn, *Französische Reflexions*, 157–58; Paul Gilbert, "L'acte d'être: un don," 278–86.

17. *PM*, 5. See the various articles by Ricoeur in Paul Ricoeur, *The Conflict of Interpretations*, ed. Don Ihde (Evanston, Ill.: Northwestern University Press, 1974); Hans-Georg Gadamer, *Philosophical Hermeneutics*, trans. David E. Linge (Berkeley: University of California Press, 1977). See also Michel Foucault, "Nietzsche, Genealogy, History," in *The Foucault Reader*, ed. Paul Rabinow (New York: Pantheon Books, 1984); Kenneth L. Schmitz, "Postmodernism and the Catholic Tradition," *American Catholic Philosophical Quarterly* 73 (1999): 233–52.

18. *PM*, 2. It is interesting to note that whereas Plato understands memory in terms of recollection, Augustine as *memoria*, Marcel as *reconnaissance* and recollection, Hegel as *Wiederholung* but more importantly as *Erinnerung* (intensively going within), Bruaire recuperates along with the concept of memory both the self and the notion of depth. In this sense, for him "memory" implies the recuperation of interiority. See *PM*, 71–85, 116–26, 183–90; "Réminiscence," 137–53.

19. *PM*, 183–90.

retical reflection and for practical use in the affairs of daily life. Thus, the common meaning of memory as recollection needs to be replaced with that of bringing back to mind the depth of what appears.[20] For Bruaire, there is no real search for the truth of being, no serious waiting *(attente)* without that attention *(attention)* which is always in tension to see without manipulating or destroying what is out there. To remember, to rest one's own gaze on the other in the double movement of appearance and depth, is, then, the capacity to recognize the *being-of-spirit* that presents itself in every phenomenon—oneself included.

Positivistic Reduction and Promethean Presumption

Perhaps one could have thought the fate of Hegel's system a convincing enough lesson to dissuade anyone from starting anew in philosophy with another pneumatological project. What is it that spirit discloses about the nature of being that would convince Bruaire of the need to retrieve the concept of the spirit? Today, "spirit" seems to be a void, meaningless concept, a forgotten reality. The forgetfulness of the spirit is, according to Bruaire, both an undeniable fact and, more drastically, the source of the cultural flattening that holds sway over contemporary man. If one is not able to recognize in a newborn infant the presence of something that makes it more than the product of blind and expedient forces of nature or the hopefully happy synthesis of its parents, there will be major difficulties in perceiving oneself as more than a "package of flesh and bones" inhabited by something noncorporeal. To forget the spirit precludes the capacity to perceive other human beings in their own infinite value. This reductive view transforms politics into the preservation of an unconfessed, but nonetheless sustained essential inequality, such that what matters turns out to be only what one is able to accomplish. Without spirit, "religions are objects whose task has been destroyed by the analysis of pathological behaviors."[21] Without spirit, there is no real freedom, no art; there is only necessity and the illusion of a free choice. The neglect of the spirit also makes "being" a void concept whose meaning is no longer comprehensible; ethics

20. Bergson's influence can be felt here. See *PM*, 186; "Réminiscence,"144.
21. *EE*, 13.

becomes a spurious discourse whose only purpose is to regulate social life in such a perfect way that one no longer needs to be free. It is indeed perplexing that in an era in which ethics and deontology are two fundamental concerns and so many are worried about what to do and how to behave, so many also forget that without a proper ontology, any ethical discourse becomes an extrinsic coercion which, if not simply disregarded, can be bent to fit one's own preferences.

Bruaire ingeniously contends, then, that the main source of the dreadful contemporary situation is indeed the forgetfulness of the spirit, a forgetfulness that reduces human inquiry to a materialistic, skin-deep glance at reality. This oblivion increases exponentially the more pervasive a gaze without *memory* becomes. Under the spell of several geniuses, says Bruaire, the world has been desacralized and reduced to sheer apparency with no real substratum. Despite the attempts of German idealism to reanimate the philosophy of nature, the positive sciences have developed the method of ignoring the spiritual dimension of each phenomenon, human and subhuman. The positive sciences have severed the being of the spirit from its manifestation, and, consequently, the latter has been reduced to what can be observed and verified. If German idealism dispensed with the Kantian distinction between phenomenon and noumenon for the sake of the former's sheer intelligibility, the outcome has been the elimination of the phenomenon due to its pure unintelligibility, resulting in its transformation into a tool at the service of man. In fact, when Fichte first denied the Kantian proposal on the grounds that there is nothing in the phenomenon which cannot be known and when, shortly after Fichte, Hegel insisted that there was no need to adopt a referential epistemology because everything is within the absolute Idea, they were also creating the space for an unprecedented materialism. According to Bruaire, then, the unequivocal outcome of the *Critique of Pure Reason* is that "metaphysics is a false problem inasmuch as it pretends to be a noumeno-logic knowledge, a knowledge of the being of the spirit."[22] Consistent with this view, Bruaire tells us that Sartre's opening remarks in *Being and Nothingness* represent a clear declaration of the contemporary denial of Aristotle's ingenious discovery of "being in potency, or the spirit within nature, the invisible within the visible." Philosophy, writes Sartre, "has taken a major step in reducing being to its external manifesta-

22. *PrMC*, 121.

tions."[23] Consequently, contemporary sciences are only able to value "data," which, as Kenneth Schmitz points out, do not lead the scientist to discover any ontological cause behind what is there because "data" are seen as something perfected and fully realized in themselves.[24] The positivistic mastery over the ontology of spirit is born from the fact that philosophical thinking is accomplished "distracted from [human] existence," and consequently it is unable to see the most fundamental evidence. The positivistic reading of being, however, gives way to its contrary: that spiritualism which claims the existence of a consciousness irreducible to sheer materiality.[25]

According to Bruaire, the main reason for the disappearance of the concept of the spirit and for the domination of the materialistic view over spirit is deep and unsettlingly simple: "the Promethean affirmation of a creation of itself by itself, which tirelessly imitates the divine in ever different ways."[26] In principle, no human spirit would claim to be endowed with the same characteristics as absolute spirit. To be born is never the fruit of one's own decision. Yet, the dominion over nature that technology and science advance, "revoking every philosophy of nature," provides the illusion that man is the origin of himself—or at least it prevents him from posing the question regarding the origin. The being-of-spirit that pursues becoming the master of being discovers that it is subject to the same laws that it bestows upon the material world and that its own being can be explained according to those parameters; its body is considered an object among others. It is possible to analyze whole philosophical systems to see in what sense and how they reflect this idea, involving discussion of different inter-

---

23. Jean-Paul Sartre, *Being and Nothingness: An Essay on Phenomenological Ontology*, trans. Hazel E. Barnes (New York: Philosophical Library, 1956), 3. See also *EdE*, 35, and *PonEs*.

24. Schmitz, *The Gift*, 37. See also Schindler, *Heart of the World*, 162–68.

25. For further development, see Bruaire's understanding of the identification between materialism and formalism in "Formalisme et matérialisme," 53–65.

26. *EE*, 45; *PM*, 238–39. For an analysis of the disappearance of the concept of spirit and its significance for philosophy and theology, see Gerald R. Cragg, *The Church and the Age of Reason, 1648–1789* (New York: Atheneum, 1961); Michael Buckley, *At the Origin of Modern Atheism* (New Haven: Yale University Press, 1990); Luigi Giussani, *Il senso di Dio e l'uomo moderno: La "questione umana" e la novità del cristianesimo* (Milan: BUR, 1994); Romano Guardini, *The End of the Modern World: A Search for Orientation* (New York: Sheed & Ward, 1956); Wolfhart Pannenberg, *Christianity in a Secularized World* (New York: Crossroad, 1989); Angelo Bertuletti, "L'Europa e il cristianesimo. Fede e modernità," in *Il caso Europa*, ed. Giuseppe Colombo (Milan: Glossa, 1991), 59–65.

pretations of language's nature, of human desire, of the task and essence of freedom, and so on. Yet, there is one element at the very beginning of one's own philosophical research that determines the subsequent steps. This decisive factor is the position adopted before the whole of being: either one upholds some form of self-creation—what Bruaire calls theomorphic or ontogenic anthropology—or one recognizes that one is given to oneself. In the first scenario, one would tend either to overlook those familiar experiences through which the spirit manifests itself to the human consciousness or to justify them in different reductive ways—emanationism and dualism being the most common forms. By contrast, the second possibility allows one to recognize the manifestation of the spirit and to be ready to listen to what it has to say. When the human spirit recognizes that it is given to itself, it is able to see that the natural order is under the same law of gift, and thus it can be rightly considered as an *other* with which there needs to be a noninstrumental, nonintrusive relationship. To say that one needs to take a position regarding his own origin, however, is not to say that truth is arbitrary. On the contrary, it is to respect that inseparability of truth and freedom which makes man's discovery of truth constitutively dramatic.[27]

It is important here to note the connection of this conclusion with what Bruaire considers to be the starting point of metaphysics: wonder. In fact, it is possible to affirm that metaphysics begins with the *wonder* which the irruption of the *other* provokes only if one postulates an anthropology for which the knowing subject is not perceived as the main source of meaning but is instead open to seeing and receiving whatever manifests itself.

27. Truth is endowed with a peculiar type of evidence that solicits human intelligence and free response. Therefore, although presenting itself as what corresponds to the human search for meaning, truth never forces the adherence of human freedom. See Hans Urs von Balthasar, *Theo-Drama: Theological Dramatic Theory*, trans. Graham Harrison, 5 vols. (San Francisco: Ignatius Press, 1988–98). In this regard, it is worth examining the proposal of the Italian School of Theology, Venegono. See Giuseppe Angelini, Angelo Bertuletti, Giuseppe Colombo, and Pier Angelo Sequeri, *L'evidenza e la fede* (Milan: Glossa, 1988); id., "Fede e sapere. Il concetto di fede teologica," *Teologia* 8 (1983): 249–70; Angelo Bertuletti, "Il concetto di esperienza nel dibattito fondamentale della teologia contemporanea," *Teologia* 5 (1980): 283–341; id., "L'assolutezza della verità e l'evidenza della fede," *Teologia* 6 (1991): 31–52; id., "La problematizzazione e la rifondazione della metafisica nell'idealismo speculativo e il dibattito teologico contemporaneo," *La Scuola Cattolica* 1 (1990): 68–89; Giuseppe Colombo, "La ragione teologica," in *L'evidenza e la fede*, 7–20; Sergio Sorrentino, "Esperienza, rivelazione e simbolo. Discussione intorno alla ragione teologica," *Sapienza* 2 (1990): 181–96; Carmelo Vigna, "Evidenza della fede. Intorno ad una proposta teorica della scuola teologica milanese," *Rivista di filosofia neoscolastica* 81 (1989): 466–77.

If this were not the case, the question regarding the truth of being would always have a negative aspect, an echo of the impossibility of responding to death's seemingly totalizing tyranny. A Promethean anthropology, with its emphasis on man's greatness, is unable to be surprised by the other because either this is there to be manipulated, or it is perceived as a menacing limit to one's own jealously guarded autonomy. It is not a coincidence that the metaphysical reflection that presupposes this anthropological understanding gives negativity a primacy over positivity.

The dialectical relation between the ontogenic anthropology and the positivistic and materialistic view of reality springs forth from the presupposition of a misconceived absolute freedom. This freedom (and not the finite freedom) is the only one which can be properly conceived as the absolute beginning of itself in the donation of itself to itself. Absolute spirit represents, on the one hand, that which makes the human spirit able to be and, on the other hand, that which sets an ontological limit that cannot be ignored. The ontological misunderstanding of absolute and human freedom gives birth to the dialectic of naturalism and theomorphism that undergirds contemporary philosophical reflection. Between the two shores of this dialectic, the being of the spirit "lies as a rotten corpse whose memory we are losing."[28]

The Concept of the Spirit and Its Manifestation

In his attempts to define what "spirit" means, Bruaire first needs to do away with the undetermined interpretations of this concept in order to give a precise account of its ontological meaning. The difficulty of the task at hand is increased by the fact that, according to Bruaire, the Aristotelian categories do not seem adequate for elucidating the concept of spirit. Bruaire contends that, whereas most of the human sciences adopt an abstract method, philosophy must proceed by the only way left open: the Platonic μέθοδος. Accordingly, for Bruaire, to pose the question, "what is spirit?" is to inquire whether spirit is a *necessary concept* or not, and whether man can retrieve it from his memory. The necessary concept is indeed the only intelligible *datum* available. In order to find spirit's being, it is

28. *EE*, 48.

thus necessary that the conceptual analysis of spirit meet these two conditions: that the *semantic analysis* of the concept of spirit reveal that there is such a thing as a nonequivocal concept, and that the concept of spirit lead us to the *being* of spirit.[29]

Theory of Recollection and Conceptual Necessity

Undoubtedly, Bruaire's understanding of "concept" is closer to that of Hegel than to that of Aristotle, for whom the intellect grasps the universal forms which the judgment needs in order for the human being to acquire knowledge through the process known by the scholastics as "simple apprehension." Hegel, instead, considers that the concept is intelligible determination *and* freedom's expression because, Bruaire says, the conceptual necessity which regulates language is originally constituted by the absolute determination of itself by itself that is presented in the form of a theological thesis in the *Logic of the Essence.* This is why Hegel clearly says that "God is not *a* concept, but *the* concept."[30]

Bruaire is indeed fascinated by Hegel's elucidation of *the* concept and by the (ontological) necessity of the concept. In fact, whenever Bruaire presents his understanding of absolute freedom, he tends to do it in terms of the absolute concept.[31] Yet, the distinction between human and divine freedom prevents him from talking about "concept," its inner cogent necessity, and "the effort of the concept" as if reality were simply the deployment of the rationality of the concept. He does not collapse absolute freedom into a human concept. In fact, intelligibility is not the overarching criterion.[32]

It is important, then, to acknowledge that when dealing with necessary concepts, Bruaire refers to the intelligibility proper to being and being's inner relationship with conceptual language and not to simple apprehension. If being can be expressed in language as its own intelligibility requires, then language is properly understood in its ontological ability to

29. *EE*, 21–22.

30. Bruaire, "Hegel et l'athéisme contemporain," 75–76. Bruaire's emphasis.

31. See *PM*, 20–30, 50–64, 139–42, 157, 273–76; *DD*, 95–96; *FE*, 83–84; *D*, 69; *LR*, 26–29, 37–45, 47–61, 73–81.

32. Contrary to Hegel, conceptual language is ill-suited to express reality fully because it cannot express the individuality, the singularity, of concrete beings and more importantly, "because the being of our spirit has its *secret* in its destiny which only the original Author of the gift can offer" (*PM*, 266).

refer to being. Looking at what Bruaire adopts from Plato will help us to perceive what the French philosopher means by the concept's ontological necessity.

Bruaire, who dedicates significant attention to some of Plato's basic tenets, sees Plato's dialectic, his theory of recollection, and his insistence upon the need for a memory of necessary concepts because they are the "only intelligible data" as decisive elements for any philosophical enterprise.[33] Bruaire, however, reads Plato through Hegel.[34] Bruaire's claim, for instance, that in Platonic epistemology concepts are seen as "the ideas inasmuch as they are understood in our propositions" echoes Hegel's absolute concept more than Plato's pure ideas.[35]

The access to truth is never immediate. On the contrary, remarks Bruaire, synthesizing Plato's epistemology, the path of conceptual language is necessary. One can access being only through rational discourse, and this implies proceeding through the discursive path, "freeing oneself from every sensible experience and every empirical support as well as every formal science which, however, are the prelude to 'dialectics.'"[36] Bruaire explains that the finality of dialectics is to bring everyone to the contemplation of the absolute, eternal ideas. In this sense, dialectics is meant to help in the conversion toward the eternal truths and away from fleeting, changing realities. Dialectics halts before the intellectual intuition, which

---

33. See Plato, *Meno* 80D–100C; *Phaedo* 72E–100A; *Phaedrus* 246D–248C, 262C–269C; *Republic* 475A–480A, 506E–509C, 517B–522D, 531D–541B. See also *D*, 10–24; *PC*, 15–53; "Réminiscence," 137–52; *EE*, 20–27. Bruaire is not proposing a return to Platonic philosophy, *tout court*. His appreciation of Aristotle and of contemporary philosophy along with his own *philosophy of the body* keeps him from such a return. Besides, as is well known, Plato's theory of recollection demands that the human soul, before having fallen and having been chained to a body, had contemplated the eternal ideas in the hyperuranian realm. Hence, once in the earthly life, human beings need to be helped to remember what they already know. This theory, while it serves to ground the human soul's possibility of an eternal destiny, fosters a dualistic anthropology which assigns to the body—and thus to the sensible world—a secondary and ultimately nonessential role. See *PC*, 167–268; *DD*, 134–41.

34. *DD*, 12; Hegel, *Die Philosophie Platons* (Stuttgart: Verlag Freies Geistesleben, 1962); id., *Vorlesungen über die Geschichte der Philosophie*, ed. Pierre Garniron and Walter Jaeschke, 4 vols. (Hamburg: Felix Meiner Verlag, 1983–86) (for an English translation, see *Lectures on the History of Philosophy*, trans. E. S. Haldane and Frances H. Simson [New York: The Humanities Press, 1974], 1–117).

35. *D*, 10.

36. *D*, 10. See also Hegel, *WL, Zweiter Band. Die subjektive Logik oder die Lehre vom Begriff*; also see *Enzyklopädie*.

alone has the capacity to see *(eidos)*—an ability which is not granted to conceptual knowledge.[37] For this reason, according to Bruaire's analysis of Plato, discursive knowledge is able to know the idea of the Good.

Plato teaches us, says Bruaire, that there is no intuition outside language, that is to say, outside the concrete expression of human being's rationality. If intuition were considered an immediate perception of the divine idea that takes place without language, then contemplation of the truth would be reduced to "an obscure sensitivity, a carnal feeling, a perception deprived of meaning." Intuition is, indeed, intelligence's "immediate grasping within language of the intelligible meaning." Yet, Platonic dialectics creates an eternal dilemma. Either dialectics is subordinated to contemplation of the Good, while remaining at the same time indispensable, or else the truth of the absolute (of the Good) is the complete other of the human being, such that, once it has brought the human being to the contemplation of the absolute, dialectics itself must then be left behind. According to the former interpretation, dialectics indeed would be unable to exhaust the depths of the absolute idea, but there would still be the recognition of a certain likeness between the absolute idea and discursive reason. If instead one follows the latter view, rational discourse would bring the human being into the silence of negative theology's dark night, in which there is no intelligibility available to human reason. If the pedagogical process of dialectics is able to teach the human being to move from the sensible world to the realm of intelligibility, then, once he has reached this level and therefore does not require the support of the experience, "what is able to guarantee that the Idea and the discursive concept have access to being? What can guarantee their power of truth?" Bruaire answers this question by analyzing Plato's theory of recollection or anamnesis, "as famous as it is badly understood"—a decisive part of dialectics, used by Plato, according to Bruaire, to reject bold idealism.[38] It teaches us that to know is to recognize and that to think is not to "create concepts," as nominalism has it. Rather, the idea is the recognition of being.

In this sense, to describe philosophy as *memory* is to attempt to show that human thought has a real, although limited, grasp of truth and that the discursive conceptual way in which human reason approaches and

37. Plato, *Republic* 533.
38. *D*, 12.

knows the truth is not sheer human invention. Bruaire does not insist upon the theory of reminiscence in order to propose an idealism inimical to empirical reality—if this were the case, he would not have devoted so much attention to those *loci* where the spirit's presence can be experienced. The emphasis upon memory and recollection entails the rejection of nominalism's fundamental tenets.

Bruaire, in fact, sees nominalism as opposed to his own understanding of the idea of "concept," and, thus, to the theory of recollection because, for him, the formation of the concept is the recognition of an ontological reality and not the forging of relative linguistic signs which ultimately are nothing but *flatus vocis*. Bruaire wishes to defend the notion that human concepts are not just a construct of the human mind. By this he does not mean that concepts are bestowed upon human beings or that there is no process of formation of concepts. If, as nominalism has it, the only possible concept of God is that formed by the human being, then the absolute is nothing but a void concept unable to grasp the reality of God. In order to protect God's absolute freedom and to explain in what sense it is possible for the human being to have a knowledge of God *in statu isto,* William of Ockham built upon Scotus's theory of univocity and attempted to explain how concepts, pure *entia rationis,* are formed by the human intellect.[39] Still, presses Bruaire, if one wants to defend God's freedom, one must adopt a

---

39. For a deeper understanding of nominalistic epistemology and its explanation of the possible knowledge of God, see Stephen Dumont and Stephen Brown, "Univocity of the Concept of Being in the Fourteenth Century. III: An Early Scotist," *Mediaeval Studies* 51 (1989): 1–129; Stephen Dumont, "The Univocity of Being in the Fourteenth Century. II: The *De Ente* of Peter Thomae," *Medieval Studies* 50 (1988): 188–256; id., "The Univocity of the Concept of Being in the Fourteenth Century: John Duns Scotus and William of Alnwick," *Medieval Studies* 49 (1987): 1–75; id., "Theology as a Science and Duns Scotus's Distinction Between Intuitive and Abstractive Cognition," *Speculum* 64 (1989): 579–99; John Duns Scotus, *Philosophical Writings: A Selection* (Indianapolis: Hackett Publishing Company, 1987); William of Ockham, *Philosophical Writings: A Selection* (Indianapolis: Hackett Publishing Company, 1989); Paul Vignaux, *Philosophie au Moyen-Âge* (Paris: Armand Colin, 1958); id., *De Saint Anselme à Luther* (Paris: J. Vrin, 1976); id., "Nominalisme," in *Encyclopédie Française,* 718–84; id., *Nominalisme au XIVème Siècle* (Paris: J. Vrin, 1948); Frank William and Allan B. Wolter, *Duns Scotus, Metaphysician* (West Lafayette, Ind.: Purdue University Press, 1995); Allan B. Wolter, *The Transcendentals and Their Function in the Metaphysics of Duns Scotus* (New York: The Franciscan Institute, 1946); Marilyn McCord Adams, *William Ockham* (Notre Dame, Ind.: University of Notre Dame Press, 1987); Armand Maurer, *The Philosophy of William of Ockham in the Light of Its Principles* (Toronto: Pontifical Institute of Mediaeval Studies, 1999).

proper philosophy of language. To claim that concepts are only *entia rationis*, a construction of the mind with no real ontological connection to being itself, implies a negative theology in which God is understood as an empty concept without being.[40] According to Bruaire, then, nominalism does not perceive that whenever one deals with thinking and language, one is also thinking of the unconditional, of the absolute, and thus it disregards the ontological roots of every philosophy of language, of every concept.

In this sense, nominalism, the precursor of contemporary positivism, proposes a philosophy of language in which "no conceptual meaning reveals any necessity and thus, every mention of the Platonic anamnesis is rejected."[41] Nominalism elaborates an epistemology compatible with an understanding of God in terms of (absolute) freedom just as Bruaire does. Contrary to Bruaire, however, nominalism proposes a theory of univocity which, according to the French philosopher, ultimately deprives God of any real being. If Bruaire's critique of Hegel consists, as we know it does, in the fact that the latter gives too much capacity to the human language—to the extent of making it able to receive and express the Word within itself—his difference with nominalism lies in the fact that it gives too little consideration to the ability of human language to express being.[42]

For Bruaire, then, to say that knowing is recognizing means that to know "is not the discovery of something new as if it were a sheer novelty at which one would arrive fantastically, without any prerequisite. *It is to discover oneself in the original truth*."[43] Thus, the memory of the concept

---

40. For further study on the contemporary discussion of "God and being," see Dominique Dubarle, *Dieu avec l'être: De Parménide à Saint Thomas. Essai d'ontologie théologale* (Paris: Beauchesne, 1986); id., *L'ontologie de Thomas D'Aquin* (Paris: Cerf, 1996); Étienne Gilson, "L'être et Dieu," *Revue thomiste* (1962): 181–202, 398–416; Jean Y. Lacoste, "Penseur Dieu en l'aimant: philosophie et théologie de Jean-Luc Marion," *Archives de philosophie* 50 (1987), 245-70; Ghislain Lafont, *Dieu, le temps, et l'être* (Paris: Cerf, 1986); Jean-Luc Marion, *Dieu sans l'être* (Paris: Quadrige/PUF, 1982); id., *L'idole et la distance*; id., *Réduction et donation: Recherches sur Husserl, Heidegger et la phénoménologie*; id., "Saint Thomas d'Aquin et l'onto-théo-logie," *Revue thomiste* (1995): 31–66; Jean H. Nicolas, "La suprême logique de l'amour et la théologie," *Revue thomiste* (1983): 639–49; Jean D. Robert, "Dieu sans l'être. A propos d'un livre récent," *Nouvelle revue théologique* 105 (1983): 406–10; Kenneth L. Schmitz, "The God of Love," *The Thomist* 57 (1993): 495–508; Henri Vergote, ed., *L'être et Dieu* (Paris: Cerf, 1986); René Virgoulay, "Dieu ou l'être? Relecture de Heidegger en marge de J.-L. Marion, *Dieu sans l'être*," *Recherches de science religieuse* 72 (1984): 163–98.

41. *D*, 39.42. Cf. *PM*, 8, 42, and 144; *EE*, 112; *D*, 39–41.

43. *RdC*, 143. Emphasis added.

of the spirit is not the creation of a new concept with which one can ultimately justify the disappearance of being. Memory is rather the discovery of what is already there for what it is. Bruaire's insistence on thinking philosophy in terms of *memory* is more than a positive counterpoint to the *oblivion* of the spirit. The advantage of emphasizing the role of memory is to clarify that the present recognition takes place within the eternal richness of being that precedes and accompanies man's discovery of it. Bruaire proposes Plato's dialectical method as that which is able to grant philosophy the cognitive access to the concept of spirit because it is through this method that being's essence is clarified. Here he finds the reason why *memory* is not an ephemeral remembrance of past events. Rather, it is that type of recollection which is bound up with being. Because Plato's method reveals the necessary relationship between human language and being, Bruaire is able to claim that rational language is the memory of being, where language is born.

According to Plato's theory of recollection, then, the human being knows something inasmuch as the idea is the *recognition* of being. Conceptual knowledge thus is not a construct of the human intellect that is ultimately oblivious to the negative metaphysics it presupposes; conceptual knowledge, rather, is that type of knowledge which "guards being and searches for its presence." For Bruaire, then, the *ontological* dimension of language is the most valuable teaching of Plato's theory of reminiscence:

> If there is an obligating presupposition of philosophical thinking, it is that the concept is necessarily destined to arrive at being by means of the original intimacy of the one with the other. This is why experience is intelligible only inasmuch as it revivifies the univocal sense in which the experience is the occasion of recollection and to which experience owes what is essential in its manifestations.[44]

It is important to stress that although Bruaire is talking about the concept of spirit, or more precisely of the being-of-spirit, he ultimately refers to the absolute and thus to the possibility of thinking being itself. In this sense, Bruaire is not claiming that every single human concept leads necessarily to being—as if every concept entailed the actual existence of what is

---

44. *EE*, 21.

thought. He is saying that conceptual knowledge is rooted in the absolute, which is also logos, and that only the necessary concept will show that intimacy. In fact, Bruaire, in a very Hegelian way, claims that the relationship between being and conceptual knowledge has its speculative mediation in the ontological proof of God's existence. The core of this proof, as we saw, is precisely being's inseparability from the concept of the absolute. Ontological recollection and ontological proof need each other. That conceptual intelligibility unveils a bond with being means, then, that while thinking pure concepts, one is able to discover that being whence they proceed. This understanding of language, sustained by the interconnection between ontological argument and the theory of recollection, allows Bruaire to affirm that conceptual analysis is the only way to understand the true *being* of the concept of the spirit.

Bruaire combines wonder (the echo of the manifestation of being in its double play of form and secret, sacredness and exteriority, which pierces through human habits, enlarges man's horizon, and beckons to him to start the search for the mystery of being) and recollection (the realization that "language is older than we are"), surprise and memory, because in order to discover the meaning of the concept of spirit, one needs to be aware of the depth of its presence. In this sense, to discover the being-of-spirit requires us to remember, that is to say, to bring to our actual awareness, the presence of the being-of-spirit. The *other* surprises if it is perceived and understood for what it is, that is, not (absolutely) "new," but familiar *and* unexpected. For Bruaire, then, the necessity proper to the concept of spirit must remain within these parameters.

Semantic of the Concept of Spirit

Bruaire identifies two senses of the concept of spirit, the unity of which alone can both make the concept of spirit *necessary* and also eliminate any ambiguous polysemy. The word *spirit* translates two Greek terms: νοῦς and πνεῦμα. The first is translated with the Latin word *mens* and the second with *spiritus*. Both meanings are included in the English word *spirit*.[45] Whereas the first sense of spirit (νοῦς) can refer either to the intelligence with which human beings are endowed or to intelligibility as such,

---

45. See *The Oxford Encyclopedic English Dictionary*, 3rd ed., s.v. "spirit." Obviously, English also translates νοῦς as mind.

the second one (πνεῦμα) refers to the rhythm of animation proper to any living being.[46] In this second sense, spirit is a symbol expressing the countercurrent balance of inspiration and expiration, "interior and exterior, contraction and expansion, systole and diastole, secret and its manifestation."[47] These two words, νοῦς and πνεῦμα, seem to be difficult to subsume under one term because they belong to different orders: one to that of the intelligence and the other to that of life itself. Although one could say that νοῦς is proper to a type of living beings and not to all, it is not easy to see in what sense one can explain νοῦς in terms of life or spiritual rhythm. This may be why it seems preferable to use the term spirit when referring to the principle of life within any living being—and in this case it would mean breath, vitality, or animation—and not so often in reference to intelligibility. The use of *spirit* in relation to intelligence seems to be a metaphor improper to a correct philosophical language. An additional difficulty comes from the fact that to understand spirit (πνεῦμα) as a living inner principle could give way to dualistic anthropological interpretations. That is to say, the spirit could be conceived solely as the opposite of matter. The former would be the "life-giving principle," while the second would be that which is in need of being "animated." This objection, however, Bruaire tells us, does not hold in the face of Aristotle's great discovery of *being in potency,* that is to say *"spirit within nature."*[48]

For Bruaire, spirit is not simply that which is in opposition to nature; on the contrary, it is nature's truth, and thus without spirit, nature cannot be comprehended adequately. Although it would be possible to see spirit as an "inner dynamic principle," a principle within nature which nevertheless cannot be identified with nature—in this sense Bruaire's understanding of spirit would not be too far from the German *Geist*—how can this notion of spirit as "inner dynamic principle" be one with intelligibility? Close attention to the meaning of both terms reveals that the difference is not an irreconcilable one.[49]

The presumed antagonism between these two senses disappears if one

46. *EE,* 22; Aristotle, *Met.* 12.7.1072b18–30.

47. *EdE,* 4. See also *PM,* 7, 139, 216–27; *EE,* 26. Schelling's influence is always present. Also, Bruaire does not conceal his admiration for Pierre Boutang's book *Ontologie du secret* (Paris: Quadrige/PUF, 1988).

48. *EE,* 23.

49. Bruaire, "Philosophie et spiritualité," 1382.

does not conceive of knowledge as a motionless vision of the pure idea. To understand what knowledge is concretely, one should not separate what is known from the way it is known. "We only think within words *(mots),* we only think within the bosom of the Word *(verbe)*."[50] Bruaire contends that the separation of language, as intelligibility's historical concreteness, from knowledge, as the capacity to know, is illegitimate. It is this breaking of the unity between what is known and the way it is known that hinders a proper comprehension of the spirit as νοῦς. In fact, Bruaire says, there is no intelligibility without a double *reflection:* on the one hand, the reflection of the sensible in the intelligible, of material sound in concept, and, on the other hand, the reflection in which thought comes back to itself, and, having become critical, puts its preconception to the test, examines its components, explores its boundaries, and re-examines the understanding of thought's main presupposition, the concept of the absolute.[51] Bruaire thinks that it is indeed possible to see that intelligibility only occurs according to that rhythm which previously was thought to be proper only to natural life. In the same way that πνεῦμα refers to the inspiration and expiration of the spirit, νοῦς also is seen as that acquisition of knowledge which is not exempt from the bipolar movement of reflection into itself and expansion outside itself in the actual expression. For Bruaire, the noetic concept of the spirit entails a fragile, but nonetheless true equilibrium in which "the two indispensable pneumatological instances counter-flow."[52] Both νοῦς and πνεῦμα follow the same rhythm, one with regard to life, and the other with regard to the mind.

This can be seen in each of the three dimensions of the logic of man's existence. The human spirit cannot be identified with intelligence or with "life" in general, although one discovers the human spirit within each of these.[53] In its original meaning, freedom is understood as the affirmation

50. *EE,* 23.

51. Nunzio Incardona rightly states that for Bruaire, "l'ontologia è tale se è critica ed è critica se riesce ad essere, per se stessa, giudizio del limite che, essendole interno, le costituisce" (Incardona, "L'*Ontodologie* di Claude Bruaire," 402).

52. Bruaire, "Philosophie et spiritualité," 1381.

53. Bruaire's fascination with human language has introduced themes that have broadened the common understanding of language: the connection between rationality and corporeality, the transformation of sound into meaning, the precedence of language to human knowing, language's quintuple structure, the rootedness of human language in the Word (a rootedness that preserves—in contrast to Hegel—the difference between the two).

of itself, thus as independence. The fact that human beings are free means first of all that they are able to affirm themselves, albeit in a limited way. Nevertheless, their own treasured autonomy would be reduced to "an abstract interiority," unreal and exhaustible, if it were not oriented toward action. In this sense, self-affirmation is oriented toward self-determination, toward disposing oneself to exercise freedom effectually in a concrete act or in a determined behavior. The contrary is also true: if a human action were not the fruit of silent reflection, then it would be impossible for it not to become violent—either toward oneself or toward others. This is why, as with the two different possibilities for *language,* only a correct equilibrium of these two tendencies, autonomy and the exercise of freedom, will keep the spiritual movement from eliminating *freedom.* The "spiritual needs," as we know, show the human being that he is not at home in nature. Nature can at most answer his biological needs *(besoins),* but not that other need *(désir)* which is always in search of *another.* Understanding desire as that spiritual dynamism which makes the human being move forward in history, as an undetermined universality, calls for the recognition of the same dynamics. This dynamism would be just a flight toward the future if, along with the emptiness that characterizes the movement toward the future, there were not also the effusive expansion of the spirit. In this sense, desire is not only the search for what is lacking but also the overflowing of the gift of oneself. There is no true desire, then, that does not also imply giving oneself. The movement of inspiration and expiration could seem here to mean something different, in that both senses of desire are oriented toward the future. It is not so, because the effusion of oneself, the gift of oneself, implies a conversion to oneself. In this sense, the greater the effusion of oneself, the more intense the desire—and vice versa.[54]

Bruaire illustrates that the concept of spirit is indissociable, that the indivisible relation between νοῦς and πνεῦμα makes the concept irreducible, and that its "necessity is verified in this unique and inevitable con-

---

Although there are still more aspects in need of clarification, a possible confusion could have been avoided: Bruaire discusses νοῦς which can refer both to the human intellect and to the divine intellect (also in the Aristotelian sense of *intelligence in itself*). His elucidation of the identification of νοῦς and πνεῦμα would have benefited if he had made this distinction more clearly.

54. In this respect, the life of sanctity is a paradigmatic example of the gift of oneself and the desire for receiving that fulfillment which one cannot give to oneself.

jugation of the two alternating senses in the same rhythm that indicates both negativity and positivity, reflection and relation, collecting oneself and effective act."[55] Thus, spirit is a necessary and determined concept because the expression keeps the reflection where the former emanates and, at the same time, the reflection is deepened by the manifestation that the reflection itself makes possible.

The concept of spirit thus leads to being, says Bruaire, because it manifests that being is *one*. There is no manifestation, no phenomenon without spirit. Although, like Aristotle or Thomas Aquinas, Bruaire sees unity as being's first transcendental property, he makes reference to both Leibniz and Hegel in stating that the diversity of phenomena presupposes a substance.[56] The pure exteriority of appearance is adequately understood in terms of infinite division: the other is always the other, and never oneself. Nevertheless, says Bruaire, the plurality of phenomena implies its opposite, unity—a substance to which they refer.[57] Otherwise, phenomena would be the apparition of nothingness—which is a contradiction because that which is not cannot appear.

Oneness is what causes being to be, not only because it identifies being in distinguishing it from other beings, but above all because there is no being *"without its uniting reflection."*[58] Bruaire's understanding of oneness is determined by that rhythm proper to the spirit. The movement of systole and diastole, reflection and expression, is what causes being to be one, to be itself. Oneness is not merely difference with respect to any other, but, more radically, it is the possibility of being-in-itself, given by an epistrophic principle of conversion toward itself.[59] This reflexivity, which

55. *EE*, 26.

56. Aristotle, *Met.* 1.2.1054a18; Aquinas, *De Ver.*, q. 1, a. 1; id., *In duodecim libros metaphysicorum aristotelis expositio*, ed. M. R. Cathala, O.P. (Turin: Marietti, 1950), X lectio 4ᵃ [lib. 10, l. 4] n. 1998 (for an English translation, see St. Thomas Aquinas, *Commentary on Aristotle's Metaphysics*, trans. John P. Rowan [Notre Dame, Ind.: Dumb Ox Books, 1995]).

57. In Leibniz's words: "I believe that he who will meditate upon the nature of substance . . . will find that the whole nature of bodies is not exhausted in their extension, that is to say, in their size, figure and motion, but that we must recognize something which corresponds to soul, something which is commonly called substantial form, although these forms effect no change in its phenomena, any more than do the souls of the beasts, that is if they have souls" (Gottfried W. Leibniz, *Discourse on Metaphysics: Correspondence with Arnauld and Monadology*, 2nd ed., trans. George R. Montgomery [Chicago: Open Court Publishing House, 1962], 17).

58. *EE*, 27.   59. *PrMC*, 122.

denies any possible disappearance in nothingness, makes the concept of spirit a necessary concept looking for its own being. Spirit, then, is *"being in its subsistence,* in its defeat of the erasing of the phenomena, precisely because it includes the uniting power" which holds together the secret and the phenomenon.[60] There is no being without oneness, and this is possible only because being is the conversion to itself, that movement of inspiration and expiration proper to the spirit. The memory of the concept of the spirit is, then, the anamnesis of its ontological reality.

Phenomenology of Spirit

When one looks more closely at the reality of spirit, one discovers that spirit is indeed the *other* of nature. In a sense, nature is both assumed and denied in spirit, which is nature's truth. Spirit is also the *other* of language: it is the principle of language, its potency of "ideality and animation," but it is not language. It is difficult to grasp what spirit is, says Bruaire, because one tends to identify it with the result of what it makes, and thus one tends to name the actions or the result of actions for what causes them. But spirit is not that which it makes, it is not language, or the expression of itself, or the fruit of the animation. Spirit is always *within* language, thought, freedom, and desire, but it is so in *abnegation* of itself. For this reason, the spirit of the human being needs to be thought in terms of potency.[61]

It appears that here Bruaire has in mind the classical dictum *operatio sequitur esse.* Under this view, freedom, desire, and language presuppose the operating potency of the spirit, but the latter cannot be reduced to the former and vice versa. Put in different terms, although there is no spirit without its manifestation, the spirit is more than its own manifestation, and thus it always remains a secret to be unfolded. The principal misun-

---

60. *EdE,* 35. See also *PrMC,* 122. Bruaire's argument that it is fitting for the concept of spirit to look for being, whose meaning is preserved by the concept of spirit, indicates the intimate connection between his understanding of concept and Plato's theory of recollection.

61. "On different occasions we have had recourse to this term, *potency* of the spirit, in order to indicate the order of thought, the free act, and human desire. In fact, it is the only one which, uniting the force of a power to the ontological virtuality, the capacity to be in potency, distinguished *that which only the spiritual being can answer for,* but to which it cannot be either reduced or identified" (*EE,* 31). Bruaire's emphasis.

derstanding behind a metaphysics that reduces spirit to a "thinking substance," like that of Descartes, consists in the fact that it identifies the self with its operations. Instead, says Bruaire, every human person is aware of this twofold reality: on the one hand, he expresses himself in what he says and does, but he is always greater than and different from what he says and does.

In trying to name what spirit is, Bruaire struggles to come to grips with a reality that has a long history in philosophy: the human soul. Bruaire purposely avoids the term *soul* because of the dualistic anthropological interpretations to which use of this term has led. He wants to forge a concept that is able to come as close as possible to the concrete particularity of the human being, while being aware that a concept can never express the individuality of a human being perfectly; it constantly escapes conceptualization. He thinks that Scotus's term, *haecceitas,* is conducive, although not perfectly, to expressing "the particularity of the essence of each spirit, which is unique without being God and is free without being the absolute initiative of its own being; which is not some-thing, but which is some-one because it is some-thing."[62] Spirit, in this first stage of Bruaire's metaphysics, refers to man's being-of-spirit—a spirit which is *other* than its own manifestations and *other* than nature itself. It is the human being in its *personal singularity.* Hence, Bruaire tells us, conceptual anamnesis invites us to recognize the being-of-spirit in the "substantial *haecceitas*" proper to the human being; the being of the spirit signifies, then, what the human being *is.* What Bruaire sets out to do is thus to think the spirit of the human being in its concreteness.

To this end, he proposes a *phenomenology of the spirit* divided into four different moments that constitute what he calls the *eidetic of the spirit,* an analysis of the concept of human spirit that lays the foundation for the ontology of gift. As goes without saying, his phenomenology is not that of Kant, Hegel, or even Husserl. He does not follow Kant because the latter's phenomenology disregards precisely that in which Bruaire is most interested: the *noumenon,* the being of the spirit, the secret in the phenomenon.

---

62. *EE,* 31. Scotus's definition of *haecceitas* is *ultima actualitas formae.* "Sic haec unitas minor de se est haec numero, non essentialiter, sed tantum denominative; sed haecceitas est numero haec essentialiter" (John Duns Scotus, *Reportata Parisiensia,* vol. 11 of *Opera omnia,* Wadding ed. [Paris: Vivès, 1891–95], 1. II., d. 12, q. 6, n. 13). The use of *haecceitas* in Scotus is not very common; it has been generalized by his school.

He does not follow Hegel because Hegel, in his dialectical procedure, applies divine logic univocally to human existence. Bruaire thus pursues the elaboration of an ontology of the *human* spirit which is not subservient to Hegel's main (theological) presuppositions. Bruaire does not elaborate a phenomenology like that of Husserl because Husserl's proposal of going back "to things themselves" means a return to human consciousness.[63] Bruaire does not want to dedicate attention to the different states of consciousness but rather to the being of the human spirit.

Bruaire's phenomenology approaches the human being in a "chronological" fashion, that is to say, from its very inception to its final destiny through the encounters and interactions with other human beings. Two fundamental phenomena need to be examined in order to discover what the spirit of the human being is. These two are not a random choice made by Bruaire but are rather two main events in life that set in motion the spiritual demands that constitute every human being: *procreation* and the first *apparition* of the child's spirit. When a new child is born, it is evident to every parent that the new human being is not just the logical result of an obedience to nature's demands. The abundance of life that a new child brings with himself exceeds the simple intervention of the parents.[64] In fact, Bruaire notes, the term used to describe this event is *pro-creation*, as if to indicate that the fruit of the human act of love is something different from the parents. What comes into the world is a whole *new* being; that is to say, it is *other* from the father and the mother. Although the newborn child comes from them, he is *other* than them. He is a whole new spiritual being who is not the synthesis of the parents—without whose involvement he would not have come to existence. The disproportion between the "natural" source of the child and the child himself forcefully states that at the very origin of that newborn lies a mystery, a deeper source from which the child proceeds. Undoubtedly, there can always be a biological reduction of this fact. Yet, as we saw, this narrow interpretation, although not devoid of true elements, is the result of an unjustified ontogenic pre-

63. *PM*, 55, 234, 242. See also Miguel García Baró, "La filosofía primera de Edmund Husserl en torno a 1900," *Diánoia* (1986): 41–69; id., *Vida y mundo. La práctica de la fenomenología* (Madrid: Trotta, 1999); Roman Ingarden, *On the Motives Which Led Husserl to Transcendental Idealism*, trans. Arnór Hannibalsson (The Hague: Martinus Nijhoff, 1975).

64. "Abundance," of course, is qualitative and ontological and not quantitative and subjective.

sumption. The birth of an infant not only implies this certainty regarding its origin, it also contains another decisive element: the child is not put into existence for *nothing*. One is not certain about the destiny the child might have, and as any other, he will have to face his own death. Nevertheless, the abundance of life, while not obviating existence's precariousness, does not overshadow the certainty that one is brought into existence for a reason. The fact that no one is able to guarantee a positive destiny does not mean that the origin, that mysterious source from which one proceeds, is either blind necessity, or more radically, nothingness.

The certitude that the newborn child is indeed *another* being-of-spirit is confirmed as truth when he shows the first signs of his own personal being. Bruaire sees in the child's first smiles the sign that the spirit *appears,* showing that he "is there," is already present. The child's smile is not just a mimicking repetition of the parents' smile. It is rather the "manifestation of a being in substantial superabundance, a being who rests in himself, jealous of the mystery of his own origin, the only holder of his own personal destination."[65]

Bruaire continues his phenomenology by pointing out that, although the child is a being-of-spirit of his own, his own being is not an already-fulfilled reality. He has to learn to be for himself, to recognize his own being while he looks for the recognition of the *other*. In a sense, being oneself is also a conquest, a "blind task" at the root of oneself. One of the first steps of this becoming aware of oneself, this assuming oneself, is the recognition of one's foreign origin. In fact, evoking Marcel, Bruaire states that there is no true self-awareness if one does not recognize that one does not come from oneself and that one's own parents cannot fully account for the origin of oneself. This is where the wonder of being spiritual lies: that the authentic self-determination of the human spirit is never self-constitutive. The being-of-the spirit is there, totally itself, but still in need of becoming itself.

The reflexive assumption of oneself never happens outside the encounter with the other. In a sense, we may say that it is only the encounter with the other that makes one discover one's own identity. Knowing another being-of-spirit entails seeing a human being through all the expressivity that his corporeality allows him, all the expressivity that he is willing to

65. *EE,* 37.

unfold. In fact, human corporeality always plays a twofold role. On the one hand, it is that which allows the being of the spirit to be encountered and to express itself. On the other hand, it is precisely that which veils the secret of its own spirit. The richness of the other's expressivity is the instrument through which the other gives himself and is at the same time what veils him. This double play of form and content shows the unsurpassable and ungraspable *alterity* of the other. The encounter makes one discover that with the other, there can be an "intuitive sympathy," which, however, does not allow us to experience what the other is passing through. In this encounter with the other, he is seen in all his ontological dependence:

> That being which does not owe his own being to himself, who, on the contrary, is given to himself, is in need of being confirmed, in restless longing for exaltation, for joy in existing. The price of the ephemeral joys cannot be measured against the deaf and consubstantial longing for an eternal dwelling place of assured subsistence.[66]

Through the other, the being-of-spirit gradually discovers his own face. In this sense, although one is not able to suffer or live in the place of others, one recognizes that they are made of the same nature. One discovers that one's own being is endowed with that double rhythm of interiority and exteriority. Bruaire uses the example of love to make his meaning clear. The loving affirmation of the other, the smile of the parents, and life with them, makes the child discover that he is also some*one* different from them. As a result of being affirmed by others, the child discovers his own limited autonomy: that he is a "self" in the full sense of the word, yet he is not the master of his own being. For this reason, his life is to be developed in this tension between the affirmation of himself and the gift of himself to the other. Although the retreat into one's own interiority is always necessary, it can only take place when two conditions are recognized: first, that the fundamental lack in oneself, one's "incurable desire," is the need for one's own other; second, that one affirms oneself only if one gives oneself to the other. In the same way that one can say "I" because someone has previously said "You" to one, one cannot say "I" without saying to the other "You."[67] Bruaire maintains that even the most radical affirmation of

66. *EE*, 39.

67. Cabada Castro, in his very fine presentation of Feuerbach's anthropology, proposes an interesting analysis of the I-Thou relationship in Feuerbach and its influence on

the other always includes the affirmation of oneself and vice versa. There is no such thing as "pure" altruism—which does not mean that there cannot be real gratuity among human beings. In fact, when the complete gift of oneself to the other does not include an affirmation of oneself, it turns out to be a sheer rejection of one's own being. To want to be the other—the human or the divine other—is a silent confession of no longer willing to be oneself. To affirm the other to such an extent that one disappears is not, ultimately, the affirmation of the other but the rejection of oneself. In this regard, the affirmation of oneself as the master of being and the rejection of oneself in a falsely "loving" affirmation of the other are identical existential positions before the mystery of being. Thus, the logic of existence implies, on the one hand, the acceptance that one is spiritual without being absolute spirit and, on the other hand, that the gratuitous affirmation of the other is made by a limited spirit who, not being the master of its own being, cannot dispose of itself to the extent of a total denial of itself. The human spirit is ontologically under the law of interior and exterior, of keeping to oneself and of offering oneself, of isolation and opening.

The infirmity one sees in the other reminds each of his own indigence, of the fact of not being his own foundation. While forcefully rejecting the philosophies of existence, Bruaire affirms that there is no true perception of one's own being if it is unable to conjugate the anguish of being-for-death and the fact that, in Spinoza's words, *experimur nos aeternos esse.* In the joy of one's own existence, these two elements remain always present: eternity and contingency. This is due to the fact that the self is given to itself completely, that it cannot but be, and to the fact that at the same time the walls of existence always seem too narrow for the breadth of the human soul. The dramatic question that death raises, not death abstractly understood, but "my own personal" death, comes from the fact that death is always a certain and inevitable destiny, while, at the same time, the existence of the spirit rejects with all its might its own annihilation. The dramatic tension between one's own mortality and one's desire for eternity makes it clear that the human spirit is made in such a way that it

Buber, Guardini, and Balthasar. Manuel Cabada Castro, *El humanismo premarxista de Ludwig Feuerbach* (Madrid: BAC, 1975). See Ludwig Feuerbach, *Das Wesen des Christentums,* vol. 5 of *Gesammelte Werke* (Berlin: Akademie Verlag, 1973). For the English translation see *The Essence of Christianity,* trans. George Eliot (New York: Harper and Row, 1957). See also Manuel Cabada Castro, *Sein und Gott bei Gustav Siewerth* (Dusseldorf: Patmos, 1971).

is in search of its own destiny: being confirmed in its own being. But how is one to pursue this destiny if one does not own his very being, if one seems unable to escape death? "Perhaps I have been promised to Nothingness, [but] I could not have sprung from Nothingness." It is to the origin of himself that the human being needs to turn in order to discover what his destiny might be. It is there that the being-of-spirit is to return to his own origin—because "it conceals my foundations."[68] To look for one's own destiny, to the possibility of being confirmed, is to look for one's own origin. If that mysterious origin is what makes the being-of-spirit be, then the secret to self-confirmation must be hidden there. For this reason, one's destiny, which should be something that lies ahead, is indeed a going back toward one's own origin. What lies ahead for the being of the human spirit is returning to its own dwelling place.[69]

Bruaire synthesizes this phenomenology of the spirit in four main points that constitute the *eidetic* of the spirit. These four elements are to be considered as forming a unity. Although the first is the most important one—in the sense that the other three presuppose its existence—none of them is to be understood separately. First, since the human spirit does not come from itself and its existence cannot be ultimately deduced from that of its progenitors, or reduced to the realm of nature, one needs to recognize that it comes from another. Here Bruaire formulates in positive terms what the systematic anthropology only stated negatively: "the human spirit is *a gift of being,* and all its existence is that of being a gift, being a *being-gift.*" Second, the being-of-spirit's way of existence is that "*of the pneumatological rhythm* of exteriorization and interiorization, of manifestation and secret, . . . in their triplicity, the spiritual potencies operate according to this rhythm of spiritual 'breath.'" Third, the being-of-spirit, in its own *haecceitas,* is not a predefined form, but rather it "is *constituted by a singular destiny.*" The being-of-spirit is given to itself and thus it is already a self, which, however, has the task of becoming itself. Fourth, the key to the destiny of the being-of-spirit is found "in the *conversion to the origin.*"[70]

---

68. *EE,* 42.

69. See the brilliant article by Leduc-Fayette, "Du retour à l'origine," *Revue philosophique* 1 (1990): 47–57.

70. *EE,* 43–44. Bruaire's emphasis. The first text in which Bruaire proposes the *eidetic* of the spirit is *EdE* (1980).

The return to the origin in order to discover one's own destiny reveals man's own source: if the human being is and he did not exist before, if man is not reducible to his biological progenitors, if his being is not ultimately attributable to nature or to social interactions, if he is different from and more than what he does or says, if he cannot close the circle of reflection, it is because he is *not* any of those elements completely. If he is *not,* then he is something *else.* If his own being is not reducible to nature or to others, if his own being cannot be deduced from any of those elements, that means that what he *is,* is *being given*—even before "having" his own being. His very being is *gift.*

CHAPTER 5

An Ontology of Gift
Finite Spirit

The outcome of Bruaire's semantic and eidetic analysis of the concept of spirit is the acknowledgment that if the collection of phenomena of spirit "forces us to use the Word *gift* to name *spirit,* it is because *gift* is, from its very beginning, its own essence."[1] Gift, then, is neither an ontological category that can be enumerated along with others, nor a name capable of describing only the being of the human spirit. Being *is* gift, in the strongest sense of the term: *"esse spirituale et donum convertuntur."*[2] To affirm that being-of-spirit is *given* is to state that it is given *to itself; it is free.* Since the gift is that of being, the human spirit disposes of itself without being its own origin, and thus being-of-spirit cannot be itself except "by the ontological reflection which converts being-in-itself to being-for-itself."[3]

The clarification of Bruaire's understanding of the human being-of-spirit in terms of gift requires us both to examine in what sense being is gift and to test whether the concept of gift is adequate to expressing being.[4]

---

1. *EE,* 53. See also Aquinas, *ST* I-I, q. 45, a. 3 and a. 7.

2. *EE,* 65. In this regard, Bruaire's ontodology considers "gift" to be the transcendental in whose light the others can be adequately affirmed. The doctrine of the transcendentals, although it can be rooted in Aristotle's metaphysics (*Met.* 3.3.998b22), is the result of the development which metaphysics underwent during the Middle Ages. With this in mind, see Aristotle, *Met.:* for truth, 6.4.1027b25ff.; for the one, 10.2.1054a18; for the good, 5.16.1021b12ff. Also see Aristotle, *Nicomachean Ethics* 1.6.1096a18ff.

3. *PM,* 263.

4. *PrMC,* 126.

The ontological reading of gift requires illustrating in what sense there could be a gratuitous return of the gift which is not abstracted from the historical and bodily existence of the being-of-spirit. This will allow us to see that, for Bruaire, being's presence is nothing but a "gratuitous and gracious gift."[5]

Giving before Having

It seems perfectly adequate, at first, to consider gift in the realm of the exchange of human possessions. In fact, there always needs to be some*one* who gives and someone who receives: for example, the bridegroom offering the ring to the bride. Some*thing* must be given in that interchange—in our example, a ring. Besides the giver, the receiver, and the actual gift, there is always a certain meaning that the gift itself symbolizes—the ring that the bridegroom gives to the bride is a sign of their mutual love and promise of fidelity. From this perspective, the possession of a good seems to be the *conditio sine qua non* for the possibility of giving. In this sense, the spouses can exchange rings because they have them and they love each other. If one approaches Bruaire's ontology of *gift* from this perspective, the first question that naturally comes to mind regards the legitimacy of talking of *being* in terms of gift, inasmuch as it initially seems more appropriate to circumscribe donation within the limits of having. In fact, one could say that a gift is given in order to be had and not in order for the other to be.

Another difficulty comes from the recognition that, even if it is true that the gift somehow carries within itself the presence of the giver and that sometimes the gift and the giver coincide, the difference between the self and the gift given seems to be an insurmountable objection to the ontological definition of gift. Except for the work of art, if the human spirit is always other from its operations—even in the gift of one's life in exchange for the other's—the relation between gift and being appears to remain extrinsic.

5. *PM*, 262. The reader should bear in mind that the main text of Bruaire which I shall be following more closely here is *EE* and that my treatment in this chapter of the theme of being as gift is restricted to the *human* spirit. The full analysis of Bruaire's ontology will be complete only when I have presented Bruaire's understanding of the absolute in the light of gift.

Bruaire considers that interpreting the logic of gift in terms of somewhat gratuitous "economic transactions" neglects the fact that the exchange of gifts discloses something fundamental about the nature of the whole, no matter how loosely connected a particular gift and being-gift seem to be. The exchange of a gift has a symbolic character that is not inevitably arbitrary because the logic of gift is grounded in the essential being-given of being. "Having" always requires and presupposes an interiority for which only "being" is able to account. For Bruaire, a "gift" can be *had* because being is *given*—and not vice versa.[6] The primary meaning of gift is thus *ontological,* and only secondarily can gift be interpreted in terms of *having.* To evaluate the primacy of "being" over "having" requires that the analysis of the concept of gift focus not so much on particular gifts and the phenomenology of giving but rather on the essence of being-of-spirit itself. This methodology affords Bruaire the possibility of justifying the truth of the logic of exchanges of gift without losing the gratuitous nature of gift. Once the ontological nature of gift has been grounded, it will be possible to reconceive adequately the dynamic of exchanging gifts.[7]

The first step that needs to be taken, Bruaire says, is to realize that the concept of *gift* does not presuppose a receiving subject to whom something is given. The eidetic and phenomenological analysis of the concept of the spirit illustrates that the human spirit is in-deducible from and irreducible to nature and thus that its very being *is* gift. If gift is to be such,

---

6. *EE,* 55. It is not surprising that there are similarities between Bruaire's position and G. Marcel's discourse on being and having. Cf. Gabriel Marcel, "Esquisse d'une phénoménologie de l'avoir," in *Être et avoir* (Paris: Éditions Universitaires, 1991), 111–25.

7. Both Marion and Derrida perceive that gift needs to be considered apart from the logic of the economy: "the gift only becomes itself by breaking away from the economy, in order to let itself be thought through along the lines of givenness. Therefore, one must re-conduct the gift away from economy and toward givenness. To reconduct is to reduce it." And reducing means "thinking the gift as gift, making abstraction of the triple transcendence . . . of the giver, . . . the recipient, . . . and of the objectivity of the object exchange" (Marion, "Sketch of a Phenomenological Concept of Gift," in Merold Westphal, ed., *Postmodern Philosophy and Christian Thought* [Bloomington: Indiana University Press, 1999], 122–43, 131). While agreeing with Marion's attempt to treat gift apart from the logic of the economy, Derrida claims that "if there is a gift . . . it must be the experience of this impossibility [for the gift to exist and to appear as such], and it should appear as impossible. The event called gift is totally heterogenous to theoretical identification, to phenomenological identification" ("On the Gift: A Discussion between Jacques Derrida and Jean-Luc Marion Moderated by Richard Hearney," in *God, the Gift,* 54–78, 59). Bruaire, by contrast, tries to prove that there is a concept of gift and that it needs to be thought ontologically.

then it cannot come *after* the existence of the receiving subject; the subject cannot pre-exist the reality of gift. Bruaire contends that the *subject* itself, and not a particular gift, is what first needs to be thought as "given." In this sense, the distinction between essence and existence is secondary to the concept of gift; that is to say, gift does not refer to the concrete existence offered to a possible essence but to the whole being, to essence and existence. For this reason, if "essence" is gift, then existence, seen in light of gift, may be interpreted according to its Latin root, *ex-sistere,* which names something that is not its own origin and that in wonder makes the discovery of being what it is.[8] "Gift is a being in and by its act of being."[9] For Bruaire, the noun "gift" and the verb "give" name one reality. Gift is what makes the subject ex-sist; it is its very essence. What is given, then, cannot be thought independently of the fact of being given.[10] The identification of being and gift provides, according to Bruaire, the correct angle from which to revisit the Aristotelian metaphysical categories.[11]

The concept of gift follows the law of "everything or nothing." The gift, to be such, needs to be given "once and for all"; otherwise, there is not re-

8. The similarities between this understanding of existence and Richard of Saint Victor's understanding of person should not pass unnoticed. See Richard of Saint Victor, *De Trinitate,* IV, 11–23 (Paris: J. Vrin, 1958).

9. *EE,* 54. The importance ascribed to gift does not deny the decisive ultimate truth of the ontological difference. According to Bruaire, the latter, however, is only adequately justified when rooted in the theological difference of absolute spirit. I ask the reader to put off assessing ontology's account of the ontological difference until I present the difference in the absolute gift.

10. Kenneth Schmitz explains: "But it is not only potency that is received [in the creating act]; the act is received as well, because the whole being (essence and existence) is received. God creates beings whole and entire, singular beings in community" (Kenneth L. Schmitz, "Created Receptivity and the Philosophy of the Concrete," *The Thomist* 61 [1997]: 362 [hereafter *CrR*]). This fine article is very useful for comparing the understanding of being as gift with the Thomistic conception of creation.

11. It is important to clarify from the outset that Bruaire adopts the Aristotelian scheme in his approach to the study of the categories. This choice implies that for him, language is not merely logical but also "leads reflection to being." Thus Bruaire, despite the palpable influence of Hegel upon his analysis of being, studies categories of being that are far from the Kantian and Hegelian schemes. The categories are neither attributes proper to the intellect nor different stages in the development of an absolute spirit that moves from objectivity to subjectivity. Instead, these genres of determination (he studies only substance, quantity, quality, and relation) refer to being; they are *ontological* categories. Cf. Kant, *KrV* A182/B 224. Kant's influence made Hegel read the problem of substance and accidents in the light of relation and perceive substance as a substratum in which attributes inhere. See Kant, *KrV* A80/B106; Hegel, *WL* I.2.

ally true gratuity. Gift cannot be held back; it cannot be given in degrees; it cannot respond to any prerequisites. The concept of gift does indeed possess a sense of destination, but the destination is first and foremost intrinsic to the gift itself and not to an already-existing subject who becomes the recipient of a gift. Bruaire contends, then, that "*only what is given to itself is gift,* in the most rigorous and fullest meaning of the term."[12]

Recalling that the German term *Bestimmung* means both destination and determination, Bruaire proposes that gift is given to itself (destination) in order to become itself (determination). This means that to give a self *to itself* is to recognize that being-gift *is free.* Being-of-spirit, inasmuch as it is being-gift, is at its own disposal in order to become itself.[13] If the gift were a fully determined subject, there would be no gratuity, no freedom, and the attempt to elaborate a metaphysics would remain instead within the realm of technology. Stating that the gift of the human spirit is called to self-determination implies, on the one hand, that it does not possess itself fully; it belongs to itself without being its own origin. On the other hand, since it is given to itself, the human spirit does not possess itself immediately. The process of determination takes place within the always already present relation to the other.[14]

Bruaire wishes to revisit the Aristotelian categories for his ontodology because he thinks that they will remain formal and neutral until they have "been appropriated, converted to the meaning of being as being, the ὄνῇὄν; until being's categories have been bent to being's essence," that is to say, gift.[15] Thinking thus of the substance of the human spirit, Bruaire says that it would be misleading to presume that to be free, to be at one's own disposal, or "to be in one's own hands," means that the human spirit has become the master of its own being. In fact, there is an ontological barrier to the realization of this possibility. If the human spirit is given to

12. *EdE,* 36 (Bruaire's emphasis). To reinforce this point, Bruaire likes to quote Aristotle, *Topica* 5.7.136b15-137b10. For a similar explanation of the problem of the identification of the gift and the giver see Schmitz, *The Gift,* 29–34.

13. *PM,* 263.

14. Bruaire warns against the assumption that "to be itself in order to become itself" is "a spiritualistic" process. That is to say, as the last section of this chapter illustrates, Bruaire is fully aware that his *ontodology* will lead to a dualistic understanding of the human spirit unless he is able to show in what sense becoming oneself is not an abstract process independent of the subject's own corporeality, in juxtaposition to the logic of existence itself.

15. *EE,* 65.

itself, its disposal of itself can never be understood in absolute terms, as if it were *causa sui,* or *ex se.* Nevertheless, it would also be a misinterpretation of the idea of "being at the disposal of oneself" to think that the human spirit is already itself from the very beginning, and, consequently that whatever came after its constitution should be regarded as secondary or juxtaposed to the true essence of the human spirit. From the very beginning, then, the human spirit as a substance, is itself (καθ' αὐτό), but it is also from another and in need of becoming what it is.

Bruaire, borrowing Hegelian terminology but modifying its content, uses the following terms to describe the movement of being-of-spirit's self-determination. The first is *inseity* (being-in-itself); this represents being-gift inasmuch as it is given without reserve. What it is, is "being-given," and existence is "coming from another." The second term is *adseity.* Being-in-itself is its own recipient; it is given to itself in order to assume itself by means of itself. This *adseity* is the potency of free personal acts. The third term is *ipseity,* which is being-gift inasmuch as it is being-in-itself through the singular reflection of itself into itself. Being-gift is given to itself in order to be itself. *Ipseity* always presupposes *inseity* because the free determination of oneself must not let go of the fact that being-gift is not self-originated. The act of being, by which the being-of-spirit is, is at the same time *in-itself* and in *potency-of-itself.* From the act of being to the freedom of the free act, "being in potency is the *adseic* assumptivity that becomes actual in the awakening of the consciousness of oneself."[16] Spiritual substance is being *in order to be subject.*[17] The human spirit is both act of being and in potency of being itself, because it is gift; that is to say, it is to determine itself and to participate in the logic proper to gift, which is further giving. This understanding of substance, which combines autonomy and self-determination, comes from the coalescence of freedom, spirit, and being. According to the first aspect of freedom (autonomy), the being-of-spirit possesses itself, it is relatively in-dependent, and it has a certain subsistence. The second aspect (determination) implies that being-of-spirit brings itself to action and to openness to others.[18]

16. *EE,* 67.
17. *PrMC,* 126.
18. As the first chapter illustrated, Bruaire's understanding of freedom ought not be thought in terms of discrete choices whose aim is to select, from several minor goods, the one which seems best to reflect the good itself. Rather, freedom is conceived of metaphysi-

The movement of self-determination proper to the being-gift of the human spirit, the ipseic assumption, is a "return" to the unknown origin, a conversion in which being-gift, "in its pure substantial identity, comes back to itself in order to be *it*-self." Gift is given to itself in order to become a subject, and in this return to itself, which "actualizes the *it* of *itself*," being-of-spirit discovers that it does not belong to the world and that it is "unrecoverable by its own origin," because if its own origin could claim it back, then it would not be truly given to itself.[19]

The proximity of Bruaire's thought to Hegel's could induce us to think that the circular image Bruaire adopts to explain the movement of self-determination follows the Hegelian movement of spirit's reflection into itself. Instead, Bruaire's contention is that the process of "conversion" needs to be placed at the ontological level, and not at an epistemological, ethical, or psychological level. In the same way that gifts are given and had because being is itself gift, so the epistemological circularity, in which the knower goes out of himself in order to know something and returns back to himself having appropriated the essence of the other and so enlarged his own, reflects the ontological act of conversion. This ἐνέργεια οὐσιώδης is the condition of possibility, reality, and necessity of the noetic conversion. For Bruaire, it would be reductive to think of substantial conversion in terms of intellectual reflection. In fact, if the being of the human spirit were to be thought as a model of total self-transparence, it would be possible to identify the movement of substance with the movement of knowing the self or the other. Instead, since being-of-spirit is given to itself, and it is given to itself in a corporeal manner, there is a difference between the acts of the spirit and the spirit itself, which precludes understanding the latter in terms of the former. The confusion between these two levels, says Bruaire,

---

cally: it is the primordial orientation toward the absolute; freedom is the decision to pursue or to reject this end. Against this backdrop, it is easy to understand both that Bruaire does not leave the realm of metaphysics when he is exploring the meaning of gift and that the substantial identity of being-of-spirit needs to be thought of within the rhythm proper to spirit's freedom of expansion and contraction, interiority and exteriority. Another distinction that needs to be made is that this primordial orientation cannot be confused with the "fundamental option." To correct this misunderstanding of freedom, see John Paul II, *Veritatis Splendor* (1978) and Livio Melina, *Sharing in Christ's Virtues: For a Renewal of Moral Theology in Light of "Veritatis Splendor,"* trans. William E. May (Washington, D.C.: Catholic University of America Press, 2001).

19. *EE,* 58.

explains how Descartes could identify "I think" with "I am a thinking substance." Here again, the theomorphic illusion underlies the affirmation that the noetic movement of reflection is the paradigm for the ontological.

The return to the origin, or the substantial conversion, does not imply that the identity of the substance is lost. Bruaire argues that identity is not to be understood as the Fichtean first principle of identity (I = I), or in the formalistic negative sense whereby substance would be defined as that which is not an accident and which subsists in itself.[20] Identity supposes *ipseic* assumption. There is no self-identity that is not constituted by the three moments of *inseity, adseity,* and *ipseity.* According to Bruaire, this identity is to be understood both in a *passive* and in an *active* sense. In its *passive* sense, substance is considered as being-given, as gift. Therefore, it cannot but be totally given to itself; it does not admit variation or degrees of any kind. For this reason, the passive sense of *gift* is what gives substance its identity; it is that by which every being-of-spirit remains what it is as long as it exists. The *active* sense of *gift* perceives being as the assumption of itself, the identification of itself in the process of becoming spiritual substance. "*The identity is of and by the spirit,* which tries to apply to things its own constitutive norm in all knowledge of nature."[21] Being-gift entails first of all the *reception* of being. The difficulty in perceiving the ontodological understanding of identity is lessened if one understands that the *passive* sense of gift (the communication of the gift) cannot be separated from the *active* sense of gift (the reception of the gift). In this sense, acceptance of the gift is the recognition that the human spirit is a *spirit* and therefore free, given to itself in order to become itself. The reception of the gift is not complete outside the acceptance of the primordial orientation toward one's own Origin and the tendency toward self-possession.[22]

Bruaire states that being-of-spirit discovers itself already in this movement of return to itself. Hence, the beginning of the conversion in which being-gift becomes itself does not depend on the free initiative of the being-of-spirit. Nevertheless, the claim that, from its very inception, the being-of-spirit is already oriented toward its origin, already in this process

20. Here Bruaire echoes Hegel's critique of the traditional understanding of substance as he portrays it in *Die Lehre vom Sein* in *WL.*
21. *EE,* 68.
22. Schmitz, *CrR,* 364–65; Balthasar, *Epilog,* 62–64.

of substantial conversion, does not mean that this conversion is a "necessary" process. Perhaps one of the greatest difficulties in this understanding of the human spirit lies in the fact that in the "ontological conversion," one discovers that one is already oneself, in a complete substantial identity, and, at the same time, that one is already turning back to one's own origin. In this respect, since freedom is to be understood ontologically, there is, on the one hand, a necessity in the sense that the being-of-spirit already is from the very beginning in return to itself, and, on the other hand, this process of conversion is not predetermined. Since being-gift is being-of-spirit, it is essentially free, and hence the development of itself is in its own hands. This is why the risk of losing oneself in the process is always present.

Bruaire does allot significant space to the description of the movement of ipseic assumption that makes the human being-of-spirit become itself. Since his understanding of substance, or of what being is, is always accompanied by the substantial conversion to its origin, it is plausible to think that Bruaire's concept of gift has transformed act into potency, dissolved being into its operation, and confused the category of substance with that of relation. Bruaire himself comments on repeated occasions on being-gift's potency to become itself, and, as we saw already, he tries to work out a philosophy of the concrete that claims to take the logic of human existence into its metaphysical account without falling into an atheistic existentialism. However, for Bruaire, *the* metaphysical category is substance and not relation. To interpret Bruaire's position as reducing gift to potency, and thus to make of Bruaire's concept of gift an "ideal," but not a "real" concept of gift, fails to take into account the fact that Bruaire always puts the ipseic assumption together with the totality of being given to itself which makes the gift to be such. In fact, the identity proper to the being-gift is never lost. Perhaps Bruaire's account of the essence of the human spirit as oscillating between Scotus's *haecceitas* and *quidditas* does call for further reflection. Nevertheless, if gift is to be given to itself, and is indeed totally given, then we are to understand the gift proper to the human being-of-spirit in terms of act rather than merely in terms of potency. Since the being-of-spirit is free, its substance is always in potency to becoming itself, to being confirmed in being—historically and eternally—but this does not necessarily mean that potency has primacy over act. Inverting this order would go against Bruaire's contention that the movement proper to be-ing is prompted, not by a Hegelian negativity, but, as we shall see, by an ultimate positivity. The final verification of this interpretation, however, depends on the explanation of absolute being in terms of gift. In the ques-tion of whether Bruaire's concept of gift is "real" or only "potential," what is ultimately at stake is the plausibility of thinking being in terms of *spirit* and not so much the issue of the primacy of act over potency.[23]

In fact, to understand why Bruaire thinks that being-of-spirit's circular movement from inseity to ipseity is best described as a return, or a "sub-stantial conversion," it is important to keep in mind that Bruaire's con-ception of substance is governed by his understanding of spirit.[24] In the previous chapter, I indicated that oneness is not "difference with respect to any other" but, more fundamentally, the possibility of being-in-itself. There I mentioned that the reflexivity proper to the spirit is the return to oneself that denies any disappearance into nothingness, the dissolution of substance in its exterior manifestations. What I am articulating now is not so much how unity can be preserved against nothingness as *what* unity itself is—Bruaire's ontodology sees in this unity the meaning of the cat-egory of quantity. In this sense, the substantial conversion is the return to the origin of being that being-gift itself is not. Being-of-spirit returns to its own origin because it is being-given to itself. Being-gift's spiritual *ip-seity* presupposes a being-in-itself whose *aseity* is potency for itself. In this sense, its becoming itself, its existence in-and-for-itself, cannot take place

23. If this is true, then the fundamental issue that secures the identity of substance is being's positivity. If what Bruaire is attempting in his ontology is to show that gift is being in its spiritual way of being, then the three different "moments" of the ipseic as-sumption are not to be thought of as "actions" that should follow "being" but rather as dimensions proper to being itself, which, as the last chapter illustrates, are to be conceived in terms of person.

24. It is important to underline that "conversion" does not mean change in the Aristote-lian sense. If this were the case, "substantial conversion" would mean the coming into exis-tence of a new being. It does not have a moral (i.e., from bad to good habits) or an episte-mological meaning. Instead, it refers to the *ontology* of the subject. In this sense, "substantial conversion" alludes to—without uncritically adopting—what Hegel described as the Spirit's movement "from substance to subject." See Schmitz's article: "Substance Is Not Enough. Hegel's Slogan: From Substance to Subject," in *The Metaphysics of Substance: Proceedings of the American Catholic Philosophical Association,* ed. Daniel O. Dahlstrom (Washington, D.C.: Catholic University of America Press, 1987), 52–68; id., "The First Principle of Personal Becoming," *Review of Metaphysics* 47 (June 1994): 757–74.

outside the discovery of that mysterious origin which constitutes it. It is, then, the very fact that being is gift that causes the human spirit not to be itself unless it becomes itself by returning to its origin.[25]

The passage from being-in-itself to being-for-itself inevitably witnesses to the impossibility of a perfect loop, a complete return to self, due to the fact that the origin *is not* the human spirit itself. For this reason, Bruaire depicts the *origin* of the human being-of-spirit as foreign, that is to say, as both belonging to another region *and* unknown.[26] The foreign origin at the human spirit's deepest core makes it impossible for the conversion to be complete.[27] In fact, "returning" presupposes, on the one hand, knowledge of the starting point and, on the other hand, the capacity to preserve the donating act that gives origin to the human being-of-spirit. Yet, the human spirit possesses neither. Bruaire claims that the return to the origin does not provide knowledge of the origin. He maintains that to identify the origin of the human spirit with the absolute presupposes a speculative or historical mediation, or even a revelation. Hence, being-of-spirit's self-assumption is an impossible enterprise if it is left to the human spirit alone. Along with its historical concreteness, and the identification between essence and determination *(Bestimmung)*, it is precisely this unknowability of the origin and destiny of the being of spirit that makes Bruaire's ontodology affirm that the *quiddity* of the *haecceity* of the human spirit remains undefinable. The substance of the human being-of-spirit is then a particularity given to its singular freedom.

Bruaire's analysis reveals the ascendancy that Schelling's rhythm of spirit has in his ontodological understanding of the category of quality. This category concerns that aspect of being-gift which expresses its most important significations: the twofold movement of inspiration and expiration. Human spirit is characterized first by reflection into itself, the

---

25. Bruaire's full understanding of "conversion" will be presented in the next chapter. So far, I have given his account of "conversion" in the realm of the human spirit. In the next chapter, this principle will be used to describe God's oneness.

26. *EE*, 56.

27. The finitude of the human spirit, according to Bruaire, cannot but be perceived within the "joyful happiness of the gift *(cadeau)* of being," and the "joy of existence." For Bruaire, gladness is the adequate echo of the perception of limitedness, because "*Geben* is the truth of *Setzen*"; being posited finds its reason in being given. See *EE*, 60; *PM*, 279. For a positive understanding of "nostalgia" for the absolute, see Aquinas, *ST* I, q. 20, a. 1; Pseudo-Dionysius, *On the Divine Names*, Bk. 4, chaps. 1 (693B–696B) and 10–18 (705B–716B).

movement in which spirit retracts into itself and assumes itself. This is freedom's spiritual norm, which accepts the fact of being-gift and then gives that gift to itself. Yet, at the same time, being-of-spirit is not only inspiration, it is also *effusion* of itself. Spirit is not only the negative movement toward itself: the truth of this retrogression is the spiritual negation of itself in the outpouring toward the other. Moreover, interior reflexivity is negation only inasmuch as it is the obtaining of spiritual energy for the effusion of self. There is no conversion to self whose end is not giving self in unlimited generosity. The qualitative movement of the spirit is affirmation of itself (negation of the exterior manifestation of itself) inasmuch as it is the triumph of gift, the promotion of the other. The logic of gift, therefore, cannot be reduced to either of these two essential qualifications. It consists in inseparable components: negative contraction into self and positive expansion of self.

Gratuitous Reciprocity

The discovery of having been given to itself coincides with the realization that, for that very reason, the being-of-spirit is also being-in-debt.[28] Although its self is truly given, and is never claimed back, the being-of-spirit, precisely because it has been given to itself, "owes" its very self. According to Bruaire, the radical identification of being-gift and being-in-debt, of "freedom—being given to itself—and moral obligation," is uncancellable.[29]

It seems however, that if being-of-spirit is bound to give back, to return the gift, then it is not free, and giving is nothing but "getting even." If to be given to oneself is to be in debt, then one owes something, and hence one is radically dependent. Undoubtedly, the human being would not owe anything to anyone if he were the origin of himself. In that case, he would be "free to give" at his own discretion. Still, if human freedom cannot be equated with an absolute abstract freedom, then for the former, freedom and dependence are co-essential.[30] There is no dependence without freedom and no freedom without dependence. The objection that be-

---

28. *EE,* 60; *FE,* 44; *EM,* 154.
29. *FE,* 27. In this regard, Bruaire maintains that the roots of ethics are ontological.
30. *FE,* 51.

ing dependent, that "having to give back," eliminates the freedom required to preserve the gratuity of the gift, is prompted by the illusion of the human being's total independence.[31] However, even without embracing such a conception of freedom, one could still say that if being-of-spirit is gratuitously given, then one cannot be "obliged" to give in return. If a gift is freely given, then no return should be expected. If something is demanded in exchange for the gift given, then the gift is not totally given and is indeed "claimed back." In this case, donation would be nothing but simple commerce, as Derrida has it.

To conceive of debt as something that one acquires and has to pay back is to shift the terms of the discussion from "being" to "having." Being-in-debt, returning the gift, cannot be imagined as giving something to someone because the recipient now finds himself *obliged* to "pay back." Instead, one *is* in *debt* and, thus, one has a debt which needs to be met. For this reason, the "debt" is not of a particular thing but rather of one's *whole being*—provided one does not think of one's own being as an object which could be given back. In this sense, when paying one's debt, one does not give "a part" or "everything" of oneself; one gives "what *one is not*."[32] Thus, it is necessary to explore what being-in-debt means in the context of the substance of the human being. To this end, we need to see first to whom the being-gift is in debt, and, second, how it is possible to pay the debt of its own being.

To understand the meaning of "debt," what needs to be seen is that whereas "being given to itself" entails the (ontological) coming-from another, being-in-debt clarifies that this being-from another is, at the same time an (ontological) being-for-another (in the sense, not of doing something for someone else, but rather of being-present-with). Being-in-debt reveals, then, the constitutive relativity of the human being to the other. Bruaire's insistence on the connection between being-gift and being-in-debt reveals that there is no assumption of itself, no being-in-itself, able to become being-for-itself outside its being-*for-another*. There is no such thing as a self already constituted which then, later on, has the possibility of entering into relation with others. The self, being-gift, is, from the very beginning, being-with-and-for others. Being-gift's substantial identity is to be

---

31. From the ontodological perspective, what distinguishes God from the human being is that whereas the latter is a being-gift which is also being-in-debt, God is gift without being-in-debt. See *PM*, 160, 279.

32. *EE*, 61. *MS*, 11.

comprehended from the outset as freely being in communion with another. The emphasis on being-in-debt introduces within the very substance of the subject its referentiality to the other (oneself, the human other, and the unknown origin from which one comes), while it clarifies that this being-for-and-with others is not at all secondary to its very essence; the subject must acknowledge and assume that relation with the other if it wants to become itself. Being in-and-for-itself is thus preserved from any solipsistic understanding. In its relationality with others, being-of-spirit becomes itself by giving itself to others. Yet, to say that being-of-spirit is not an "empire with closed borders" does not mean that the category of substance is dissolved into that of relation, or that there is no real, although relative, substantial identity. To justify the ipseic assumption of finite being and the reality of its being-given fully, Bruaire would turn to the Trinitarian absolute. If the human being is created in the Word, then the substance of finite being resembles that relationality proper to the Word—with the obvious reservation that finite substance does not subsist in itself and that the relations between finite beings are not to be understood hypostatically.[33]

Awareness that one is in debt to another cannot override the unknow-

---

33. Obviously, without falling into Hegel's absorption of substance into the category of relation, Bruaire does move away from the Aristotelian and Thomistic conception of relation. See Aristotle, *Categories* 7.6a35, Eng. trans. *Categoriae and De Interpretatione*, trans. E. M. Edghill, in *The Works of Aristotle*, vol. 1 (London: Oxford University Press, 1955); *Met.* 5.14.1020b26–1021b11. St. Thomas said that the being of *relation* is *imperfectissimum.* Cf. Thomas Aquinas, *Summa Contra Gentiles* IV, 14 (hereafter *SCG*). For a reading of Bruaire's ontodology contrary to mine see Emmanuel Tourpe, *Siewerth "après" Siewerth. Le lien idéal de l'amour dans le thomisme spéculatif de Gustave Siewerth et la visée d'un réalisme transcendental* (Louvain: Louvain-La Neuve, 1998), 415–17. Tourpe's insightful analysis, hampered perhaps by a limited knowledge of Bruaire's entire oeuvre, claims that relation is the fundamental ontodological category because Bruaire's gift is a potential and not a real category. For further reflection on a conception of substance which includes relationship but does not dissolve the former into the latter and which is able to forge a new concept of the human *person,* see David Schindler, "Norris Clarke on Person, Being, and St. Thomas," *Communio* 20: 580–92; W. Norris Clarke, "Response to David Schindler's Comments," *Communio* 20: 593–98; id., *Person and Being* (Milwaukee: Marquette University Press, 1993); Schmitz, *CrR,* 360–71; id., "Selves and Persons: A Difference in Loves?" *Communio* 18: 183–206; id., "The Geography of the Person," *Communio* 13: 27–48; Joseph Ratzinger, "Zum Personenverständis in der Theologie," *Dogma und Verkündigung* (Munich: Erich Wewel Verlag, 1973): 205–23 (for an English translation, see "Concerning the Notion of Person in Theology," trans. Michael Waldstein, *Communio* 17: 439–53); Hans Urs von Balthasar, "On the Concept of Person," *Communio* 13: 18–26; Karol Wojtyla, "The Structure of Self-Determination as the Core of the Theory of the Person," in *Tommaso d'Aquino nel suo VII centenario* (Naples: Edizioni Domenicane Italiane, 1975–76), 37–44.

ability proper to the other. In this sense, there is more "apophatic" thinking in Bruaire's sometimes excessively rationalistic approach than he is willing to admit. In fact, Bruaire's philosophy attempts to acknowledge that the very origin of being-gift is unknown to itself because being-gift is not the origin of itself. Within itself, there is a mysterious presence, which is not the human spirit and which is more intimate, more fundamental to its own being than even itself. The origin is "and remains *unknown*," so much so that the task to return to it is blind. It is only from the not-knowing derived from its being a "spiritual orphan" that being-gift, in search of its own destiny, sets out toward the unfulfillable assumption of itself, fulfilling the debt, that is, its own being.[34] There is also a certain way in which the human other remains "unknown." According to the logic of *ontodological* identity, the other is also being-gift and remains *other*. There is, therefore, always an ultimate, particular singularity that cannot be absorbed, comprehended, or neglected. Of course, this individuality does not transform the other into an individual insularity making the relationship to others ultimately nonessential and relativistic. Otherness is what makes others encounterable and, at the same time, unassimilable to one's self.

In discovering the other, and in pouring oneself forth toward the other, one gives not what one has but, as Bruaire writes, "what one *is not*." From what has been said so far, "being-in-debt" cannot mean giving something one owns and has at one's disposal to offer freely to another. Rather being-in-debt regards what one *is*. To be sure; but how can one give what one *is* if one cannot give *being*? Furthermore, how can one give if one does not know the other that is latent within the intimacy of the human spirit and that is the ultimate source whence one's own being proceeds? What does it mean to give what one is not?

When Bruaire says that the finite spirit is to give what "it is not," he is not saying that the human being cannot give. He is not thinking quantitatively, in the sense that the expression "it is not" would be still something that human spirit can indeed return. It is one thing to say that, at the level

---

34. *EE,* 62. As the parable of the prodigal son teaches, it is only in the return to the Father that one discovers oneself. Let us remember here that this sense of "incompleteness" is not unknown to Thomism either. For Aquinas, the human soul is not a complete substance. See *ST* I, q. 75, a. 2, ad 1. This unknowability remains valid within a philosophical approach, and, relatively speaking, also within a theological one.

of the human spirit, the (ontological) gift cannot be returned and another to say that the human being cannot give at all. The ability to return the gift would eliminate the logic of gift, would "neutralize" it, so to speak. This is why, to "return" the gift, to give back what one is not, needs to have the form of a gratuitous reciprocity.

To pay the debt is the acknowledgment that the being-of-spirit has been placed within a logic of gift that is left at the hands of every human subject. In this regard, to be-in-debt is that property of gift which calls for giving further, freely.[35] Since being-of-spirit is given to itself to assume itself in the return to itself, the first way of giving further regards the subject itself, and it means to accept being-gift. Before giving any concrete gift, to "return the gift" is to welcome the gift which being-of-spirit is. The logic of gift excludes every *quid pro quo,* and it is for this reason that Bruaire says the debt cannot be paid. To be-in-debt is not a matter of giving the other what he rightly deserves but rather of an initial gratuitous acceptance of the gift. Gratuity only likes to be welcomed gratuitously.

That this interpretation of Bruaire's notion of being-in-debt as gratefulness is accurate is evidenced by the fact that, for Bruaire, to give oneself to the other is to recognize him and to affirm him for what he is, a free subject. For Bruaire, to give oneself to the other, to give what one "is not," is to *honor* the other, to recognize him for what he is. In this regard, Bruaire comments, for example, that to educate is far more than the communication of a body of knowledge in the hope that it will turn out to be useful later on. To educate is "truly giving *oneself* to the *other* and honoring the other as such."[36] Obviously, honoring the other is not a merely intellectual recognition. Affirming the other for what he is, a task which is decisive for the spirit's ipseic assumption, is, I contend, a most difficult and demanding action: it implies the recognition of the other in his otherness and, for that reason, the dramatic affirmation of the other's freedom and of his own particular history of becoming himself.[37] To give what one is not, at least on this anthropological level, is to honor alterity "in spirit and in truth," as Bruaire was fond of repeating.[38]

Being-in-debt is not, then, a constriction imposed from outside but, on

---

35. "Le don donne à donner" (Bruaire, "Le Dieu de l'histoire," 7).
36. *FE,* 28.   37. *FE,* 54–55.
38. This expression is taken from Jn 4:23.

the contrary, the free dynamic of love which gift brings about. It is true that a gift that is given with the expectation of a return is not truly a gift. Nevertheless, "pure" gratuity cannot imply the oblivion of the loving relation that ontologically constitutes the subject. Within the logic of love, gift implies both gratuitous receptivity and further giving. The rejection of being-in-debt in the name of a "pure" logic of gift implies a rejection of the dependence that characterizes the being-given of the being-of-spirit. To claim that the gift-of-spirit is not "in-debt" is to affirm implicitly that being-of-spirit is the origin of itself and to empty the nature of gift which, as we shall see, is infinitely fruitful. Being-gift is being free *and* being-in-debt. "He who has received, gives; he who has lived in freedom, fights for it; he who has been hosted, welcomes; he who has been recognized, affirms the other."[39]

The intrinsic relation between being-gift and being-in-debt, says Bruaire, grounds ethics in ontology. Bruaire, always interested in ethical issues and engaged in political debates and activities, strove to explain how what man does is always dependent upon who he is. As his analysis of Hegel's *Philosophy of Right* helped him to discover, "only an ontology of spirit capable of reanimating the certitude of the truth of each freedom's being would be able to secure the cornerstone of ethics, i.e., the ground of [moral] obligation."[40]

Without drawing distinctions between ethics and morality, Bruaire sees

---

39. *EE*, 63. Bruaire's explanation of "being-in-debt" enables him to explain the meaning that subsistence has within *ontodology*. The subsistence that is ascribed to substance is not the capacity to continue in existence in spite of losses, or even in spite of the possibility of death. Subsistence cannot be understood as security or self-sufficiency, as that which stands-underneath the qualities and preserves the identity of the subject through different changes. All these characterizations of self-subsistence tend to obscure the reality of the gift's being-given. Subsistence means first and foremost that being-gift is totally given to itself once and for all; it means that being-gift is given in order to be *and* cannot be claimed back. If we cannot properly understand subsistence when we forget that being is given from the very beginning, we must admit that there is no guarantee of eternal subsistence either. Being-given inaugurates the logic of gift and sets in motion the dynamic of giving. It is this being-in-debt of the gift which is the very root of the desire for eternity, an eternity in which one can recognize the source from which one comes and honor it properly. Being-in-debt also represents the native fragility of the gift and the need for an eternal confirmation of one's own being. Nevertheless, both the knowledge of the origin and the eternal confirmation of being-gift are only promises which cannot be guaranteed. "Gift is not such if it is not given once and for all. But the spirit of each one is the *absolute non-right* of being and of being that which one is" (*EE*, 69).

40. *PdD*, 102.

the understanding of the meaning of moral *obligation* as the key problem of this reflection.[41] The natural presupposition behind this starting-point is that there must be an adequate reason in order for man to act and to respect certain laws and socially assumed behaviors. To this end, two requirements need to be met. No ethical obligation, says Bruaire, can be such if it is imposed from outside itself, regardless of whether the human being has interiorized this constriction or not. At the same time, every ethical obligation ought to precede our free acts.[42] Moral obligation cannot be born from human decisions; it cannot be at their mercy. Of course, it has to be *for* human freedom and assimilated by it, and in this sense be *of* freedom, but it has to be so without being freedom's effect.[43] Bruaire contends that human feelings, previous engagements, or even human decisions can no longer be seen as the root of moral obligation. Kant erred in placing moral obligation in the rationality of will, because "one would still need to prove that the human being is under obligation to reason, to the rational form of my maxims, in order for their imperative character to be secured."[44] Bruaire holds that moral obligation must not come from outside but from inside the human spirit, and if human moral rationality (as understood by Kant) lacks binding force, then the grounds of this obligation are to be found in the human *spirit.* Nevertheless, again in counterpoint to Hegel, Bruaire claims that "the free spirit" cannot be thought of in the same terms as the (Hegelian) absolute freedom. Indeed, the ground of moral obligation is to be found in the human spirit, but only inasmuch as its being-free is understood in terms of being-gift. For this reason, says Bruaire, "because the ontology of spirit is an ontology of gift, it is also the ground of ethics. . . . [B]eing-gift, being because of the gift and for the gift, is moral obligation, at the beginning and at the root of every ethical norm."[45]

The reason for man's obedience to a certain law or to certain behavioral codes needs to be determined by what the human being is. And, since being-of-spirit is being-gift, and being given is also being-in-debt, this *debt of being* is what makes the human spirit give itself, "pay with its own person," according to the logic of gift which is constitutive of its existence. This, according to Bruaire, is the *only* ground of moral obligation.[46] In fact,

41. *FE,* 47.
43. *MS,* 11.
45. *PM,* 282.
42. *PM,* 283.
44. *EdE,* 37.
46. *EM,* 154.

Bruaire says, if one were the origin of oneself, one would not be obliged to anything or anyone. In that case, every moral constraint would be extrinsic to what one is and, for that very reason, would remain ultimately powerless. The fact of having been given to oneself grounds an inseparable unity of freedom and obligation. Being-of-spirit is a gift which owes its own being and which exists in the ontological necessity of giving.[47] For Bruaire, then, being free and being under obligation is another way of saying being-gift and being-in-debt. This truth of the human *being* is what roots morality in ontology, before any religious creed but without ignoring the "intimations of Christianity."[48]

The relationship between being-in-debt and being-gift also explains why, according to Bruaire, ethics cannot be reduced to random choices. If morality did not stem from ontology but came after it, it would be fragile and relative to each individual freedom. Moral duty would fade away, and its link with ontological truth would be lost. On the contrary, if what the human spirit is cannot be traced back to itself but only to the fact that it is given to itself, then it is under the obligation of giving back "in the totally poor substitute of the gift of oneself," which is what one gives or does.[49] Since this obligation is rooted ontologically, it is not inculcated or fabricated; rather, "it is discovered in the vivacity that measures the discovery of oneself, of the present *(cadeau)* of being which I am."[50]

Phrasing the relation between being-gift and being-in-debt that grounds morality in ontology in our own terms, we can say that, for Bruaire, morality is the echo of the original gratuity of being given; it is to reciprocate the gift given gratuitously. This is why, for him, to be "moral" is to recover a childlike attitude; that is to say, it is to recover the simplicity of joyfully recognizing the gift of being-given with the certainty that at the origin of self there is Another, a certainty that is able to generate a culture that does not destroy the human being.[51]

---

47. *FE*, 51.   48. *EM*, 155.
49. *EdE*, 37.   50. *PM*, 284.
    51. Bruaire, "Le problème éthique de la culture," *Axes* 10 (1970): 17. Inspired by Nietzsche, Bruaire suggests that the being-of-spirit needs to undergo the famous triple metamorphosis in order for the human being to become childlike again and so to recover and live in the "native freshness" which comes from the "inexhaustible discovery" of being-gift. See *RP*, 103. On this same theme, see Hans Urs von Balthasar, *Wenn ihr nicht werdet wie dieses Kind* (Freiburg: Johannes Verlag, 1998); Ferdinand Ulrich, *Der Mensch als Anfang. Zur philosophischen Anthropologie der Kindheit* (Freiburg: Johannes Verlag, 1970); Gustav Siewerth, *Metaphysik der Kindheit* (Freiburg: Johannes Verlag, 1957).

A Perilous Existence

Bruaire is compelled to clarify the relationship between the concept of gift and his understanding of the logic of human existence in order to avoid falling into a body-soul dualism that would undermine the basic tenets of his ontology.[52] In fact, he affirms that it is only in its relations with nature, with its own corporeality first and foremost, that the logic of being-gift of the human spirit can be adequately grasped. Bruaire understands being in terms of spirit, and the conjunction of these two is most adequately described as *gift*; thus, it is necessary to examine in what sense there is a true *human freedom* and what it means for the human being to be free, that is, to be at its own disposal in order to become subject. The two terms whose relation needs to be properly thought out in order to give a complete *ontodological* account of the human spirit are therefore freedom and (human) nature.

The *ipseic* assumption takes place within the life to which human freedom has been entrusted. The issue of freedom's simultaneous dependence upon and independence of nature is decisive for verifying whether being-of-spirit is truly given to itself. In fact, if being-of-spirit is given to itself and, in this respect, possesses itself, then it has to be able to take the initiative to actualize its own potencies, or, more simply, to act. In order to truly *be* a gift, human spirit needs, on the one hand, to respect its own ontological passivity because it is given and it is not the origin of itself; on the other hand, it has to be able to constitute the *beginning* of an action, to be able to take the initiative. In this regard, says Bruaire, human spirit is both linked to its own corporeality, through which the human spirit awakens to itself and to the world, and, at the same time, free from its own nature. This is the *paradox* (and not the contradiction) of the human being: that the human spirit is given to itself to be itself by itself means that being-of-spirit is both free from itself without being its own origin and free of its own freedom. Human spirit, as being-gift, is act that possesses the potency to act without therefore being the *absolute* origin of its own action.

If we call to mind Bruaire's analysis of Schelling, we can see that human freedom is conceived as analogous to absolute freedom. Absolute freedom is its own beginning, the absolute commencement of itself from

52. The foregoing analysis refers back to the presentation of this issue given in chapter 1 of the present book and clarifies its overall rationale.

itself. In this sense, if there is such a thing as *human* freedom, it also has to be thought in terms of being its own beginning—although with the ontological limitations which its own being-gift entails. It is the being-of-spirit itself which is the origin of its own actions. This is so, says Bruaire, because the human spirit is a particular singularity; that is, it is substance in order to be subject. If human spirit were *pure* singularity, it would be the absolute beginning of itself. In this case, we would no longer be talking of human spirit but of absolute spirit.

If being-of-spirit were only a *particular* without being singular, it would not be able to take the initiative to perform free acts, because it would not be given to itself. Human spirit is given to itself without being the origin of itself, and for this reason, it is *particular* and *singular.* For Bruaire, this affirmation has a threefold implication: being-of-spirit is *in act* and able to dispose of itself in its *ipseic* reflection; being a reflection *in act,* being-of-spirit is the initiator of free *acts;* and lastly, "a free act is the act of the potency that is available for the *ipseic* being itself."[53]

Whereas one could say of other beings that they are also given, that they are also a gift, one cannot say that they are given to themselves to the extent that they can determine themselves and hence, be free. Their essence is already totally determined from the very beginning. The human spirit is at its own disposal in order to assume itself, to become subject. This provides the vantage point for understanding all the actions of the human spirit. Since becoming a subject involves freedom, language, and desire, Bruaire needs to illustrate in what sense the being-spirit is free in each of these elements. Because it is *free,* being-of-spirit is able, first of all, to commit itself to, or relinquish, a certain action. Being-of-spirit is always responsible for its own actions and has the power to bring them to completion or not. Thus, there is no external coercion that can replace the movement of freedom itself. On the other side, one cannot force another person to be free if he does not want to be free or has decided to give up.

The reflective assumption also means that the spirit *knows* itself in order to know itself as free from its own acts. Being-gift comes back to itself and, in so doing, partially completes the conversive return to self by means of reflective self-knowledge. The singular spirit knows itself

53. *EE,* 76.

through the universal dimension of the spirit. What holds for all of the other realities that fall within the reach of human knowledge also holds for self-knowledge: there is no knowledge of the particular outside the universal. This is why the human spirit transforms language in order to manifest itself within language. But "thought comes to freedom only if the latter adopts it," and there one discovers that although "free for the knowledge that is given to itself, freedom can destroy its meaning by forgetting itself." This remark is a fundamental one. The knowledge of oneself that one acquires in the reflective assumption, although it is a certain and true knowledge about the meaning of oneself and of the other, does not eliminate being-of-spirit's freedom to dispose of itself, because it does not eliminate freedom's ability to cancel knowledge by ignoring what one discovers. In this regard, forgetfulness is not the manifestation of a feeble memory but rather freedom's decision.[54]

For the human spirit to be at its own disposal in order to accomplish an act means for it to be endowed with an inexhaustible energy, the energy of desire that "captures life in order to animate the spiritual breath (inspiration and expiration)." Because being-of-spirit is being-gift, *desire* is fundamentally determined by the being-in-debt of the human spirit and is thus both "avidity of giving and longing for the Other. Demand of effusion and infinite and indefatigable request of return to the Origin."[55] Still, as happens with reason, desire offers its *neutral* indetermination to freedom and is at the mercy of the latter. In this sense, freedom can measure it, deviate it, or corrupt it.

The issue regarding the "being-free" of the finite spirit at the three different levels of freedom, language, and desire addresses the deeper matter of the reciprocal relation between being and existence as a whole. Although

54. In a certain sense, one could say that the most important discoveries must always be accompanied by the motion of freedom. Of course, there are always those discoveries such as logical or mathematical truths whose evidence is such that freedom's adhesion is not called into question. For those discoveries that regard the *meaning* of one's own being and of being in general, however, the participation of freedom in the dynamic of knowledge is coessential. In this sense, although Bruaire does not say so explicitly, there can be no "knowledge" of the absolute without the involvement of freedom, i.e., without freedom's characteristic movement of self-determination. In this respect, the above-mentioned studies by the Venegono School (Italy) on the nature of "evidence" and the relationship between freedom and knowledge are very fruitful.

55. *EE*, 78.

being-of-spirit's freedom puts it at the "risk of an uncertain existence," being-of-spirit nonetheless subsists in spite of "happy or unhappy choices, fortunes or misfortunes." Gift, the essence of being-of-spirit, is totally given to itself and cannot be claimed back. Ex-istence is, in this respect, the being-of-spirit which takes charge of itself inasmuch as being is given to itself, given to acquire (relative) *ipseic* autonomy. Being in act actualizes itself and informs itself with that "singularity to which it is originally pre-formed." Personal existence is the truth of being-gift, though not the *ultimate* truth, because substantial conversion does not reveal the unknown origin whence being-of-spirit comes. Because of the relation between essence and existence, as ontology has it, the human spirit is *"auto-vulnerable."* While preserving the "identity *of the player, of the play, and of the risk (enjeu),"* being is at stake within existence.[56] Spiritual existence is being at the mercy of itself, a historical assumption of itself which does not eliminate the risk of wounding itself, of losing the gift—something which, however, can always be regenerated.

This relationship between being and existence shows that, for Bruaire, the movement of interiority and exteriority that determines the way in which being-of-spirit follows its own essence in its existence is not exempt from risk. Without dissolving spirit's identity in the movement of substantial conversion, the return to the origin takes place within the interplay between desire, freedom, and language. It is in this interplay that, according to Bruaire, one risks one's existence. This dialogue between desire, freedom, and language captures the root of the ever-present risk of the loss of gift.[57]

In *The Affirmation of God,* it seemed that the syllogistic analysis yielded a notion of a self-balanced human existence called to be and to live in dialogue with the absolute. However, after more than twenty years of systematic reflection Bruaire grounds the main threat to human existence metaphysically. The ruin of the "logic of human existence" takes place when the human spirit deserts the present of its existence and renounces the logic of its own being-gift. It is then that the being-of-spirit falls into either an

56. *EE,* 80. Bruaire's emphasis.

57. The logic of gift, by which being is given in order to give of itself, according to which identity opens to alterity (one's own alterity and the other's), is at the mercy of that freedom which weaves it and can therefore be accepted or refused. In terms of spiritual ontology, it is here that the promotion of being as good and its annulment in evil is confirmed and grounded. See *EdE,* 37.

atrophic or hypertrophic existence. In the first case, the universal dimension that language brings into human existence is reduced, and the assumption of self, instead of being an *ipseic* conversion in search of its own origin, becomes the abstract singularity of a being that "stops itself, rejects itself, closes itself in total indifference, . . . [and] sinks itself in the nostalgia of an intimate past." In this instance, human existence takes the form of what Bruaire calls an "abstract freedom," or an "insular humanism," or an "aestheticism."[58] In hypertrophic existence, on the other hand, the substantial conversion neglects its ontological limitedness and the human spirit tries to live its own being-gift in the exaltation of itself.[59] Therefore, according to Bruaire, lurking behind the delicate rhythm of the logic of human existence (though without destroying it altogether) is the "hidden desire to be God." To obtain this end, one would change the meaning of the absolute and call it "the Immobile Foreigner, the All-Powerful, the System, the Fascinating Eros, the Unique One, the Realized Absolute: such are the disguised emblems of a spirit that knows of the un-depreciable price of its own being, but *refuses being a gift, and does not allow itself to give.*"[60]

Bruaire's *ontodology,* then, claims to forge an ontology that is not abstract and that is able to express the being proper to the human spirit. This intention is what brings him to the realization that ontology must not be withdrawn *a priori* from the existence of the being-of-spirit. *Ontodology,* however, would remain drastically incomplete if it did not attempt to enter into the realm of absolute spirit and there verify whether *gift* is a category able to name *being,* or a term adequate only to describe the human spirit. Bruaire has shown in what sense *esse spirituale et donum convertuntur;* if he wishes his *ontodology* to be perceived as a proper *metaphysics,* he must now explain in what sense *esse infinitum et donum convertuntur.*

58. *AD,* 22–48, 81–94.

59. The forms that human existence takes in this second case are "the will to power," the thirst to subsume existence into an omni-comprehensive system, and the delirium of prophetism, in which one gives oneself over completely to the power of language. See *AD,* 49–80.

60. *EE,* 82. Emphasis added. This *ontodological* reading of the logic of human existence confirms my interpretation of Bruaire's systematic anthropology as leading to this concept of gift, which, although not fully developed, Bruaire presupposes to such an extent that it gives its own form to his systematic anthropology.

CHAPTER 6

Altogether Gift
Absolute Spirit

The ontological examination of being as gift undertaken so far appears to be too anthropologically burdened to allow for a concept of absolute gift. In fact, if being-gift is being-given and being-in-debt, then it does not seem possible to formulate a concept of gift which, while remaining *one,* is nonetheless able to embrace the similarities and the differences between the being-given proper, on the one hand, to the human spirit and, on the other, to absolute spirit. Nevertheless, only if the latter is gift can Bruaire validly argue that gift is the metaphysical name for being—and not merely its anthropological or theological representation.

Bruaire's conception of absolute spirit in terms of gift is presented in two main steps. The first explains how, for him, "absolute," "spirit," and "being" name the same reality. Since this issue has already been partially discussed, the present account is limited to exploring how Bruaire's *ontodology* completes his understanding of absolute spirit. The second step follows Bruaire's striking characterization of the absolute as the *infinite,* the *creator,* and the *eternal.* Although each of these issues could be treated separately and in greater detail, I shall limit this chapter to the examination of Bruaire's claim to think being-of-spirit in terms of gift.

The Absolute Principle

Grasping Bruaire's understanding of the absolute gift requires seeing both how the concept of the human spirit leads him to that of the absolute spirit and also the sense in which, according to him, the absolute must be conceived in terms of spirit and being.

The Mediation of the Concept

Understanding the finite being-of-spirit in terms of gift requires, as we know, both a "destination" (given to itself) and an "origin," a "source." Thus, one could claim that there has to be a giver who gives the human spirit its very being. If this were the case, the movement from finite to infinite spirit would be the classical *analogia entis:* beginning from one "effect," the human spirit, one could move to its principal cause, absolute spirit. Yet, Bruaire forcefully rejects this reading of his *ontodology* because the movement from the gift to a potential giver would entail acquaintance with the unknown origin.[1] *Ontodology* is not a "hidden theology." The anonymity of the gift, which makes it a "reference without referent," is enough to prevent Bruaire from thinking that there is either a "personal or impersonal author" behind the gift of the human spirit.[2] The concept of (finite) gift compels Bruaire's ontodology to acknowledge an unknown and mysterious origin, but that does not mean that the gift of the human spirit permits an immediate evidence, an innate idea, or a direct perception of

1. *EE,* 94. Bruaire's rejection of a "known origin" should not be understood as a rejection *tout court* of the *analogia entis.* Bruaire is not claiming that the *analogia entis,* which presupposes the ontological difference or the Thomistic *compositio realis* (*De Ver.,* q. 27, a. 1, ad 8), would lead us to the "theological difference" between God and creatures because the analogy of being presupposes it. He is not implying that the *via eminentiae* presupposes a knowledge of God that is ultimately closed within the boundaries of onto-theology. There is a certain knowledge of the source from which the gift comes, but there is no positive knowledge regarding the identity of this source (*ST* I, q. 45, a. 3). Only once it has been proved to be absolute spirit and creator could there be a clearer understanding of what the mysterious source is, always in a *major dissimilitudo.* As I see it, Bruaire's insistence on the ignorance of the "giver's identity" is a rejection of *ontologism* and a defense of philosophy's autonomy with respect to theology.

2. This statement should not deceive the reader into thinking that Bruaire rejects causality. Quite the contrary, Bruaire believes that *ontodology* is also the truth of causality, although he never explains it in detail. He succinctly states that gift is the spiritual truth of causality because it gives to causality its fundamental unity. Formal causality expresses the constitutive essence of being-gift and material causality its substantial material. Final causality is the destiny to which being-gift is destined and efficient causality is that according to which being-gift is posited in existence. For *ontodology,* final and efficient causality coincide. Gift says causality in its spiritual *unity.* (See *PM,* 276–77). In *EE,* Bruaire does not talk about material causality. For an adequate and suggestive response to this question see Schmitz, *The Gift.* In a sense, one of the main objectives of Schmitz's book is that of reproposing a new understanding of causality. The main difference between this beautiful book and Bruaire's *ontodology* is that in the latter, gift is a category used to describe the absolute itself.

the source. The movement from the finite to the infinite spirit is therefore done by means of the *speculative* mediation of the concept. While preserving the difference between finite and infinite gift, Bruaire thinks that the concept of spirit is a univocal one and is thus able to name both of them. Thus, he claims that *"it is the spirit that sends back to the spirit"*; that is to say, it is the *concept* of spirit that leads to the absolute spirit.[3]

The semantics of the concept of spirit illustrates that an unavoidable duality remains in the human spirit. This "unity of two" results in the human spirit's inability to "say itself" completely in what it does. There is always an unbridgeable distance between what one is and what one does. The difference between that "hidden potency" which is the spirit and the different faculties (language, freedom, and desire) in which it can be seen makes this "distance" abundantly clear. Furthermore, finite being-of-spirit is being-gift because it is "totally given to itself," it is not "the origin of itself," and it is also "being-in-debt" by the very fact of being-given. If one tries to find all three of these characteristics in the concept of absolute spirit, one ends up with a spirit in which there is no distance between being and doing, which does not proceed from another, and which therefore is not in debt to any higher principle. If one is unwilling to give up all hope of finding a univocal concept of gift, and that is the only meaning that the concept of spirit has, then it seems that only two roads remain open to ontodology: either to accept the risk of anthropomorphization and thus to ascribe to the absolute what is proper only to the human spirit (as Feuerbach did), or, with Plotinus, to surrender *de facto* to the much maligned "negative theology" and concede that there is nothing that can be said about absolute spirit.

Surprisingly, in *Being and Spirit,* Bruaire inaugurates his remarks on absolute spirit by stating that this *pure* concept of spirit is free of any anthropomorphic reference. According to him, in the absolute spirit there is no difference between νοῦς and πνεῦμα. On the contrary, the two realities are identical because absolute spirit is "the living absolute freedom which is in absolute knowledge of itself."[4] Absolute spirit does not owe its own being to anything but itself. Bruaire therefore states that it is possible to conceive of spirit without the characteristics proper to the human spir-

3. *EE,* 90; *FE,* 76.
4. *EE,* 88.

it. This fact, which he considers to be an "evidence," is justifiable only by means of the development of the concept. The "speculative thread" needs thus to be followed independently of any phenomenological data. In this sense, whereas the study of the concept of the human spirit issues in the *eidetic* of the spirit guiding the recognition of the presence of the spirit in its most proper manifestations (i.e., procreation; the first appearance of the presence in the child of a spirit opposed to nature and different from that of the parents; language), the exploration of the *pure* concept of spirit is devoid of any "spiritual experience" and does not lead to any phenomenology of the spirit.

Although, as we know, the speculative mediation of the concept finds its most proper expression in the ontological argument, my main concern here is not to re-present Bruaire's demonstration of God's existence. What matters now is to understand why this absolute needs to be thought in terms of spirit. In fact, if the absolute were not conceived in terms of *spirit,* it would be difficult to grasp the validity of the ontological argument, the creation of finite beings, and the real difference between absolute and finite spirit. We will now attend to Bruaire's understanding of the concept of the absolute. The examination of Bruaire's analysis of Plotinus's and Heidegger's conceptions of the absolute will shed light on Bruaire's contention that the pure concept of the absolute demands to be thought in terms of being and spirit. The subsequent sections will respond to the question why absolute spirit is gift, even though it is not given to itself from another.

The Inaccessible Absolute (I): Plotinus

Besides Bruaire's critique of Kant's rejection of Anselm's ontological argument (because Kant failed to see that the absolute is spirit), there is another possible way of understanding the absolute by trying to think its concept as deprived of spirit and being.[5] Would it be possible to dissociate

5. Bruaire holds that the root of the difficulties affecting the ontological argument was identified by Hegel: the ontological argument is conceived in a Christian world and thus presupposes the understanding of God which revelation conveys (*EE,* 108). Christianity brings to light that the absolute is spirit and that there is no spirit that does not manifest itself. Bruaire comments that, on the one hand, the *negative* conclusion of the ontological argument states simply that to think of the absolute as non-existing is the same as not thinking it at all. On the other hand, the *positive* conclusion of the argument, which is the ontological affirmation of God, remains "latent precisely because the affirmation remains the in-formed and determined waiting *(attente)* for the manifestation of absolute spirit which [the ontological

the terms "absolute" and "spirit" so that one could somehow talk about an ultimate reality without ascribing to it either intelligibility (νοῦς) or the pneumatic rhythm of reflection (πνεῦμα)? Is a non-spiritual absolute conceivable? And if it is, how can one account for the multiplicity of what exists? According to Bruaire, the philosophical system that tried to offer a concept of the absolute radically dissociated from that of the spirit is the system of Plotinus. Coming to grips with his philosophy will show why the absolute is also a spiritual being. Plotinus, a man "who seemed ashamed of being in the body," attempted to construct a rigorous account of that other which, taking the spatial image for what it is worth, is "beyond" being and spirit: the One.[6]

Plotinus, like Bruaire and some of the major idealists, is a philosopher of the absolute.[7] Plotinus tries to offer a radical understanding of the absolute from the perspective of the absolute itself, in a supreme effort to strip his reflection of any trace of anthropomorphization. As Giovanni Reale shows, *The Enneads* deals with two decisive issues. The first regards the absolute itself: Why is there an absolute, and why is it what it is? This question is radically new and cannot be found either in Plato or in Aristotle, for whom the first Principle "is the *unconditioned*," that is to say, that whose essence cannot be called into question. The second question is why and how the many come from the One.[8]

---

argument] expresses" (ibid., 92). The identity between the absolute and spirit is the cornerstone that upholds the delicate yet powerful argument first proposed by Anselm.

6. Porphyry, "On the Life of Plotinus and the Arrangement of his Work," in Plotinus, *The Enneads*, trans. Stephen MacKenna (New York: Larson Publications, 1992), 1. All subsequent citations from *The Enneads* refer to this translation. The two main texts in which Bruaire deals with Plotinus are *EE*, 95–107, and his article *PrMC* ("Problème de la métaphysique et conversion)," 121–26.

7. Luigi Pelloux classifies the readings of Plotinus's *Enneads* into two main groups: the metaphysical and the religious. Hegel, Rosmini, and Ravaisson belong to the first; Inge, Underhill, Guitton, and Maréchal to the second. See Luigi Pelloux, *L'assoluto nella dottrina di Plotino* (Milan: Vita e Pensiero, 1994), 9–18. Let me also mention here the importance that Plotinus had for Hegel (Hegel, *Vorlesungen über die Geschichte der Philosophie, Teil 3 Griechische Philosophie II. Platos bis Proklos*, 176–88) and Schelling. See Xavier Tilliette, "Vision plotinienne et intuition schellingienne," in *L'absolu et la philosophie*, 59–80; id., *Schelling: Une philosophie en devenir*, 2 vols. (Paris: J. Vrin, 1992).

8. Giovanni Reale, "I fondamenti della metafisica di Plotino e la struttura della processione," in *Graceful Reason: Essays in Ancient and Medieval Philosophy Presented to Joseph Owens, CSSR*, ed. Lloyd P. Gerson (Toronto: Pontifical Institute of Mediaeval Studies, 1983), 153–75, 158. This article is also an interesting illustration of the rationale behind the contemporary rejection of the classical reductionist interpretation of Plotinus as "emanatistic." My

For Plotinus, the One, that "by which everything which is exists,"[9] is nothing but the "index of the uncategorizable."[10] Plotinus insists that the Principle cannot be described as Aristotle would have it; neither can it be identified with the Good *tout court* (Bonaventure), or with Being (Aquinas's *Ipsum Esse*), or with freedom (Schelling). Instead, the only name that can be given to it is the *One*.[11] Unity, for Plotinus, is that attribute which accounts for every being and apart from which nothing can be. In the *Enneads*, Plotinus tries to think the absolute, that which is beyond thought itself, not primarily because of a deficiency in man, but because the One "is" totally other.[12]

When thinking unity in *itself*, one needs to be on guard against introducing any principle of division. The principle of unity cannot be the "soul" *(psyche)* because, although the soul is able to confer unity, it confers it only because it receives this unifying principle from another in the same way that "the beauty of a body is borrowed."[13] Nor can the One be the intellectual principle (νοῦς). In fact, to introduce intelligence into the One is to plant in it the division between the knowing subject and the known.[14] If such were the case, the One would be divided into itself (it would have the Idea of itself within it).[15] But, in order to know itself, it would have to leave

---

account of Plotinus is indebted to the work of both Pelloux and Reale. See also John M. Rist, *Plotinus: The Road to Reality* (Cambridge: Cambridge University Press, 1967); Maria Luisi Gatti, *Plotino e la metafisica della contemplazione* (Milan: Vita e Pensiero, 1996); Leo Sweeney, S.J., "Are Plotinus and Albertus Magnus Neoplatonists?" in Gerson, *Graceful Reason: Essays in Ancient and Medieval Philosophy*, 177–202.

9. Plotinus, *Enneads* VI, 9, 1.

10. *EE*, 97.

11. The issue of naming this first principle as "good" will be dealt with shortly.

12. If the One is "totally other," then, one could ask, how is it possible to talk about it? In Plotinus, there are two combined approaches that arrive at the same understanding of the absolute and present it not only as the end point of his metaphysics but also as the starting point and guiding principle of living. The first is the rational analysis, which proceeds to show in dialectical terms how, turn by turn, one thing and its opposite could be said of the absolute. This dialectical approach aims at allowing the human being to "see" the transcendence of the One. On the other hand, complementary to the rational, is a mystical way, which offers a deeper insight into the "nature" of the One. "The main source of the difficulty is that awareness of this Principle comes neither by knowing nor by the Intellection that discovers the Intellectual Being, but by a presence surpassing all knowledge" (*Enneads* VI, 9, 4). See also Pelloux, *L'assoluto nella dottrina di Plotino*, 98–105.

13. Plotinus, *Enneads* V, 9, 2.

14. *Enneads* III, 4, 9; V, 1, 8.

15. In this sense, the One is not self-knowledge, because this would presuppose, says Plotinus, a prior moment of ignorance. "Yet its absence of self-knowing, of self-intellection,

a difference within itself. Hence, one could talk about the Idea of the One, and of its capacity to know, but one would be far from absolute oneness. Thus, the One is neither soul (spirit), nor intelligence (*nous*), nor being or the totality of beings.[16] In fact, as Bruaire remarks, Plotinus would find it impossible to accept the Mosaic revelation of "I am who am," because in order for the One to be, it would need to know itself.[17] Of course, to say that the One is not "being" does not mean that it does not exist. It is the supreme existent, yet it is beyond being and existence itself. This nonbeing of the One, however, is not to be conceived as the dialectical opposite of being. Obviously, if the One is beyond being, its "nonbeing" is beyond "nothingness," understood as that which is not. The "nothingness" proper to the One is, in a sense, "absolute."

It would be possible to describe the One as Good, since it is the cause of everything. Yet this is only a description *quoad nos*. The One can be perceived as good because things proceed from it, but in itself, the One is not the Good, it is only the One. The One, says Plotinus, is beyond whatever is good, because what brings to existence whatever is good cannot be "Good"; it has to be totally other.[18] So, although in a sense it is possible to say that the One is the Good, such an affirmation must be made with this reservation in mind.

The real difficulty in saying what the One is, then, comes from its absolute indeterminacy. The One transcends every name, category, and genus in which the human mind tries to encapsulate it. Plotinus contends that there is no name, no concept that can function as anything more than a merely fleeting indication of something that cannot be grasped at all. Even to think of the One as God is "to think too meanly" of it.[19] The One "is not." Although the One is the principle of the existence and of the intelligibility of everything, the principle without which nothing can exist or be understood, the One is for the human intellect nothing but "a perfect

---

does not comport ignorance; ignorance is of something outside—a knower ignorant of a knowable—but in the Solitary [One] there is neither knowing nor anything unknowing. Unity, self-present, it has no need of self-intellection" (*Enneads* VI, 9, 6).

16. *Enneads* VI, 9, 2.

17. *EE*, 96–97. Plotinus, *Enneads* VI, 9, 3. See Gilson, "L'être et Dieu," 181–202, 389–416; Paul Vignaux, *Dieu et l'être: Exégèses d'Exode 3:14 et de Coran 20:11–24* (Paris: Études Augustiniennes, 1978).

18. Plotinus, *Enneads* VI, 9, 6; VI, 7, 41; V, 3, 11.

19. *Enneads* VI, 9, 6.

night" of complete darkness in which nothing can be seen.[20] The One enables seeing, itself transcending any light. Yet, to say that the One is not
does not transform this first principle into a sheer vacuity. On the contrary, it is simply to affirm that it is totally Other.

The One, for Plotinus, is utterly impenetrable, and Plotinus's metaphysics of the absolute is, as a result, purely negative: nothing can be said about
the One because the One is not.[21] Is one then condemned to the absolute indeterminacy that Plotinus postulates? "For this One is utterly a self-
existent, with no concomitant whatever. This self-sufficing is the essence
of its unity. Something there must be that is supremely adequate, autonomous, all-transcending, most utterly without need."[22] What characterizes
the One, then, is its *self-sufficiency* and *indifference* with regard to everything that is not itself.[23] The One is beyond everything else. As Luigi Pelloux
affirms, "while Aristotle seeks whether act is the principle of reality, Plotinus goes further: he wants to find the principle of act, and this leads him to
the One."[24] There is no other "explanation" of the One besides this absolute
simplicity whereby the first Principle suffices to itself.[25] Since, according
to Plotinus, the absolute needs to be understood as self-referential, as that
principle which is *causa sui,* then the One could be understood as absolute
freedom, something which, surprisingly, does not destroy its simplicity.[26]

20. *EE,* 98.

21. Plotinus, *Enneads* V, 3, 13; V, 4, 1.

22. *Enneads* VI, 9, 6.

23. *Enneads* VI, 8, 7.

24. Pelloux, *L'assoluto nella dottrina di Plotino,* 118.

25. John Bussanich notes that Plotinus attributes an inner self-relationship to the One
that does not shatter its absolute simplicity (see *Enneads* VI, 8, 8). He also believes that the
famous passage in which Plotinus claims that the One is cause of itself (*Enneads* VI, 8, 13.
14, 16) is better "construed to mean that the One has no cause, that is, that it is a necessary
being whose being is completely self-derived" (John Bussanich, "Plotinus's Metaphysics of
the One," in *The Cambridge Companion to Plotinus,* ed. Lloyd P. Gerson [Cambridge: Cambridge University Press, 1996], 45).

26. Plotinus, *Enneads* VI, 8. For this reason, it can be said that "if there had been a moment from which He began to be, it would be possible to assert his self-making in the literal
sense; but since what He is He is from before eternity, his self-making is to be understood
as simultaneous with Himself; the being is one and the same with the making, the eternal
'bringing into existence'" (*Enneads* VI, 8, 20). According to Pelloux, this insistence on the
One as freedom is such that "il significato del Bene nei confronti della libertà, rappresenta
peraltro il massimo sforzo che l'antichità abbia compiuto per asserire il carattere personale
dell'Assoluto" (Pelloux, *L'assoluto nella dottrina di Plotino,* 115). See also Reale, "I fondamenti
della metafisica di Plotino," 159–63; Gilles Leroux, *Plotin. Traité sur la liberté et la volonté de
l'Un (Ennéade VI, 8)* (Paris: J. Vrin, 1990). Bearing in mind the great differences between the
two thinkers, it is interesting to note the proximity between Plotinus and Bruaire as regards
the idea of absolute spirit.

If the One is so entirely other than the world, and it does not need anything but itself in order to be itself, how can we explain the existence of the multiple, of the not-one? Why did the One not remain alone with itself? In response to this question, Plotinus explains that the first hypostasis, the Divine Mind, is born because "all that is fully achieved engenders: therefore the eternally achieved engenders eternally an eternal being. At the same time, the offspring is always minor."[27]

The One, then, begets out of its own perfection, out of necessity, that which is not itself. It begets that other which is called to "love the begetter."[28] Bruaire emphasizes that the great value of Plotinus's work lies not only in the radicalness with which he conceives of the absolute but also in the way he explains how the world proceeds from the One. It is not by effusion, alteration, or ontological emanation. The formula Plotinus uses to describe the coming to be of what is from what is not is already familiar to us: "the Good gives what *it does not* have."[29] To give what one has would imply change and alteration on the side of the One. On the contrary, in giving what it does not have, the One remains what it is without any shadow of alteration. This is what, according to Bruaire, brings Plotinus's thought so close to the idea of creation. What does it mean for the One to give what it does not have? If something comes from the One, then it is not the One; it is thus *other* with respect to the One. Bruaire explains that the One does not give what the One is; rather it *gives* "other." Because the other is not the One, it is much less than the source whence it proceeds. The emanation is "less good, that is to say, less self-sufficing." And what is less self-sufficing than the One is the not-One, that is to say, "multiplicity striving toward unity; that is to say, a One-that-is-many."[30]

Although Bruaire uses the term "to give" to indicate the procession of the many from the One, he is aware that Plotinus does not interpret this procession in terms of donation. Plotinus offers an illuminating example that clarifies the sense in which the procession of the many from the One is to be understood. The procession from the One happens as in the case of fire. The activity of fire is twofold: on the one hand, there is a proper ac-

---

27. Plotinus, *Enneads* V, 1, 6.
28. Ibid.
29. Bruaire quotes *Enneads* V, 3, 15, and VI, 7. Emphasis added.
30. Plotinus, *Enneads* V, 3, 15.

tivity by which the fire is what it is, that is, heat; on the other hand, there is another activity that occurs while fire remains what it is, that is, the communication of warmth.[31] Interpreting this famous and much-debated passage, Reale points out that the activity by which the One remains what it is, is "auto-creative freedom," absolute freedom, and the activity that comes from this first activity is in a certain sense a "*sui generis* necessity" that is a type of "willed necessity."[32] In a sense, then, the hypostasis and the many are "necessarily wanted" by the One. Bruaire clarifies that it is precisely this necessary character of the procession that leaves Plotinus without any "giving positivity," any generosity, any "spiritual gift."[33] Furthermore, for Bruaire, the fact that there is no gratuity implies ultimately that Plotinus fails to explain the intelligibility of the procession. Bruaire implacably reiterates that if the One is the only reality that "is" beyond being itself, it "is not," and so whatever proceeds from it cannot "be" as well. Recalling Plato's admonition in the *Parmenides*, Bruaire affirms that "if the One is not, nothing is." Therefore the upshot of that "willed necessity" is nothing but sheer appearance. If the One is not, then what comes from it is not "being," as Plotinus would have it, but "nothing."[34]

Following the second hypothesis of Plato's *Parmenides,* Bruaire affirms that "if, and only if, the One *is,* then something can be said about the first Principle."[35] Still, says Bruaire, since for Plotinus the One is not and thus is utterly impenetrable, Plotinus's metaphysics is nothing but the purest form of negative theology, the result of which is not only that nothing can be said about the One but also that no valid explanation can be offered of the existence of finite beings. Bruaire postulates that only if one respects the identification of the absolute with spirit is it possible both to affirm that the absolute is and to justify finite spirit.

31. The more abstract formulation is offered before the example just quoted: "There is in everything the Act of the Essence and the Act going out from the Essence: the first Act is the thing itself in its realized identity, the second Act is an inevitably following emanation from the first, an emanation distinct from the thing itself" (*Enneads* V, 4, 2).

32. Reale, "I fondamenti della metafisica di Plotino," 162.

33. *EE,* 101.

34. Plato, *Parmenides* 164B–166C. At this point, we understand Plotinus's rejection of his own corporeality and his desire "to give back to the Divine in myself, to the Divine in the All." See Porphyry, "On the Life of Plotinus," chapters 1 and 2.

35. *EE,* 97. Cf. Plato, *Parmenides* 142B–155E.

The Inaccessible Absolute (II): Heidegger

Still, there is another possible reading of the relationship between the One and the many that ends up defending a type of absolute very much in the line of Plotinus's thought. According to Bruaire, this is what happens when, instead of speaking with Plotinus of the "One and the many," one follows Heidegger and uses the terms "being" and "beings."[36] One thereby distinguishes between "presence" and "present" and introduces a radical separation between the ground and what is grounded. Viewed in this light, being is best understood as the conceptual and etiological ground of beings *(entia)*. This perception of being unveils what Heidegger describes as the onto-theological constitution of metaphysics, which, however, ultimately isolates being on the very level of reality at which Plotinus places the One.

The connection that Bruaire perceives between Plotinus and Heidegger is not without justification. In both authors, the human intellect strives to reach that "ultimate ground" from which everything comes. In Heidegger, as in Plotinus, being *(Sein)* is always beyond, and the human being tends to remain trapped in his perception of beings *(Seiendes)* while attempting to reach this ultimate ground. Heidegger points out the propensity to project onto that unfathomable Mystery which we call "being" what is proper only to beings. Regrettably, in his critique of the ontological difference, Bruaire simply states the similarities between Heidegger and Plotinus. His tendency not to provide detailed justification undermines his lucid and cogent insight into Heidegger's philosophy. Furthermore, it is my opinion that Bruaire's criticism ought to have referred more specifically to Heidegger's understanding of "onto-theology" than to the "ontological difference" in general.[37] Perhaps Bruaire's preoccupation with defining being as gift, and

36. *EE*, 103.

37. I think that there is a valid understanding of "ontological difference" that does not necessarily coincide with that of Heidegger. The ontological difference is formulated in the famous question which Heidegger asks in his *Was ist Metaphysik?* (Frankfurt: V. Klostermann, 1981): "Warum ist überhaupt Seiendes und nicht vielmehr Nichts?" (1). Let me call the reader's attention to the Heideggerian terminology. He asks about "Seiendes" and not about "Sein." Although this question does not seem to imply an equiprimordiality of being and nothingness as Heidegger would have it (cf. *Being and Time* §44; *Vom Wesen der Wahrheit* in *Wegmarken* [Frankfurt am Main: Vittorio Klostermann Verlag, 1967], 73–97), but rather a predominance of nothingness over being, the question itself can also be read

with explaining the priority of this concept over any distinction between essence and existence, prompted him to disregard the "ontological differ- ence" *in toto*.[38] Nonetheless, this distinction would have made Bruaire's ar- gument clearer.

Jean-Luc Marion explains that "it is because of its onto-theological con- stitution that any metaphysics is unable to access being as being, but only being *(être)* as *ens (étant)*."[39] Onto-theology thinks being as such only in its relationship with beings. According to Heidegger, this intimate connection has not prevented a leaving behind of the *entia* in order to reach being it- self. The representation of the divine being is shaped by the way of being of the finite *ens* as it appears to us in the ontological difference—understood again in Heideggerian terms. This is why God, when considered as *esse*, is in reality perceived as one being among beings, while any causal efficiency that could be reasonably ascribed to God determines not only "created" be- ings but also God himself.[40] Moreover, from the perspective of Heidegger's onto-theology, God must be *causa sui* in order to ground other beings; that is to say, in order to be the foundation of other beings, he must be self- constituted.[41] Beyond beings, beyond the absolute itself, lies that Mysteri- ous Source from which everything comes and which, like Plotinus's One, "escapes any ontological order," because for Heidegger, as for Plotinus, the

---

as *the* question that sets philosophy and religion into motion (cf. Hans Urs von Balthasar, vol. 1 of *Herrlichkeit. Eine Theologische Ästhetik,* 7 vols. [Freiburg: Johannes Verlag, 1961–69]; Verweyen, *Ontologische Voraussetzungen,* 159–206). Kant was the first to use the term *onto-* theology (see Kant, *KrV,* B660). Nevertheless, Heidegger gave the term a new meaning, which is the one Bruaire addresses here. See Martin Heidegger, *Identität und Differenz* (Stuttgart: Neske, 1999), 45.

38. *EE,* 190 n. 1.

39. Marion, "Saint Thomas d'Aquin et l'onto-théo-logie," 32.

40. "Created beings" is in quotation marks to indicate that in Heidegger there is little room for a creation *ex nihilo.*

41. The literature on the Heideggerian notion of ontological difference is immense. Let me mention here some of the most significant texts: Max Müller, *Existenzphilosophie im geistigen Leben der Gegenwart* (Heidelberg: F. H. Kerle, 1949); Erhard Albrecht, "Identität, Unterschied und Widersprüche in der Problematik von Sprache und Denken," *Hegel Jahr- buch* (1979): 89–92; Gianni Vattimo, *Le avventure della differenza. Che cosa significa pen- sare dopo Nietzsche e Heidegger* (Milan: Garzanti, 1980); John D. Caputo, "Heidegger's 'Dif- ference' and the Distinction betweeen *Esse* and *Ens* in St. Thomas," *International Philosophi- cal Quarterly* 20 (1980): 161–81; Hans Kimmerle, "Différence et contradiction," *Tijlschrift voor Filosofie* 43 (1981): 510–37; J. Grodin, "Réflexions sur la différence ontologique," *Les Études philosophiques* 3 (1984): 337–47; Virgilio Melchiorre, ed., *La differenza e l'origine* (Milan: Vita e Pensiero, 1987).

absolute is not *spirit*. Bruaire emphatically states that, given this ontological framework, it does not seem possible to make sense of participation, creation, or even emanation. The drastic separation between true being and beings nullifies "every attempt to reconcile Heidegger's ontological difference with the divine creative act as Aquinas understands it."[42] Furthermore, Heidegger's ontological reading wrongly condemns Aquinas and classical metaphysics to *Seinsvergessenheit*. In this sense, as Balthasar would say, Heidegger elevates the ontological difference to absolute status; it is no longer the distinctive sign of the creature. Thus, from the difference between Being and beings, Heidegger retreats to the identity in which being manifests itself because of its need for the human being. This is so, continues Balthasar, because when the "immanent analogy between the *actus essendi* and *essentia* does not deepen in being's transcendental analogy, it eliminates itself and dissolves itself as identity which attempts to reconcile contradictory terms."[43]

Bruaire is not interested so much in offering a detailed elucidation of Heidegger's ontological difference as he is in explaining what he thinks is the main principle underpinning his onto-theology. According to Bruaire, the reluctance of the Plotinian and Heideggerian philosophical systems to recognize that the absolute is spirit is due to a pre-judgment that absolute spirit is *inaccessible*. This mistake originates not in the infinite distance between the absolute and the human being but in its utter proximity. In this respect, Bruaire, following Marcel and Fessard, affirms that the other of the human spirit, absolute spirit, must not be thought in spatial terms as that which is totally beyond the human being.[44] Bruaire likes to repeat St. Augustine's axiom *"interior intimo meo"* to argue polemically that absolute spirit is not only the wholly other but infinitely more spirit than the human spirit and that it is "immediately unknown by the total proximity of its presence" to the human spirit.[45]

42. *EE,* 103.

43. Hans Urs von Balthasar, *The Realm of Metaphysics in the Modern Age,* vol. 5 of *The Glory of the Lord: A Theological Aesthetics,* trans. Oliver Davies (San Francisco: Ignatius Press, 1965), 449.

44. Gabriel Marcel, *Journal métaphysique,* 281; Fessard, *Dialectique des "Exercices",* 164–77.

45. Augustine, *Confessions* III, 6, 11: "Tu autem eras interior intimo meo et superior summo meo." This statement also has its methodological formulation: "noli foras ire, in te ipsum redi; in interiore homine habitat veritas" (Augustine, *De vera religione,* XXXIX, 72).

Even though the absolute can never be adequately "grasped in the ideal identity of the conceptual form," it nonetheless offers itself to our intelligence.[46] No matter how great the difference between God's essence and our comprehension of it, the inseparability of language and the pneumatic life prevents us from thinking that the absolute is inaccessible. *Inaccessibility* is an unjustified assumption whenever one attempts to tackle the issue of God's *quiddity.*[47]

Bruaire intends, in his reading of the ontological argument and his rejection of Plotinus's and Heidegger's conception of the absolute, to illustrate the negative consequences that an inaccessible absolute has for the understanding of both the absolute and the finite spirit. If the absolute is not spirit, then it is not, and the existence of finite being remains inexplicable. The proximity of the divine and the human word witnesses to the need both to reconsider the absolute in terms of spirit and being and to acknowledge man's limited capacity to know. In fact, since spirit implies the double connotation of νοῦς and πνεῦμα, intelligibility and spiritual rhythm, there is no realm of intelligibility that does not denote the presence of the spirit. According to Bruaire, because the *absolute is spirit,* it can manifest itself, express itself, and, within a *major dissimilitudo,* let itself be

46. *EE,* 105. Without wishing to emphasize similarities between the two thinkers when there are in fact very few, I recommend attention to Marion's analysis of Ex 3:14. One reason Marion advances for the priority of love over *esse* in naming God is precisely the fact that God *gives* his name. In fact, even before analyzing the answer that God gives to Moses, "I am who am," Marion points out that in the historical revelation, God is saying who he is by "offering his name." The perception of God as *being* must not obscure the fact that God first *gives* an answer. See Jean-Luc Marion, *L'idole et la distance,* 178–89. Cf. Ghislain Lafont, "Mystique de la croix et question de l'être. A propos d'un livre récent de Jean-Luc Marion," *Revue théologique de Louvain* 10 (1979): 267.

47. In this sense, although Bruaire's thought is distant in some respects from that of Aquinas, we can find in Thomas the same tension between man's way of signifying God through limited concepts and God's way of being. It is both the latter (God's *modus essendi*) and our limited capacity to understand that limit our comprehension of God. Nevertheless, regardless of our limited understanding, what man knows about God is "something," and therefore one would not do justice to the reality of the case were one to adhere to a radical negative theology. On the one hand, God "cannot be defined" (Aquinas, *Quaestiones Disputatae De potentia,* q. 7, a. 3, ad 5 [hereafter *QDP*]; *SCG* I, 25; *ST* I, q. 3, aa. 5 and 6). (Albert the Great, from whom Aquinas learned the value of a negative approach to God's essence, has an understanding similar to Aquinas's—although the latter swerves away from the former in the last part of his work. See Albert the Great, *Super Dionysium: De divinis nominibus* in *Opera omnia* 37/1, ed. P. Simon [Cologne, 1972], #3.) On the other hand, there is a name that can be positively attributed to God (*ST* I, q. 13, a. 11, and *QDP,* q. 7, a. 5, ad 3).

known to the human being. What is needed, then, to affirm fully that there is indeed a concept of absolute spirit, is to rediscover both in what sense the infinity proper to the absolute principle refers to that absolute spirit which is immanent because transcendent and in what way "gift" is an adequate name for both finite and absolute spirit.

Absolute Gift: The Infinite, the Creator, and the Eternal

To unfold the meaning of "gift" proper to absolute spirit, Bruaire takes into account both his previous philosophical reflection and the intimations of Christian revelation. As we shall see, his ontodology proposes a Trinitarian ontology in which the absolute, God, is perceived as characterized by such a superabundant positivity (infinite), that he is not only able to give himself to himself eternally, he also gives what he is not, that is, he creates.[48]

Infinite Spirit

Since Bruaire's ontology begins with the human spirit rather than with an abstract "being" and perceives being in light of alterity, it characterizes the absolute spirit as the *other* of the *finite* human spirit and hence as *infinite* spirit. If the triad which so far has guided Bruaire's *ontodology* is finitude, spirit, and being, the central triad is now infinity, spirit, and being.[49]

Whenever one undertakes the task of elucidating the meaning of the infinite, the weight of negation (*in*-finite) tends to hold sway over all rep-

48. For the elaboration of an ontology in the light of the Trinity, see August Brunner, *Dreifaltigkeit. Personale Zugänge zum Geheimnis* (Einsiedeln: Johannes Verlag, 1976); Klaus Hemmerle, *Thesen zu einer trinitarischen Ontologie* (Einsiedeln: Johannes Verlag, 1976); Gisbert Greshake, *Der dreieine Gott* (Freiburg: Herder, 1997); Piero Coda and Andreas Tapken, eds., *La Trinità e il pensare: Figure, percorsi, prospettive* (Rome: Città Nuova, 1997); Piero Coda and L'ubomír Zák (eds.), *Abitando la Trinità: Per un rinnovamento dell'ontologia* (Rome: Città Nuova, 1998); Bruno Forte, *Trinità come storia* (Cinisello Balsamo, Milan: Edizione Paoline, 1985); Mario Serenthà, "La teologia trinitaria oggi," *La Scuola Cattolica* 118 (1990): 90–116.

49. Bruaire, "Philosophie et spiritualité," 1385. Bruaire's *ontodology* thinks of the *pure* concept of absolute spirit as always in counterpoint to that of the human spirit. This decision has the advantage both of unmasking any unrecognized anthropomorphization and of better illustrating that *gift* is a category applicable not only to the human spirit, but also to being itself.

resentations of this concept. The infinite thus appears to be that which is not limited by any type of quantitative or qualitative determination, and hence it appears to be totally undetermined. Bruaire argues that when infinity is understood in spatial terms, there are only two possibilities for representing what the infinite is: "either the infinite is the *other* of the finite, lying beyond or beside it, and then this infinitude, since it is limited by the finitude which it itself excludes, denies itself; or the infinite is absolutely without limits and can be differentiated from the finite only by including it within itself."[50] Hegel chooses the second term of the equation and, according to Bruaire, remains a prisoner of the prejudice of a spatial understanding of the infinite. Bruaire instead maintains that the negation of the finite implied in the concept of the infinite works in two directions: outwards and inwards. "It is impossible to think of surpassing the greatest without thinking of the utmost intimacy of the smallest: *interior intimo meo et superior summo meo.*"[51] To negate the finite means to change both our idea of the beyond (negation of determination) and our idea of the intimate. Bruaire corrects Hegel's idea of the infinite, because Hegel "infinitizes" (by making it unlimited) only the first term, that is, the beyond. But, since the infinite is an infinite *spirit,* the movement cannot be only the unilateral negation of the negation. It must also affect our understanding of the finite.

Bruaire—who takes from Marcel the image of the human spirit conceived as a being whose center is obscure (in opposition to the clear center of a human spirit supposedly in complete possession of itself) and from Fessard the explanation of Hölderlin's elucidation of the epitaph commemorating the first centenary of St. Ignatius's death: *"Non coerceri maximo, contineri tamen a minimo, divinum est"*—explains that the finitude that the infinite negates is double: the inward finitude of the limit of intimacy and the outward finitude of the limit of the sublime.[52] The positive

---

50. *AD,* 255. In *AD,* 252–66, Bruaire offers his understanding of the absolute infinite and its relationship with the human desire for God. See *EE,* 120.

51. *EdEES,* 72.

52. Let us listen to Fessard's explanation: "Plus profondément encore que l'intelligence n'est-elle [la liberté] pas, quelle que soit l'étendue de sa domination, faculté du possible, 'mouvement pour aller plus outre' et négation des limites? *Non coerceri maximo.* Et d'autre part, plus son bût est lointain et immense, plus il lui faut, pour l'atteindre ou seulement progresser vers lui, se déterminer dans le plus immédiat, dans le plus prochain. *Contineri a minimo.* Ces deux mouvements contraires dont l'opposition ne peut que croître parce

result of the negation in-finite, therefore, is to be understood, not according to Hegel, but after the manner of Schelling, as the *spiritual rhythm* of absolute self-concentration and self-expansion. "The divine spirit is greater than any greatness and, in the unity of its act, more interior than my extreme interiority."[53]

Once he denies the validity of this spatial image on account of its unilaterality, Bruaire is careful not to confine the infinite to a *kinetic* image that would reduce it to a movement of interiority and exteriority. In fact, the spiritual movement of interiority and exteriority needs to be read in terms of the *ontology* of spirit in which the limitation of the finite is understood as ontogenic impotence and the infinite is understood as the omnipotence proper to being. On the one hand, "the effusive expiration *infinitizes*": absolute spirit is "the total affirmation of itself in an act that actualizes itself without any limit of indetermination." On the other hand, "the infusive inspiration *infinitizes*": absolute spirit "confirms itself in the determination of its own act, by identifying itself with its own absolute origin." For this reason, Bruaire continues, the formal negation of the infinite is the affirmation of the "absolute potency *in* the pure act."[54] While the movement of interior and exterior conveys a more adequate understanding of the infinite, we must not be deceived by Bruaire's dialectical interpretation of this movement precisely because, for him, these two inverse significations are identical. This is the real usefulness that Bruaire sees in the term *act:* it respects the ontological reading of the infinite by bringing the two elements into a nonconfused unity.

If human finitude were only a matter of (physical) extension or of intellectual and moral limitedness, absolute infinity would be conceived only as "spiritual" (in opposition to matter) and as pure intellect or sheer goodness. Instead, for Bruaire's ontodology, the being of the human spirit is limited first of all because it is given to itself in order to become itself.

---

que, loin de se détruire, ils s'engendrent l'un l'autre, Ignace a compris tout de suite qu'ils se touchent et se réunissent à force de s'être éloignés, et se retrouvent en Dieu et en Dieu seulement. *Divinum est*" (Fessard, *Dialectique des "Exercices"*, 173).

53. *DD*, 121–22. The Augustinian *interior intimo meo* returns here as the undeniable reminder that the human spirit is not the author of itself and that it must discover its mysterious origin (*EdEES*, 73). This is why the *interior intimo meo* cannot be understood as a back door opened to pantheism.

54. *EE*, 122.

This not-being-its-own-origin is what characterizes human spirit's fini-tude and what gives birth to all other forms of finitude: spatial, physical, ethical, and intellectual. Hence, infinite spirit is pure act in the sense that it does not owe its own being to anything besides itself. Infinite spirit is *unlimited potency,* that is to say, absolute plenitude. For Bruaire, infinite power or "unlimited potency" cannot be imagined as a precarious begin-ning which nonetheless has the capacity to fulfill itself and bring itself to its own plenitude. Infinite spirit is not a potency called to give way to actuality. It cannot be distinguished from the pure act that is its perfect accomplishment. In this sense, *infinity* can be equated with pure act and perfection—provided one does not interpret "per-fection" as a rigid and rhythmless absolute spirit.[55]

Likewise, in contrast to the human spirit, absolute spirit can be con-sidered as an infinite freedom that *is* its own initiative. If the former is gift because totally given to itself and so endowed with an ontological passivity that determines its own being, the concept of absolute spirit, precisely as spirit, invites us to think of the infinite as a "gift of itself to itself" to which, contrary to what happens in the case of the human spirit, no passivity can be ascribed. Infinite spirit is the absolute initiative of itself. In this respect, the absolute gift of itself to itself leaves no room for any form of being-in-debt. It not only does not owe anything to anyone, it also does not need anything besides itself in order to be. If it did, it would be dependent and so not truly absolute; its relation with the nonabsolute spirit would then be that of Plotinus or of Hegelian necessity. In addition to this, for ab-solute spirit, which is pure act, the return to itself is not a disappointing enterprise.[56] Absolute spirit is, then, "the absolute potency in act of its own being," an act which includes the identical effusion and infusion of itself.

What needs to be borne in mind in this delicate movement of dona-tion of itself to itself is that absolute spirit is infinite; that is to say, it is

55. Aquinas has a similar understanding of God's infinity: "since the divine being is not a being received in anything, but He is His own subsistent being as was shown above [*ST* I, q. 3, a. 4], it is clear that God Himself is infinite and perfect" (*ST* I, q. 7, a. 1).

56. I have already indicated the problems in Schelling's understanding of the absolute beginning and the way Bruaire attempts to answer them. In order to have a more complete response to this delicate issue, two things are required: an idea of beginning and movement from the beginning to the end, on the one hand, and an adequate understanding of eternity, on the other. The latter will be discussed in this section and the former in the section that follows.

infinite potency without being in potency. It is *perfect act* and, as such, is the negation of any limitation. Hence, whereas the difference between operation and *esse* in the human being can never be bridged because the human being is not pure act, there is no ontological distance between them in the absolute. In this sense, the absolute freedom of the infinite spirit is the *identity* of "its ontological self-positing that transgresses every limitation in the actual *expression* in the absolute knowledge of itself" and "the collection *(recueillement)* without remainder, the return to the unconditioned origin."[57]

To think of the absolute in terms of *spirit* requires using the category of "expression" because spirit is *nous* and this *intelligibility* is characterized by the term *word*. At the same time, spirit is also *pneuma*, and, for this reason, there is no spirit that is not endowed with that twofold rhythm of expression or manifestation of itself and recollection of itself in a single word. Absolute spirit cannot be thought as a self-contained entity, after the manner of a Leibnizian monad. Infinite spirit is self-determination and thus is also pure expression of itself—together with recollection into itself.

To understand better what this absolute expression of itself means, Bruaire proposes a consideration of the intimation of Christian revelation that suggests the timeless actualization of the infinite power as the expression of itself as Word. The difficulty of conceiving this adumbration, of the self-manifestation of absolute spirit (self-expression) in the Word, comes from the fact that the human word is never the complete expression of the human self. By contrast, in the case of the infinite spirit, infinite potency in act, the Word is identically "manifested and gathered" in its own Origin. What does it mean to say that the infinite spirit expresses itself in the Word? One can answer this question if

> one is able to accept the claim of the "generation" of the Word: "Begotten, not created": *creation gives that which the Creator is not; begetting is* gift *of the whole being of its Principle, infinitely.*[58]

Infinite *spirit*, which is pure act, expresses itself, gives itself, begets the Word. This manifestation of itself in the Word does not follow necessarily from the divine Origin. That is to say, the first principle does not need

57. *EE*, 125.
58. *EE*, 127. Bruaire's emphasis.

to express itself in the Word in order to become itself, as if there were something lacking in it. The expression of the Origin in the Word is not required in order for the former to know itself; the Word does not offer a knowledge that the Origin does not have. The Word reveals all the full omnipotence of the Origin that *gives* itself completely without any limit.[59] Nevertheless, the Word cannot be thought as proceeding from the Origin, as if the latter were "completely itself" without the former and the former were subordinate to the latter. The expression of the Origin in the Word does not follow upon a prior decision of the former, as is normally the case for the human spirit. The Origin "begets" or "gives" a Word because, as infinite *spirit*, it does not exist without its manifestation. If the Word is the truth of pure act, then, Bruaire says, *the gift of itself* is the truth of its begetting. Infinite expression is nothing but the *gift of the absolute power of the gift*. In this gift, the Word expresses the Origin perfectly without the latter's losing itself.

To give itself to itself in the perfect expression of itself therefore implies an introduction of *alterity* into the *oneness* of the principle. Nevertheless, Bruaire claims that this otherness within the infinite does not destroy its *unity*. Both sameness and otherness need to be maintained because the *identity* of the expression with the infinite power, "which is everything that it can be because it is infinite, is by means of the *difference* between the giver and the gift, a difference in which the giver gives itself."[60] The unity is then preserved, because *infinite* spirit is the absolute freedom which gives *itself to itself*. The "Word" *contains* all of the gift—with the difference that it is given. Therefore, since the expression is identical with what is expressed, it cannot but return the gift without holding anything back.

According to Bruaire, one needs to make the effort of thinking the absolute in itself in order to see that the relationship between the infinite spirit and its expression is like the seed that brings within itself the fruit which its power generates. Infinite spirit is the pure act which is the absolute gift of itself, a gift without origin, without debt, and without a destination "outside of itself." Two things must therefore be preserved in order for

59. Bruaire thinks of the absolute in terms of pure act and omnipotence. In order to remain faithful to this reading, Bruaire decides to couple pure act with infinite potency, an unhappy terminological choice which is often misleading.

60. *EE*, 129.

this donation to be "absolute." On the one hand, it must hand itself over completely to the other, without keeping anything of itself. On the other hand, in giving itself in the Word in this way, the infinite spirit reciprocates the gift in a way that eliminates any passivity proper to the finite gift. For its part, the Word, without holding anything back, gives everything in return. In fact, had the donation in the Word not been a *generation,* then the "Word" would not have received everything from the source and would not be identical with it. In this sense, the "Word" would be "outside" absolute spirit and would be a limited spirit. If this were the case, then the so-called Word would be in ignorance of the giver and would be under the obligation to return the gift to an unknown giver. Instead, Bruaire insists, what is given is everything: since the gift is the *absolute* gift of itself, the gift cannot be lost. The Word expresses the source completely and, in so doing, returns the gift.

Although illuminating, the analysis of absolute spirit as *infinite* still leaves two questions unanswered. First, one could argue that when Bruaire reviews the Aristotelian categories, he says that substance should be understood in terms of donation, and its most proper characteristic is that of being "totally given to itself" and so unable to be claimed back. It seems, then, that what is given is totally given in the case of both absolute spirit and human spirit. Where then is the distinction? Bruaire argues that the answer to this question lies in the difference between *generation* and *creation.* Since both the Word and the human spirit are *given* completely to themselves and cannot be claimed back, Bruaire is forced to place the difference between generation and creation in *what* is given in each case. In the generation of the Word, absolute spirit gives *itself;* in creation, absolute spirit gives what *it is not:* finite spirit. In this sense, the *absoluteness* that *begetting* entails refers both to the way the gift is given and to the gift itself. This distinction between the being-given of the absolute and of the finite spirit might end up jeopardizing the univocity that Bruaire would like to ascribe to the concept of gift, regardless of his intention.

The second question regards the *gratuity* of the absolute gift. In order to provide an adequate answer to the question, one needs to look at the gift both in terms of the source of the gift and of the gift itself. With respect to the first, the question could be formulated in these terms: If absolute spirit must be understood as infinite act in which the Origin necessarily manifests itself, what gratuity is left in the gift? From the side of the gift-given, the question could be formulated as follows: Does not the identity between the gift and the giver, which makes the gift give itself completely back to the giver, eliminate the gratuity of the absolute gift? Addressing this second question requires discussion of God as creator and as eternal.

Creator Spirit

Under the title *creator*, Bruaire deals in *L'être et l'esprit* (*EE*) first with absolute spirit as creator spirit and, second, with finite spirit and the world as a whole as created reality.[61] By approaching these interrelated matters, Bruaire hopes to deepen his revision of the study of being, and more specifically of its categories, in light of *ontodology*. To this end, he deems it necessary to explore the meaning of the idea of absolute spirit as *ground (fundament)* or *principle*. The unusual status that Bruaire gives "creation" in his treatment of absolute spirit is prompted by his desire to explain that to conceive of absolute spirit in terms of gift is to see how God gives himself to himself. At the same time, donation in God (the begetting of the Word) should be thought along with the donation outside God of what he is not (creation). "All of God's omnipotence is necessary in order to give that which he is not. All the same, in order to give without reserve what he is, something infinitely more is needed: God's omnipotence. Here, then, is the difference between begetting and creating."[62]

It is important to indicate that, while Bruaire places creator spirit between infinite and eternal spirit, his exposition would have benefitted had he not followed the structure of Hegel's *Lectures on the Philosophy of Religion* and inverted the order of exposition—that is to say, had he first presented the sense in which the act of donation within the absolute requires difference within the unity of the absolute principle and the sense in which the donating act between the giver and the gift does not annihilate the logic of gift. Not having explained adequately the distinction and

---

61. *EE*, 129–44. Bruaire also deals with the idea of "creation" in other places of his work, although nowhere as thoroughly as in *EE*. See *PM*, 100, 144–51, 167, 193–94, 256. Bruaire also envisions his metaphysics as a metaphysics of creation: see *PM*, 280; Bruaire, "Création et inspiration," *Communio* 7 (1982): 3; *FE*, 110–11; *DD*, 73; and *LR*, 113–31; Renée Toussaint, "Le don, l'envers positif du 'ex nihilo.' Le concept de création chez Claude Bruaire" (Ph.D. diss., Institut Supérieur de Philosophie of the Catholic University of Louvain, 2001).

62. *FE*, 112.

the unity among the divine persons, or the role of the Holy Spirit in the Trinity and in creation, Bruaire allows the difference and the similarity between begetting and creating to remain veiled by a twofold ambiguity: on the one hand, approaching creation in relation to the begetting of the Son makes the gratuitous nature of creation more difficult to understand, and, on the other hand, it is more complicated to elucidate how the creation of the finite spirit is an act entailing the whole of the absolute spirit.

At the Source of Creation

Bruaire contends that gift needs to be understood in terms of *creation*, a concept that, regardless of its Biblical origin, is also philosophical with "full legitimacy."[63] Remaining faithful to his method, Bruaire does not demonstrate the philosophical validity of creation by presenting the need for a universal cause that gives the ultimate reason for the world's contingency. Nor does he explain creation in the classical terms of participation or "emanation."[64] He believes that all the other meanings of creation (causality, *causa sine ratio*, ground, etc.) are included in, and enhanced by, the concept of gift and that gift offers the proper comprehension of the concept of the *infinite* and its relationship to the finite spirit, which undergirds

63. Although in a different way from Aquinas, Bruaire also maintains that "creationem esse non tantum fides tenet, sed etiam ratio demonstrat" (Aquinas, *In II Sent.*, d. I, q. 1, a. 2; id., *QDP*, q. 3, a. 5). Scotus, who in some respects is closer to Bruaire's mind, establishes a greater demarcation between philosophy and theology. This is done in such a way that, as Leo Cardinal Scheffczyk explains, the result is a more ambiguous understanding of the philosophical breadth of this term: "tout en continuant à soutenir qu'on pourrait connaître par la philosophie la création à partir du néant (*Op. Oxon.* II, d. I, q. 2, n. 3, 4: ed. Wadding t. VI, I, 30), Duns Scot pense qu'on ne pourrait prouver de façon évidente à partir de la création, une causalité toute-puissante (*Op. Oxon.* I, d. 42: t. V, 2, 1350). Mais l'idée de création intégrale incluant celle de toute-puissance, ce n'est que relativement qu'il peut admettre le fondement rationnel du concept de création, dont le caractère propre ne peut découler que dans la foi" (Leo Scheffczyk, *Création et Providence*, trans. P. Prévot [Paris: Cerf, 1967], 163–64). For the possibility of knowing God as creator, see *DS* 3004 and 3875. The biblical texts are: Gn 1:1–2; 2 Mc 7:28; Prv 8:22–31; Rom 4:17. See also *DS* 285, 455, 790, 800, 851, 1333, 1442, 3002, 3021–25 (First Vatican Council), and in the recent *Catechism of the Catholic Church*, 296–97, 338.

64. Creation is not an *emanatio totius entis a causa universali*. See Aquinas, *ST* I, q. 45, a. 1. Cf. *ST* I, qq. 44–49; *SCG* II, 15–18. See also Cornelio Fabro, *Partecipazione e causalità secondo S. Tommaso d'Aquino* (Turin: Società Editrice Internazionale, 1958); Rudi A. te Velde, *Participation and Substantiality in Thomas Aquinas* (Leiden: E. J. Brill, 1995). I must remind the reader that this way of approaching the issue of creation does not entail a rejection of causality.

the identification of gift and creation.[65] Bruaire, referring to Scotus, affirms that the concept of creation is not deduced *a priori* from God. To do so would be to eliminate any gratuity and to make gift necessary. The entire necessary speculative process heretofore presented rules out this reading of Bruaire's argument as illegitimate.[66] At the same time, the concept of creation cannot be inferred *a posteriori* from the world, as if creatureliness were something that could be found in the definition of substance.[67] With Scotus, Bruaire says that the concept of creation was offered with God's revelation as Christianity understands it, and, at the same time, he argues that it can be proved rationally.

As we have seen, the movement from finite to infinite spirit proceeds by means of the analysis of the pure concept of the spirit. This method allows Bruaire to show that absolute spirit is the *other* of the finite spirit, with the result that whereas the latter is characterized by its ontological indigence, by the passivity of being given, the former denotes only ontological fullness, donation without ontological passivity. The reverse path, from infinite spirit to finite spirit, now leads to the concept of creation and enhances the understanding of the being-gift of the human spirit. If absolute spirit was described previously as infinite because the absolute is the *other* of the *finite* spirit, the finite spirit is now considered as the *other* of the *infinite* spirit—which is its principle. For this reason, if the infinite is pure gratuity, the finite other of that sheer gratuity cannot be conceived

65. I would like to bring the reader's attention to the fact that Bruaire does not reduce causality to *efficient* causality. Instead, he insists that it is the four causes that are to be comprehended within the concept of donation. This reading of creative causality in terms of *efficient* causality was mistakenly attributed to Aquinas and it ignores texts such as *ST* I, q. 44, and *In III Sent.*, d. 10, q. 10. This reading is to be found in Suárez. Cf. Jean-François Courtine, *Suárez et le système métaphysique* (Paris: PUF, 1990). Angelo Scola notes that the attempt to explain creation in terms only of *efficient* causality has had drastic consequences for theological reflection: (*a*) it does not acknowledge divine Being's Trinitarian character as revealed in Jesus Christ; (*b*) it does not consider how the freedom of the three Persons intervenes in the creative act; (*c*) it does not explain how, along with divine efficiency, there is the communication *ad extra* of the Trinitarian being through the mediation of Jesus Christ. See Angelo Scola, Gilfredo Marengo, and Javier Prades López, *La persona umana: Antropologia teologica* (Milan: Jaca Book, 2000), 89.

66. Interestingly enough, Bruaire accuses Scotus of failing to exploit his (Scotus's) understanding of creation to elaborate an anthropology enhanced by the concept of gift (*EE*, 132-44).

67. Aquinas, *ST* I, q. 45, a. 3.

of in terms of degradation but in terms of totally *positive* donation. Hence, finite spirit is another (being) given to itself.[68]

Bruaire has shown that infinite spirit is total gift of itself *(communicatio sui)* and, at the same time, it is totally reciprocated in its Word. This original donation is the beginning without beginning, or "commencement without commencement," to use an older formula drawn from Bruaire's study of Schelling. Since the infinite is *spirit,* its unity is constituted by way of the *inner* difference between the source and the expression, a difference which, however, "disappears" because the absolute gift of itself of the infinite spirit is nothing but "the absolute positivity of the ontogenic power in act."[69] If the first principle is conceived of in terms of absolute gratuity, then the mysterious source of the human spirit, the *interior intimo meo,* should be conceived of accordingly. For this reason, Bruaire says, all the formulas modernity has forged in order to avoid "whispering" the created nature of the world, for example, noumenon (Kant), Ur-grund, Un-grund (Schelling), sufficient reason (Leibniz), ground (Heidegger), need to be modified and the anthropomorphic presumption undergirding them corrected.

If infinite spirit is "sheer positivity," then donation cannot but be gratuitous, that is to say, *absolute.* This means that gift is not the *result* of a pro-

---

68. Bruaire's reference to time and eternity focuses on the understanding of time proper to the absolute, and only secondarily to that of the human spirit. Bruaire never enters into the much debated question among the scholastics concerning the demonstration of the beginning of the world in time. Aquinas denied the possibility of proving such a beginning rationally and concluded that the commencement of the world in time "sola fide tenetur, et demonstrative probari non potest" (*ST* I, q. 46, a. 2). Bonaventure considered absurd the simultaneous affirmation of creation and denial of a creation in time (Bonaventure, *Breviloquium* II, 1, 1 and 3); also see Scotus *Op. Oxon.* II, d. 1, q. 3.

69. *EE,* 130. I emphasized the term "inner" to avoid suggesting that the divine Origin's donation of itself presupposes a movement *outside* itself. See *ST* I, q. 27, a. 3. Following Hegel, Bruaire says that the Spirit is the activity of self-manifestation (*Enzyklopädie* §378 and §§383–84). Nevertheless, with O'Regan, we need to acknowledge that this movement in Hegel is a process of becoming and finitization. For Bruaire, by contrast, the manifestation does not imply a finitizing of the spirit. See O'Regan, *The Heterodox Hegel,* 44–63. "Disappears" is in quotation marks to prevent any modalistic reading of the donating act within the absolute spirit. Bruaire does use this term *(effacer);* nevertheless, I think that it is more a polemical and imprecise way of underscoring that difference does not rupture the unity. Any judgment of Bruaire's presentation of the intra-Trinitarian movement of donation as "modalistic" would require the study of two issues which we still need to explore: the idea of person and the concept of the confirmation of the absolute gift by the Holy Spirit.

cess, a change, or a movement. The being-gift of the human spirit is *totally* given to itself. Bruaire finds in the exploration of the adverb *"totally"* the door that opens to the proper understanding of *gift*-of-spirit. The terms "totally given" and "absolute gratuitous donation" do not mean only that gift is given once and for all and cannot be claimed back (as the eidetic analysis shows); these terms also indicate that there is no precondition that somehow forces the act of donation itself and that there is nothing from which this gift could be given. If this were the case, then gift would be given in order to complete an already existent reality and would not be a *total* gift. Ontologically speaking, for a gift to be truly a gift, not only must it be given freely, without expecting anything in return, there must also be absolutely no conditions that prompt or require the donating act. The only "adequate and univocal" term to describe being-of-spirit's gift is creation, and since this donation is "total," creation cannot but be "ex nihilo."[70]

The nothingness of *ex nihilo*, Bruaire says, emphasizes the fact that creation (both as *verb*, act of creation, and as *noun*, created reality) does not presuppose any precondition, since this would contradict the absoluteness of the gift, a contradiction which would entail "the rejection of creatureliness." Bruaire contends that every trace of an imaginative representation of the term *"nihilo"* must be acknowledged and then rejected. There is no pre-existent reality which could have been used to bring finite gift into existence, not even the Leibnizian *praetentio ad existendum*. In this respect, Bruaire would also say that the preposition *ex* of *ex nihilo* does not mean a "material cause" or a "something"—which, strangely, would be called "nothing"—from which the gift is to be given.[71] To relativize the gift is to eliminate its gratuity, and this implies the destruction of its ontological reality. If gift cannot come from any nondivine reality, then the created spirit is bound to come from absolute spirit itself, which, as infinite, is utter positivity. "*Ex nihilo*," then, does not mean that nothingness is original or equiprimordial with being. Nothingness is not originally a relative term that is somehow needed in order to understand being. In a certain sense, it comes only after the position of the absolute, that is, that timeless donation of itself to itself. It is only from the point of view of the human spirit that one could conceive the two terms "being and nothing" as equi-

---

70. *EE*, 131; *PM*, 238.
71. Cf. Aquinas, *ST* I, q. 44, a. 1, ad 3.

primordial. Since Bruaire approaches "nothingness" from gift, he is able to disclose that the meaning of nothingness is the absolute spirit's rejection of the possibility of not creating another infinitely different from him. As Rolf Kühn elucidates, Bruaire regards the nothingness of the *ex nihilo* as the rejection of being *simpliciter*.[72] The affirmation of this superabundant love as the source of the created cosmos is the positive translation of the meaning of *ex nihilo*.[73]

Ex parte Dei, then, nothingness expresses both the fact that the reason for creating is to be found solely in the absolute itself, which is sheer gratuity, and that the absolute does not use anyone or anything to bring forth into existence that which did not exist before.[74] Therefore, if one wishes to acknowledge the full radicalness of the term "totally given to itself," one also needs to admit that created being is different from its source and that this difference is rooted within God himself. At the same time, just as God is absolute and does not refer to anything in order to create, after the creative act he *remains* non-relative, non-dependent on the creature. Hence, the creative act, in order to be totally given, must not change God's nature; that is to say, God must not need the created spirit in any way. If this were the case, then the human spirit would not be truly given to itself. It would instead be created out of a certain constriction or as the result of a degradation; in both cases, God would no longer be God, and the finite spirit would not be truly free.[75]

---

72. Kühn, *Französische Reflexions*, 162.

73. It seems that the most adequate term that combines "freedom" and "gift" is *love*. This word is able adequately to portray the ultimate reason for creation, eliminating the objection of the "necessary donating act." Although the term love appears only on rare occasions, especially in his description of the "logic of mercy," Bruaire's *ontodology* could also be described as an attempt to ground a metaphysics of charity. Cf. *PM*, 163–65, 210, 216–31, 249–52.

74. The Arian controversy makes clear that Christ's mediation cannot be understood in terms of a demiurgical activity. Cf. *DS* 126. The negation, *ex parte Dei*, does not mean that God can deny himself. In this sense, God's incarnation and descent into Hell cannot be seen as a self-denial but must be seen as a paradoxical form of love. Cf. Balthasar's polemical book *Mysterium Paschale* (Grand Rapids, Mich.: Eerdmans, 1993) with select bibliography.

75. Unlike Hegel, who does not give the *otherness* of the human spirit its full due, Bruaire says that the Other of the finite spirit does not presuppose anything in bringing the latter into existence as an absolutely (ontologically) different *other*. Chapelle, whose work on Hegel and religion Bruaire uses to support this judgment of Hegel, explains how even Hegel's reading of creation in terms of speculation and not of representation is unable to ground adequately the difference between the absolute and creation. Cf. Chapelle, *Hegel et la religion*, vol. 2, 146–77, 195–99. See also O'Regan, *The Heterodox Hegel*, 169–87.

To understand this second meaning of creation from nothing it is decisive to grasp that Bruaire affirms, on the one hand, the radical ontological difference between created and absolute gift, which is totally given to itself, and, on the other hand, the similarity between creating and begetting. In the same way that one could perceive an analogy between God's being and man's being, it is possible to see an analogy between God's *gift* of himself to himself and his *gift* to the other. Bruaire struggles to define the *ontological* difference between absolute and finite spirit because, although wishing to give full autonomy to the being-of-spirit, he wants to avoid eliminating the similarity between begetting and creating. This similarity, he says, lies in the *communicatio* of being understood formally: both finite spirit and infinite spirit "are given." I said just now that giving is understood formally. Nevertheless, we must not think that Bruaire adopts the term "gift" as an empty concept to which he then gives one specific content when he talks about the human spirit and another when he talks about absolute spirit. Creation's being-given implies the *act* of being-given, and it implies that *what* is given is also, in a certain sense, gift. The speculative distinction between *act* of giving and the *content* given cannot be read as if there were no similarity, however minimal, between the two "gifts."

Therefore, no matter how radically one may conceive of the *ontological difference* between absolute spirit and finite spirit, it is illegitimate to push it so far as to rule out any similarity between the *donating* act known as *begetting* and the *donating* act known as *creation*. In fact, Bruaire says, the ontological concept of gift can open an explanation of the nature of creation (finite gift) only in terms of the difference and the similarities between these two acts of giving being.

In order to tackle this delicate issue, Bruaire begins by posing the question radically. Unlike Aquinas, Bruaire contends that the creative act needs to be understood in the same way as the act of begetting.[76] Bruaire thinks

76. I think that Bruaire would have benefitted from a more thorough reading of Aquinas. This would have allowed him to discover that Thomas maintains an objective unity between the *potentia generandi* and the *potentia creandi*. Although there is some evolution in Aquinas's thought, it is clear that in his latest works, Aquinas holds that God's creative potency finds its root in the Trinitarian processions. Aquinas explicitly says that "processio personarum divinarum est causa et ratio processio creaturarum" (*ST* I, q. 45, a. 6 and a. 7, ad 3); see also *QDP*, q. 2., a. 5, ad 6: "The generation of the Son and the formation of creatures are of the same kind, not univocally indeed, but only by analogy. Thus Basil (*Hom. de Fide XV*) says that the Son receives in common with all creatures." In this sense he is called the

that Aquinas is correct when he describes the donating act as an *absolute act* because being is not given proportionally; every being is *datio totius esse*.[77] Nevertheless, Bruaire believes that Aquinas fails to see—or did not consider it necessary to show—how "the act of being is identical both in God and in creation." Aquinas did not know how to reconcile "the *actus essendi* with the alterity of created being."[78] Bruaire tries to explain that the gift of being—"being in act of the spirit's infinite power"—is twofold: the gift of being of its potency which is absolutely expressed in the Word *and* the being given to itself in creation. In exploring the *act* of giving (donat-

---

Firstborn of every creature (Col 1:15), and for the same reason his generation may be placed under one common head with the production of creatures. Cf. *QDPD*, q. 10, a. 2. See also Javier Prades López, "De la Trinidad económica a la Trinidad inmanente. A propósito de un principio de renovación de la teología trinitaria," *Revista española de teología* 58 (1998): 333–38; Gilfredo Marengo, *Trinità e creazione* (Rome: Città Nuova, 1990); Francesco Marinelli, *Personalismo trinitario nella storia della salvezza. Rapporti tra la SS.ma Trinitá e le opere ad extra nello Scriptum super Sententiis di San Tommaso* (Rome: Libreria editrice PUL; Paris: J. Vrin, 1969); Gilles Emery, *La Trinité créatrice: Trinité et création dans les commentaires aux Sentences de Thomas d'Aquin* (Paris: J. Vrin, 1995). Bruaire is not affirming that created and absolute spirit are of the same "nature." In fact, while one might wish for more precise language, Bruaire strove throughout his philosophical career to affirm the difference between absolute freedom and human freedom. To this end, he shows on several occasions that Hegel, Feuerbach, and Schelling fail to make this difference sufficiently clear and so end up either absorbing the infinite in the finite or conceiving the infinite in terms of the finite. As we shall see, the similarity rests on the action of giving and on a certain "commonality" between human spirit and absolute spirit (which attempts to explain philosophically in what sense the human being is created in the image of God); the dissimilarity, on the fact that God creates, i.e., he gives what he is *not*. It is also important not to forget that there is a true, although analogical, sense in which the divine processions serve both to distinguish persons within a single nature *and* to produce creatures, which nonetheless does not necessarily lead to a confusion between begetting and creating. In addition to the texts of Aquinas cited, also see *In I Sent.*, d. 26, q. 2, a. 2, ad 2. For a contemporary theological application of "Creation from the Trinity," see Hans Urs von Balthasar, *The Last Act*, vol. 5 of *Theo-Drama*, 61–188. What is missing in Guy Mansini's rejection of Balthasar's enterprise is the possibility of validly conceiving of substance and time in non-Aristotelian terms. Cf. Guy Mansini, O.S.B., "Balthasar and the Theodramatic Enrichment of the Trinity," *The Thomist* 64 (2000): 499–519. See also: August Brunner, *Dreifaltigkeit. Personale Zugänge zum Geheimnis* (Einsiedeln: Johannes Verlag, 1976); Ghislain Lafont, *Peut-on connaître Dieu en Jésus-Christ?* (Paris: Cerf, 1969); Marie-Joseph Le Guillou, *Le mystère du Père* (Paris: Fayard, 1973).

77. *ST* I, q. 45, a. 1. Bruaire is reading his own understanding of substance into the cited text. In the text which Bruaire quotes, Aquinas refers to the creation, not of singular individuals, but of the whole of being. Aquinas treated the philosophical progress from thinking of the causes of single corporeal beings to the consideration of being as such in the previous question, *ST* I, q. 44, a. 2.

78. *EE*, 137.

ing) being, Bruaire believes that what is donated is the same type of act of being. He asks, "how is a *communicatio entis* possible if it is not a *communicatio sui?*" Can God give himself to the other (i.e., finite spirit) without giving himself (infinite spirit)?

> The absolute exchange [between the Father and the Son] is *identity in absolute difference,* a difference which preserves the inaugural priority of the absolute ontological initiative with regard to the reciprocity, the rendering of the gift to the gift. Contrariwise, creation means *difference in the identity of being-given,* the alterity of the gift when the giver no longer gives himself in it and hence, limits himself in it.[79]

Only insofar as the donating act of the infinite spirit is constituted by three different moments is it possible to think of this as a different and yet identical act. A careful examination that anticipates a later explanation calls these three moments *donation, reddition,* and *confirmation.*[80] The first, which is already familiar to us, expresses the fact that absolute spirit is the *infinite* potency which is pure act and which gives and expresses it-

---

79. *EE,* 138. Bruaire's emphasis. Please note that in the previous quotation Bruaire talked about a *communicatio entis* and not a communication of *esse.*

80. A terminological explanation is here in order. Bruaire uses the term "reddition" in order to describe the Son's return of the gift. As the Father *is* the donation of himself to the Son, the Son *is* the return of himself. Although the common translation of the French term "reddition" is "surrender," I think that Bruaire is referring to the Latin root of "reddition" which is *reddere,* that is, *re-dare. Reddere* has three meanings: "(1) to give back, to restore, to reflect, to re-express; (2) to place, to give in return or in reply; (3) to give up as due, to render" (*Chambers Murray Latin-English Dictionary,* s.v. "reddere"). These three meanings, along with the positive understanding of gift which Bruaire postulates, compel us not to translate "reddition" as "surrender." In fact, "surrender" is first understood as "giving up," and not as "giving back"—which is what the context of Bruaire's *ontodology* seems to suggest.

I would like to retrieve the old English term "reddition" and not to use either "surrender" or "restitution." The last of these has the advantage of preserving the idea of "giving back," and it does so while preserving the connotation of "necessity and gratuity" proper to the absolute return of the gift which the Son is. Nevertheless, "restitution" has two connotations that do not respect Bruaire's main intention. "Restitution" means to give back to the "rightful owner" what he "has lost." This connotation seems to jeopardize the personhood of the Son because it implies that the Son does not adequately possess the divine nature. In fact, he would have to return what is not his. The second misleading connotation is that "restitution" is conducive to interpreting donation in terms of "having" and not in terms of "being"—which goes against Bruaire's understanding of "being" as "gift." "Reddition" reflects the Latin root of the term *(reddere),* which means to give again, and it avoids the negative implications which characterize the verb to "surrender." In addition, it allows us to translate the ternary "donation, reddition, confirmation," without using a circumlocution.

self. *Reddition* is the return of the gift to the origin (without loss of either difference or identity). When the act coincides totally with its content, the expression of the gift cannot but return the gift. *Confirmation,* which was earlier described as *mercy,* is the double donation of the gift, which secures its absolute gratuity. In theological terms, the first is the Father who begets the Son, from both of whom proceeds the Holy Spirit. To explain the reality of the finite spirit, Bruaire first underlines that the "movement" from donation (Father) to reddition (Son) is that of *giving* and thus of *gratuity,* and then he proposes to think these three "moments" by abstracting from their undeniable and timeless unity. According to Bruaire, this is the best possibility we have for discovering the difference within the one act of total donation.

If one could conceive of a distance between the second and the third moment (reddition and confirmation), it would be possible to conceive of a donation from the absolute power which gives but which does not give itself, that is, which *creates* another. Of course, this answer should not lead the reader to suppose either that the three different moments in God happen "in time" (as if they were not a donation of the divine nature itself), or that there is no real difference between them (a difference which, however, does not eliminate their unity). Bruaire maintains that the distance between these three moments is a "fictitious" one that happens in a "fictitious time," which nonetheless *really signifies* being pure and simple, a being "which is *available* in order to be the other of being, the being given to itself as finite spirit." Bruaire describes this *mysterious* donating act (creation) in these terms:

> Being without the Self of the infinite spirit. Being of the Expression without the Expressed, neutral being which nonetheless is omnipotence's plenary act, being in which infinite spirit has not confirmed *itself,* being of the gift that is 'on hold' where the reddition is the act in exchange. Being in which the infinite gives itself since gift's initiative is inexhaustible within the reddition itself, the difference of itself in the identity of itself.[81]

We would not do Bruaire justice were we to think that the expression of the Father in the Word is incomplete until the Holy Spirit confirms the donating act. We still need to look at this point more carefully, how-

---

81. *EE,* 139. In *DD,* 101–5, Bruaire places the "fictitious distance" between the first and the second moment and not between the second and the third.

ever, because for Bruaire the Holy Spirit does not make the Son be the Son; the Spirit does not give the "self" to the Son, as though the donation from the Father were not the total donation of all of himself. In theological terms, one could say that the divine nature is identical to the three divine persons. Bruaire maintains that creation is possible because of the intra-Trinitarian difference. The "real difference," says Bruaire, between the "Reddition to the Beginning *(Principe)* and the Confirmation of Itself in the *rhythm* of the Holy Spirit" is what makes creation possible.[82] To think of the creation of the human spirit *in* the Word, says Bruaire, the most adequate approach is to affirm that the human spirit is given by the absolute spirit in the same way as the Son is given from the Father.[83] Nevertheless, begetting and creating cannot be identified. Bruaire draws a distinction between the *act* of donating and *what* is being donated. "Begetting" expresses first of all the identity between the giver and the gift and, second, their difference. In this sense, the Father would be of the same nature and differ only in the fact that he is the begetter and the Son is the begotten. This mysterious act of being (giving) has its ultimate reason in absolute spirit's infinite nature. Absolute spirit *is* this eternal giving—which does not mean that God is in the process of making himself; he *is* absolute gift. At the same time, Bruaire also sees that the "spiritual effusion is also profusion of spiritual beings." God not only gives himself to himself (Donation, Reddition, Confirmation), he also gives what is not himself, that is, he creates *another*. Contrarily to begetting, creation describes first a *difference:* finite spirit *is not* absolute spirit; it is *other*. There is *"no analogy"* between begetting and creating. As I mentioned before, there is a *communicatio entis* but not a *communicatio sui*. The difference resides, then, in *what* is given. Bruaire struggles to make a clear distinction between the two. "God does not distribute himself analogically, and the being-given [of the human spirit] does not have any proportion to him. God creates."[84] It is only the infinite spirit which can give *all* of itself to itself and give what is not itself, that is, create the other.

---

82. *EE,* 140. Emphasis added. Although Bruaire never quotes Bonaventure, the famous passage from the *Hexaemeron* XI, 9, seems surprisingly close to Bruaire's understanding of creation. See St. Bonaventure, *Collationes in Hexaemeron,* vol. 5 of *The Works of Bonaventure,* trans. José de Vinck (New York: St. Anthony Guild Press, 1970), 161–62.

83. Bruaire mentions here the passage in St. Paul's epistle to the Ephesians (Eph 1:3–14). God creates man *in* and *for* the Word.

84. *EE,* 141.

Bruaire believes that only begetting implies a *communicatio "sui."* Yet, without ignoring the "ontological difference" between them, Bruaire explains the *commonality* between absolute gift and created gift in terms of the *identity* of the gift, an identity between the *act of giving* and *creation.* This identity, he explains, is the dialectical equivalence between the "yes" that creates the human spirit and the refusal of the latter to be erased in pure exteriority, in spiritual nothingness.

Bruaire's brilliant analysis allows us to see that the *act* both of begetting and of creating can be perceived in terms of *donation.* The Father gives all of himself without reserve to his other; he eternally begets the Son. At the same time, his gratuitous omnipotence creates another, different from him, who resembles him. Finite spirit is not gift in a lesser degree. The need for both donations to be total makes Bruaire underline the radicality of creation from nothingness. In this regard, he affirms that finite gift is *other* than absolute spirit, which means that, although both of them are gift, the being-gift of the finite spirit is not ultimately the same as the divine reality. Since Bruaire wants to preserve the identity of the being-given of the Son and of the finite being-of-spirit, while not forgetting the difference, he wants to see in the concept of gift a univocal concept. It does seem, however, that even though both the Son and the finite being-of-spirit are totally given to themselves, the difference between them requires an analogical concept of gift, rather than a univocal one. An analogical concept of gift would have eliminated some of the ambiguities present in Bruaire's reflection while respecting his original intention. We still need to see what Bruaire considers to be the role of the Holy Spirit, not only *ad extra* in the creative act, but also within the absolute spirit. This will allow us to give a more comprehensive answer to the question regarding the possibility of a univocal concept of gift.

Created in the Word

If the human spirit is created in the Son, who is the expression of the Father, then the human spirit is in a sense an "image" of its other. To be the image of the Son entails that the human spirit first *is*, then that it is *another,* and finally, since it has been created by absolute freedom, that it is *free.* Bruaire holds that a certain resemblance of creatureliness may be found in man's artistic capacity. In this sense, one could say that the artist is also a *creator,* since he brings to existence something new and different from himself that somehow resembles him. Nevertheless, artistic creativity, a privileged locus of the discovery of the being-gift of the human spirit, is not sufficient for a discovery of its being created. Procreation is another locus for the discovery of the creatureliness of finite being. Still, the same objection arises here as well. The being-of-spirit of the child is being-gift because of a divine creation, and not by virtue of human action.[85] Neither the work of art nor the begetting of a child can be presented as signs in which we can recognize creation. According to Bruaire, only *language* is an adequate sign of the creatureliness of the human spirit. Bruaire does not hold this because he believes that language is the most sublime result of human creativity. This belief would presuppose a very meager reading of the human being's procreative act and an overconfidence in man's capacity to know. As explained previously, Bruaire's fine analysis of language shows that, despite man's capacity to change and modify it, language is not a human invention. If language is understood as the "reflection of material being into the intelligible idea," as rationality, one cannot but acknowledge that "thought is given to us for us to think."[86] Bruaire is not looking to demonstrate that the human being might have a certain creative capacity, no matter how faint. His point, in other words, is not to argue that if infinite spirit is also creator spirit and if the human being, as its other, is finite spirit, then it must be possible to establish that, somehow, finite spirit is also a creator spirit. Rather, language expresses the memory of being, and, because of it, language imposes its own meaning on man and man is given the possibility of discovering the meaning that language implies. That finite spirit is enabled to participate in language (rationality) means that finite spirit, with the gift of itself, has received the "gift of being in communion with the pure ideality of absolute spirit, which, in its Word (*Verbe*), thinks itself by begetting itself, reflects itself by expressing itself."[87] Bruaire's suggestion that human language precedes the being-of-spirit—

85. *EM,* 76–77.

86. Bruaire's choice of language over procreation as a sign of creatureliness reflects both the ultimate ambiguity of the procreative act (which, however, is not subject to the objection that God's intervention is superfluous for the conception of a new human life) and Bruaire's rationalistic tendencies.

87. *EE,* 142. Obviously this statement is, so to speak, "after the fact." It is not possible to "ascend" from language's rationality to participation in the Word.

and thus encounters itself within it—finds its full meaning in light of his metaphysics of gift. Since finite spirit is created *in* the Word, its discovery of the truth is a participation in being's intelligibility.

The participation in the ideality of absolute spirit is not merely a spiritual action. The human spirit is corporeal; finite spirit does not "inhabit" a body that is secondary to its very self, although a certain distinction between oneself and one's body may be drawn. Finite spirit's capacity of participating in the divine being is not given outside its relationship to its own body, and through the body, to all of nature. As we have seen, Bruaire maintains that human existence does not occur without the natural world; there is no language, no single act of freedom, no spiritual entreaty, without the natural world.

Following Bruaire's analysis, we need to acknowledge that subhuman beings, and thus the cosmos, do not have a substantial being which becomes itself in the *ipseic* assumption of itself by itself. In this sense, not all beings are given to themselves as the human spirit is, and, consequently, they cannot be seen in terms of gift, in the strict sense of the term. Yet, they are not mere "appearances" either. The cosmos is relative to the human being-of-spirit; it is created for the created finite spirit. In this sense, the being proper to the phenomena transcends them and requires that of the human spirit. Absolute spirit's creative act not only posits finite being in existence as its other, it also sets the world, "nature deprived of spirit," into existence as the *other* of the human being.

It is now possible to understand why Bruaire pays so little attention to the description of the being-gift of the natural world. The being of the created world is almost completely relative to that of the human being. Nature is never *expressive* by itself; it is only a sign of the divine, in which the "ontological source is transparent."[88] Nevertheless, it is a sign *for* the human spirit. Inasmuch as it is a sign, the created world has its own beauty and its "independence" with respect to the human being. Still because it is a sign, it is a sign *for* another and not for itself—and in this sense it is secondary to the human spirit, to whom it is given so that he, the Holy Spirit, might return them to the Father.

Without denying the validity of this reading of the created world, it seems to me that the presentation of the symbolic or "sacramental" value

88. *EE,* 144.

of reality needs a much more detailed elucidation. Here again Bruaire's philosophical method suffers from the excessive influence of Hegel's *Lectures on the Philosophy of Religion*. Thus, he is unable to explain in what sense reality is a sign—and hence a gift. It would have behooved him to explain in more detail how it is possible to be "a substance" without being "to itself"—something proper only to the finite spirit. On the other hand, it is not clear in what sense the created world, with the exception of the finite spirit's own body, is necessary for the human substance to become subject. Without denying the value of Bruaire's understanding of the created world, I think that this lack of explanation weakens the radicality Bruaire intends to confer upon the concept of gift. This deficiency also seems to diminish the understanding of spirit that Bruaire is proposing. Although very fruitful for the comprehension of the human being and absolute spirit, Bruaire's reflection could have developed in greater detail that sense in which there could be interiority in the created world. If spirit is understood as *nous* and *pneuma,* and if intelligence cannot be ascribed to the natural world, the only way to retrieve the spiritual dimension of the subhuman world—and hence its being—is to make the link to human consciousness much stronger.

Eternal Spirit

St. Augustine acknowledged with great simplicity the uneasiness everyone faces when dealing with the issue of time: *Quid ergo tempus? Si nemo ex me quaerat, scio; si quaerenti explicare velim, nescio.*[89] Since the dawn of human thinking, eternity has normally been understood in contrast to time. Greek philosophers, who perceived the sublunar world in opposition to the eternal universe, grappled with this concept. Parmenides and Heraclitus, and, in a different way, Plato, Aristotle, and Plotinus, dealt with this issue.[90] Nevertheless, as Matthew Lamb suggests, the notion of eternity is properly grasped only within the context of revealed religion.[91]

---

89. Augustine, *Confessions* XI, 14.

90. Plato, *Phaedo* 80B–84B; id., *Timaeus* 29E–40D; Aristotle, *Met.* 4 and 12.7.1072a25–b 24; Plotinus, *Enneads* 7, 3.

91. Matthew L. Lamb, "Eternity and Time," in *Gladly to Learn and Gladly to Teach,* ed. Michael Foley and David Kries (Lanham, Md.: Lexington Books, 2002), 195–214. See also id., "Divine Transcendence and Eternity," in *Continuity and Plurality in Catholic Theology,* ed. Anthony J. Cernera (Fairfield, Conn.: Sacred Heart University Press, 1998), 77–106.

Although many Christian philosophers used Aristotelian categories to explain divine eternity, they did so according to a perception of divine transcendence unfamiliar to the Greek world. The large majority of Christian thinkers tried to propose a concept of eternity starting from that of time understood as the measure of movement, that is, the "measure of before and after." In this sense, if time is the measure of becoming, eternity is not only an unlimited duration without beginning or end but, above all, duration without any change. Eternity is that type of duration which analogically measures a reality that is not affected by the imperfection proper to change. Following this basic intuition, eternity is described as "totum esse praesens,"[92] "*interminabilis vitae* total simul et perfecta possessio,"[93] or "omnino extra motum."[94]

Following this classical path, Bruaire explains eternity as that type of duration which is not affected by change;[95] similarly to St. Augustine, he approaches the issue of time from an existential perspective.[96] Being-of-spirit's *ipseic* assumption, its return to the origin, entails both facing its own personal death and longing for eternity concretely, that is, desiring to be eternally confirmed in being. Since Bruaire's negative anthropology circumscribes the presentation of eternity to the ontological realm, *eternal*

92. Augustine, *Confessions* XI, 10–13.

93. Boethius, *Philosophiae Consolationis* V, 6. I emphasize the phrase "limitless life" because it is very easy to fall into the misunderstanding that timeless eternity means lifeless eternity, or what is the same, unending boredom. Instead, for the classical thinkers, eternity as changeless duration does not mean that eternity is incompatible with history. On the contrary, it is history's complete fullness. See Ambrose, *Tractatus de Misteriis*, 8–16, quoted in Lamb, "Eternity and Time," 5. The confusion of eternity with an absolute concept derives more from late medieval thought. Cf. Bernard Lonergan, *Verbum: Word and Idea in Aquinas*, ed. F. Crowe and R. Doran (Toronto: Toronto University Press, 1997).

94. *ST* I, q. 10, a. 1. For Aquinas see also *SCG* I, 15; cf. Brian J. Shanley, "Eternity and Duration in Aquinas," *The Thomist* 61 (1997): 525–48; Bonaventure, *Itinerarium Mentis in Deum*, 5, 7.

95. Before the publication of *PM*, Bruaire dealt with this delicate matter in several contexts, particularly when he unearthed the roots of political philosophy. As I have shown, Bruaire contends that only an adequate conception of eternity is able to ground human justice. *RP*, 243–63; *PM*, 204–15, 216–27; *DD*, 142–51; *SQ*, 63.

96. For Augustine, the only answer to the existential drama of "time and eternity" is offered by Christian revelation. Since the mystery has entered into human history ("Et descendit hic ipsa vita nostra et tulit mortem nostram et occidit eum de abundatia vita sua ut redeamus hinc ad eum" [*Confessions* IV, 12, 19]), our nature is able to participate in the eternal life the human being longs for ("sed aliud est ipsa cuius partecipes efficimur vita aeterna; aliud nos qui eius partecipatione vivemus in aeternum" [*De Trinitate* I, 6, 10]).

spirit is that which is not subject to the same tragic human law as the human spirit. Still, rather than surrendering to unreflected presuppositions and siding with those who imagine God as an abstract entity incompatible with the flux of history, we must rediscover the understanding of time which *ontodology* requires and, having done so, unmask those fallacious images of divine stillness by proposing a positive understanding of eternity.

Considering time from the point of view of the ontology of gift, Bruaire sees the beginning of the human being as a creative act which is instantaneous, that is to say, "atemporal," but which, nonetheless, is immersed in that noneternal flow of time which is human history. Creation is not in the time of the world but the "gift of the temporal world to the being-gift which is a-temporally created."[97] From the heart of its own existence, human spirit, which is being-gift, longs for the eternal existence that can only be given it.

If one thinks of eternity according to this conception of time, the result is a negative sense of timelessness. Absolute spirit, gift of itself to itself, does not have a beginning in time because it is its own beginning. There is no ontological infirmity to be found in the creator spirit. Nevertheless, Bruaire, always wary of letting any negative theology compromise an adequate perception of the absolute, points out that the absence of a beginning and an end and the lack of change do not necessarily require a "motionless" absolute. Far from proposing an infinity that, in order to be itself, needs to change or to acquire something which it does not already have, Bruaire warns against a conceptualistic reduction of the absolute in which sempiternal presence is understood as stillness and an antihistorical changelessness. He argues that *eternal* spirit cannot be imagined to be an "ineffable thing," an "unalterable Spectator," or a "hypostasized duration." Eternity does not mean rigid identity. Only a Parmenidean absolute calls for a rigid, ineffable, motionless divinity.[98] None of these images can obscure Bruaire's awareness that God is absolute *spirit* and hence, that the eternal is not an isolated (relationless) unity. The transformation of a decaying time into a changeless eternity presupposes an erroneous inference: that a timeless eternal is an ahistorical eternal.

97. *EE*, 149.
98. *PM*, 220.

The consequences of the misleading extrapolation characterized above also affect the idea of human historicity; along with the absolute, human existence is also disfigured. If in an intensification of apophatic negation, the absolute is indeed supposed to be "history-proof," what value do human actions have? If human endeavor cannot be conceived of in relationship with the eternal, not because eternity does not exist, but because by nature it remains ontologically indifferent to human affairs, do not "good and evil, love and violence" become equivalent? If eternity is impermeable by history, then all human toiling remains "without a possible tomorrow."[99] Furthermore, does not this way of thinking limit absolute freedom, preventing it, if such were possible, from entering human history?

Bruaire finds that the best way to correct this apophatic understanding is to propose a *positive* concept of eternity. To this end, he uses what for him is one of Schelling's most decisive contributions to the history of human thought. Under the intimations of Christian revelation, Schelling advances a unique conception of eternity, which, when corrected of its basic deficiency, says Bruaire, is able to provide a notion of eternity which is not anti-historical but, on the contrary, meta-historical. Eternity is no longer seen as history's contrary but rather as its truth.[100] Let us look now more closely at how Bruaire understands Schelling's conception of eternity.[101]

Schelling, Bruaire tells us, does not think of the eternal absolute as a pure void but rather as that which is most concrete, the infinite, the "source and the end of everything." For Schelling, the absolute, which is absolute freedom, is constituted by three inseparable moments: an original "no," an original "yes," and the unity of both. The priority of the "no" makes it possible for there to be that contradiction which allows movement, life, and progress. There is no free "yes" which does not negate a "no" by sublating it

99. *EE,* 151–52.

100. According to Bruaire, these are Schelling's three main contributions: (*a*) the absolute understood as freedom; (*b*) the absolute commencement; (*c*) eternity as the "plenitude of time." Bruaire considers that Schelling allows an understanding of *eternity* which might "very well be able to generate a renewal of today's speculative philosophy" (*SQ,* 13, 66–67).

101. It is beyond my intention to give a detailed account of Schelling's idea of time. This presentation is limited to Bruaire's account. Acquaintance with the *Weltalter* witnesses to the accuracy of Bruaire's account. Perhaps we are now in a position to understand Tilliette's observations à propos of Bruaire's philosophy: "Un métaphysicien de la trempe de Claude Bruaire, par surcroît hégélien de formation, a trouvé de lui-même dans Schelling ce qu'il désirait: l'Absolu-Esprit avide de se donner parce que capable d'être moins que lui-même" (Xavier Tilliette, *Schelling* [Paris: Calmann-Lévy, 1999], 414).

in itself. As indicated, the negative movement has a certain priority within the rhythmic *circumincessio:* the beginning without beginning is the denial of the divine withdrawal into itself. This commencement is the result of an immemorial decision which can take place "only when a violent power blindly breaks the unity in the jostling between the necessity and the impossibility of being."[102] It is according to those three moments that time and eternity need to be thought.

Within Schelling's philosophy, the consequence of this notion of the twofold freedom of the absolute for the understanding of time is that time is considered to be "subjective"—not in the sense of "relative," or of a "subjective category of the intellect," but in the sense of "subject," where subject means substance. This position, comments Bruaire, has two main implications. First, for Schelling, there is no such a thing as "time" but only "times": the times of every singular and substantial being. Second, if time is subjective, and so is not merely a measure, it *does not mean finitude.*[103] Bruaire explains this apparent paradox by appealing to Schelling's *System of Identity.* In this work, one can see that, for Schelling, the finite—whether the objective finite of the order of nature or the "ideal" finite of free spirits—is constituted by the identity of the "Object and the Subject, the Self and being." This means that the infinite is always present in the finite because the former is that absolute freedom which contracts itself in the finite in order to know itself. Finitude contains within itself "the infinity of love proper to the [infinite's] expansion in created beings."[104] The main consequence of this way of perceiving the presence of the infinite in the finite is that "time is that state where the infinite is masked, forgotten." The temporal is the eternal "diverted and lost," and, in virtue of the law of eternal progress, set in motion by contradiction. The temporal is thus the way to return to the divine.[105] Therefore, under this view, history cannot be perceived as incompatible with eternity, because only in the latter does human history find its fulfilment.

If, according to Schelling, the finite spirit finds its truth in the eternal

102. Friederich W. J. Schelling, *The Ages of the World,* trans. Jason M. Wirth (New York: State University of New York Press, 2000), 13.

103. *SQ,* 64.

104. *PM,* 222. Obviously, this pantheistic understanding poses the problem both of the difference between the finite and the infinite and of the presence of the eternal in that which is only temporal.

105. *SQ,* 94–95.

spirit, then one is to think of eternity through an ontological reflection on the act of freedom. Following this insight, Bruaire underscores that, within their equilibrium, the three principles mentioned above ("no," "yes," and "the unity of both") constitute the absolute act which cannot but be understood as *eternal* spirit. Exploring the spiritual rhythm of absolute spirit, one attains the basic structure which constitutes eternity. This triad, which follows a Trinitarian scheme, has as its first moment God's self-restriction and withdrawal into himself: this is the eternal Past (the Father). However, the truth of this concealment is the effusion, the expansion of himself, that is, the denial of the withdrawal into himself. This is what Schelling calls the eternal Present (the Son).[106] Although it seems that this movement of the negation (Son) of the first negation (Father)—which is the immemorial decision of being—threatens to rupture the unity of the absolute act, as Schelling says, "they ['no' and 'yes'/Father and Son] come together in one and the same because the negating force can feel itself as negating only when there is a disclosing being, and the latter can be active as affirming only insofar as it liberates the negating and repressing force."[107] The original act cannot be offered by the negative and the positive alone; a third moment (Spirit), consisting of the unity of the Past and the Present, is necessary. This third moment is required by the absolute divine decision that determines to give itself to itself, and in the "Spirit the original power makes itself indistinguishable from absolute freedom."[108]

Contrasted with this eternal movement, which Schelling calls the "plenitude of times," is human existence, which knows a relative beginning where memory weakly tries to guard some of its past and where it awaits an uncertain fulfillment. Eternity is the truth of history, because it is that "Life and Force" which finite human existence longs to reach and which it cannot give to itself. Schelling, says Bruaire, helps us to see that "eternity and victory" are the same word, and as such, "eternal history" is the prom-

---

106. It would be helpful to call to mind Schelling's own example: "Hence, the day lies concealed in the night, albeit overwhelmed by the night; likewise the night in the day, albeit kept down by the day, although it can establish itself as soon as the repressive potency disappears. Hence, good lies concealed in evil, albeit made unrecognizable by evil; likewise evil in good, albeit mastered by the good and brought to inactivity" (Schelling, *The Ages of the World,* 18–19).

107. Schelling, *The Ages of the World,* 18–19.

108. *PM,* 222.

ise of fulfillment for this feeble human history—not in the sense that the finite would be absorbed and eliminated in it but, on the contrary, that while "remaining finite, [the human spirit] will be nonetheless conformed to eternity."[109] This is why, Bruaire says, finitude is better explained ontologically than chronologically.

No matter how brilliant Schelling's refined analysis of time and eternity is, there remain crucial difficulties that prevent Bruaire from implementing *tout court* Schelling's reflection in his *ontodology*. The first is the simple fact that the *circumincessio* of the three principles leads only to the "perpetual escape of the *effective* act." As I indicated briefly before, the only possibility of bridging the gap between possibility and factuality is the immemorial decision of the beginning. Nevertheless, "eternity has its conceivable positivity only by means of the inconceivability of its non-beginning."[110] It seems that the "blind force" which Schelling discovers at the heart of the immemorial decision is not able to account for the whole of the divine positivity that comes to light through the spiritual movement from itself to itself.

More importantly, Schelling's study suffers from an excess of anthropomorphism, as Tilliette has indicated.[111] Bruaire notes that Schelling, like Hegel, unilaterally applied the same type of logic to both the absolute and finite spirit. Whereas for Hegel the error consisted in the absorption of human logic into divine logic, which generated the illusion that human language could express absolute knowledge, in the case of Schelling, human freedom is ascribed to absolute spirit. Bruaire explains that Schelling's priority of the "no" over the "yes" is something proper to human, not divine, freedom. The human being is given to himself, and the ontological passivity of his not being his own origin makes "in-dependence" an original reality for him. Of course, Bruaire does not understand independence in the sense that the human being does not need any other being in order to account for his own existence—there is nothing further from his ontology than such a "positive" anthropology. Perhaps forcing language somewhat, Bruaire wants to stress the "primary power of the 'no'" by hyphenating the

109. *EE,* 153–4.
110. *EE,* 153–4.
111. See Xavier Tilliette, *Le système vivant,* vol. 1 of *Schelling: Une philosophie en devenir,* 599–605, where he shows accurately the tension between the anthropological and the theological model in Schelling's *Weltalter.*

word in-dependence. For the human spirit, where it is not possible to say "no," it is not possible freely to say "yes." He who cannot refuse cannot give. It is because the human spirit is a "gift-*given*" that in-dependence, or ontological passivity, is primordial. One must not forget, however, that, besides this meaning, the "no" entails also that nothingness has been rejected in order for the human spirit to be. The human spirit is neither God nor the natural other.[112] Whereas it is true for the human being that affirmation is a negation of the negation, Bruaire claims that it is not the same for the absolute spirit. No trace of ontological passivity can be discovered in it; even the reception of the gift by the Son is an active reception—so much so that Bruaire calls it "reddition."[113]

What defines absolute spirit for Bruaire is the positive and not the negative element, precisely because absolute spirit is the absolute gift of itself to itself. If gift gives itself to itself *as such (communicatio sui)*, that is, if it "gives the infinite potency which gift is," then the divine "Gift is eternally positive." The Father cannot be understood as the contractive "no" of absolute spirit but as sheer positivity. The Son is not the negation of the Father but the reddition of the absolute gift, and the unity of the two is not determined by blind necessity but by the outpouring gratuity of the absolute gift. Absolute spirit is *eternal* spirit because it is the *gift* of itself to itself in the complete lack of ontological passivity. Hence, Bruaire's ontology of gift, while adopting the ontological analysis of divine freedom to explain the *positive* meaning of eternity, corrects the negative metaphysics lurking behind Schelling's understanding of eternity and makes possible a rereading of the three dif-

112. This negative sense of in-dependence includes the three meanings of creation *ex nihilo*: God does not have any other reason to create finite spirit besides his own goodness; nothingness is the rejection of the possibility of not creating; it is the "no" said to the being-other of the human being, i.e., the human being is finite spirit.

113. Although I agree with Bruaire's criticism of Schelling, I do not think that Bruaire's understanding of freedom does full justice to a "negative" anthropology. If the human spirit is gift, then neither divine nor human freedom can be understood in negative terms. Human freedom is given to itself to become itself in the return to its origin. Hence, human freedom's ultimate truth is not in-dependence but adherence to the good. What is given is a positive reality. In the same sense, precisely because the human spirit is created in the image of the Word, human freedom is first "yes" and only then "no." Obviously, both options (the "yes" and the "no") need to be there in order for the human being to adhere freely, but just as what is first for the human being is the divine yes that creates him, so, too, what is original and more adequate to human freedom is the acceptance of this gift (himself) and not the rejection of it.

ferent (Trinitarian) moments that represent absolute spirit's inner life. Let us look at Bruaire's analysis in the decisive pages of *EE*.

In his ontodological rereading of Schelling's concept of time, Bruaire wants to present an adequate understanding of the absolute *principle* which is utterly *positive* and which, while escaping any trace of *anthropomorphization,* can be perceived as *metahistorical,* that is, as the truth of human history. To this end, he adopts Schelling's terminology, although he pours into it a new content. Hence, the Father is also called the "eternal past," the Son the "eternal present," and the Spirit the "eternal future." Since Bruaire is interested in explaining the absolute principle, it is important not to read this terminology as oxymoronic. Emphasis is placed more on "eternal" than on "past, present, future." This "chronology," adequate only to human history, is adopted in order to present the three dimensions of gift. Therefore, they cannot be represented as implying either "succession," as if there were indeed a past without a present or a present without a future, or as suggesting an "abstract simultaneity," as if there were no origin or source. Without confusing them, then, these "moments" are to be conceived as "immediate" to one other. There is a real distinction between the three of them, yet always within the identity of the gift. The immediacy of "present, past, and future" is first of all ontological, and in force of that, "chronological." Eternity thus includes the fullness of time without succession.

Bruaire's exposition does not begin with the past but with the "eternal present." It is the expression which leads us to the source. The eternal present is the "perfect expression of the infinite power," and it "carries in itself the whole of freedom." For this reason, the Word (the gift *given*) is immediately "transfigured in the Act of the Giver." Bruaire explains that, for the human being, it is radically impossible to "give one's own being over *(faire passer)* to the present of our initiatives." The eternal divine present, by contrast, is "infinitely the absolute donating effusion." The gift-given (expression) in the interplay proper only to absolute love "returns" the gift, that is, not in the sense of "paying back a debt" or of "rejecting" the gift given, but, more adequately, in the sense of the absolute loving co-respondence of the Son.[114]

114. The term "absolute loving co-respondence" is mine. "Co-respondence" is hyphenated in order not to lose sight of the fact that the person of the Son remains himself in this divine procession, while being of the same divine nature. This term liberates the expression "return of the gift" from the economic linguistic register.

The "eternal past" is the Father, that is, the infinite original power, which immediately passes "into the present of its act." The "past," then, is to be thought as the *gift* given to its gift, given "without passivity." Bruaire warns us against interpreting the "eternal past" in anthropological terms. For the human being, the past has only a weak presence in the present through memory; in itself, it is essentially gone. This illegitimate procession could make one think that talking about the "past" implies describing a succession. Yet, if this were the case, the present would not be the perfect expression of the past; it would be another, completely different being. One attempt to avoid this error might be to think that, since the present is the perfect expression of the past, and there is no distinction in nature, then past and present are simultaneous. Instead, Bruaire invites the reader to avoid seeing the immediacy of the past and the present in terms of "abstract simultaneity." There is a past because there is an origin that gives. Nevertheless, this origin cannot be thought of as pre-existing the gift. The "reddition of the gift to the Beginning, the deposition of the Self," is nothing but the "confession of its being second in its given primacy."[115]

The expression, the eternal present, gives itself immediately to the origin, thus to the eternal past, which does not exist without immediately giving itself (to the Son). Nonetheless, eternity knows also of a third irreducible moment: the "eternal future." Just as there is no divine origin without its expression, and no expression without the origin, so there is no eternal past and present without the eternal future. As with the other two moments, Bruaire tries carefully to eliminate any intrusion of human time into the conception of absolute eternity. Eternal future is the full and immediate realization of the present, not "the anticipation" of something that is yet to come. Hence, the eternal future is the definitive fulfillment of the gift, the "eternal persistence of the gift of itself." Persistence does not suggest that the absolute gift is some sort of feeble donation in danger of disappearing. It is rather the already accomplished, eternally fulfilled donation which makes "overabundant the effusion of the gift." Whereas the human being lives in the uncertain but ardent expectation of being eternally confirmed, the eternal absolute gift of itself to itself is confirmation already fulfilled. The "eternal future" represents a decisive moment

115. *EE*, 156–57.

of the loving interchange between the source which gives itself and the expression which returns the gift. The eternal future is the confirmation of the superabundant and fathomless positivity of the gift; it is not merely something that is yet to come.

Bruaire is aware that this way of perceiving eternity could be read in terms of "negation and of negation of the negation." He explicitly takes another course by changing these terms into those of the "donation, affirmation, and confirmation" of the gift. The importance of this third moment for Bruaire's thought cannot be overemphasized. The Holy Spirit is the "eternal future," the conclusive eternal affirmation of the gift, and not the incomplete "not-yet" of an eternal which is always in need of becoming itself. It is thus that Bruaire frees his *ontodology* from the accusation of constituting merely, in the end, a fictitious gift (as with Schelling's understanding of eternity) and so of postulating a false eternity.[116]

This *positive* meaning of eternity allows us to understand the latter as an eternal and complete "happening."[117] Eternity is the truth of history, not because in the latter the eternal has lost itself and strives to return to itself, but because it is the final confirmation of the ontological fragility of the human being, its final and definitive confirmation. This is why the human being's "return to the origin" has a vital importance and, consequently, human actions (which could swerve from this path) have to "carry the weight" of the eternal, so to speak. Nevertheless, philosophy cannot go any further than thinking of this eternal confirmation of history as a *possibility* (something which does not necessarily invalidate the reality of both time and eternity) but not as a necessary conclusion to the end of the human being's life. In the same way that there is nothing necessary in the creation of the human being, there is nothing necessary in his eternal confirmation.

116. *EE*, 156–57.
117. In this regard, I think that Bruaire's view of eternity (and creation) is not very far from Balthasar's. Cf. Balthasar, *The Last Act*, 66–98.

CHAPTER 7

God's Unfathomable Love
The Confirmation of the Gift

A persistent question regarding the gratuity of gift remains unanswered. As the previous elucidation has shown, Bruaire's ontology perceives gift as the proper name of both absolute and finite spirit, and not only for creation. Considering the absolute spirit in terms of gift requires a conception of its oneness in terms of multiplicity; that is to say, while remaining one, its nature as absolute determinate spirit makes it relational within itself. Therefore, God, out of his own goodness, begets the Word, the perfect expression of himself. If God's essence is *gift,* and the Word adequately expresses what the Father is, then the Son must be understood in terms of absolute gift as well. Of course, in the Son, the gift is unconditional receptivity of the gift of the Father, which—precisely because it is an *absolute* receptivity—is, at the same time, the reddition of the gift to the Father, "the perfection of the mutual love."[1] The difficulty lies in how one is to conceive of this loving exchange between the Father and Son. If the movement were merely twofold, it seems that there would be no *real* donation, only a *necessary,* non-gratuitous exchange. If one thinks of this interchange in formalistic terms, then it seems that the reddition annuls the original gift: if the source (Father) gives all of himself and the expression (Son), in a loving response, returns the gift, then the original dona-

---

1. Bruaire, "Philosophie et spiritualité," 1385.

tion would be "balanced," so to speak, by the Son's reddition of the gift.[2] If the total gift given by the Father (donation) is answered by the total return of it (Son; reddition), what place is there for that "giving without return" which characterizes the logic of gift? As already disclosed in the illustration of the creative act and of eternity, Bruaire believes that to affirm the ultimate positivity of the gift requires acknowledging that the absolute movement of donation is threefold, and not simply twofold. Hence, along with affirmation and reddition, one must talk about confirmation, or, which is the same, about the presence of the spirit within absolute spirit. Therefore, what now needs to be examined is whether the confirmation of the gift is able to undergird absolute gratuity.

Addressing this issue clarifies that absolute spirit is not merely a faceless self-determining substance. Rather, the absolute's movement of self-determination asks to be understood in terms of relations of donation, and the affirmation, reddition, and confirmation of the gift are thus nothing but a way of presenting the divine processions that constitute the absolute as three persons in the one person-gift. Building upon Aquinas's concept of person, Bruaire presents his conception of absolute gift's real positivity in counterpoint to Hegel's account of the Trinitarian mystery because, as John Milbank also recognizes, "it remains the case that Hegel *(hélas!)* is the most profound modern meditator upon the identity of the Holy Spirit."[3]

Love's Ruse: The Ultimate Positivity of Gift

The logic of gift requires that we conceive of donation precisely as that absolute freedom which is not its own act unless it "expresses itself generatively, ontogenically; [unless] it is the gift of itself, and, by force of the same spiritual logic, all its dismissed omnipotence is given back to it."[4] If this logic holds, then what needs to be corrected is our conception of the divine interchange. We need, therefore, to move from a representational (imaginative) or dialectical way of thinking to the speculative.

The movement from the Father to the Son and from the Son to the Fa-

---

2. See *EdEES,* 74; *EE,* 181; *FE,* 112–13; *EdE,* 38; "Philosophie et spiritualité," 1385.

3. John Milbank, "The Second Difference," in id., *The Word Made Strange* (Cambridge, Mass.: Blackwell Publishers, 1997), 183.

4. *EE,* 181.

ther cannot be imagined in terms of a process, as though there were an infinite distance between the source and the Word. It is thus that Gnosticism
and subordinationism conceive the passage from one to the other. This
representational way of conceiving the divine procession is ultimately unable to see either the original donation of the Father, which is transformed
into an unknown and unattainable transcendent source, or the role of the
Son within the Trinity. The second model, which I have called dialectical,
conceives the relationship of donation in the absolute spirit as an infinite
alternation whose fulfillment is entrusted to a future that never arrives.
The expression is uttered and the word speaks the source, which, in turn,
by pronouncing the word, initiates an eternal circular pendular movement
that is unable to attain what it promises.[5]

Bruaire then encourages leaving this way of thinking behind and moving to the speculative understanding of gift. Echoing Schelling's *Weltalter,*
he proposes that the spiritual rhythm of donation involves not only two
moments, that is, affirmation and reddition, but three: affirmation, reddition, and confirmation. Contrary to what it may appear, the third moment (confirmation) is not extrinsically called upon so that the logic of
gift may break the alternating rhythm of donation. Bruaire's point is that
the Father's donation to the Son requires that absolute spirit also be spirit within God; otherwise the donation will not be *real.* Bruaire does not
thereby imply that the spirit in God is also responsible for the begetting
of the Son—which would be absurd; he insists only that the begetting of
the Son mysteriously presupposes the existence of the spirit in God who
confirms the donation of the Father to the Son. Hence, it is the donation
of the Father which must be thought as a double act, or, to use an image
dear to Bruaire, like "a hair-triggered gift."[6] On the one hand, there is the
expression of the Father; on the other hand, there is the "ruse of love" of
the Father (the Holy Spirit), which redoubles the gift, gives it back without
receiving anything in return, and thus secures the infinite gratuitousness

---

5. *EdE,* 38; *EE,* 182. Bruaire suggests that the positivity of the dialectical movement of
absolute spirit in Hegel is made possible by what could be described as "all the power of the
Spirit," which, as we shall see, is nothing but sheer negativity (*D,* 70). See also *Enzyklopädie*
§82.

6. Bruaire borrows the expression "à double détente" from military language, where it
refers to a rifle that releases two bullets at a single pull of the trigger. *EE,* 186; *FE,* 112.

of the gift and testifies to the superabundance of divine love.[7] Therefore, there cannot be a true and real donation in the absolute spirit unless it is *at the same time* confirmed. For this reason, the processual or dialectical representation of the spiritual movement is always incomplete. Thus, the whole of the foregoing analysis of the self-donating movement needs to be seen in this new light. The movement of donation cannot be understood as complete until the third movement is recognized as "necessary" for there to be a donation. There is no donation and reddition without confirmation. It is only in this way that "the positivity of the Spirit is eternal victory over the [fictitious] Nothing of the rejection of itself."[8]

Confirmation's Transgressive Root

The presentation of Bruaire's understanding of gift has made it clear that he always follows the "speculative force of the concept." It is the analysis of the concept of spirit that demonstrates that the human being needs to be understood in terms of donation. The concept of the human spirit requires a phenomenology of the spirit, which is possible because the analysis of the concept enables recognition of the presence of the spirit. It is the same logic of the concept that guides Bruaire to the recognition of the inseparable unity of being-gift and being-in-debt. As shown, this analysis brings him from finite spirit to absolute spirit. At this second level, the logic of the *pure* concept of the spirit proves its existence and the necessity of conceiving it as one, being, and spirit. The exploration of the concept of absolute spirit offers three main categories in which to glimpse the essence of the absolute: infinity, creator, and eternity.

I have indicated that Bruaire attempts to apply the logic of the concept univocally to both human and absolute spirit. As I discussed above, this objective is jeopardized by the fact that, although in both cases Bruaire tries to show that the concepts of finite and infinite gift respect the same methodological requirements, his analysis arrives at two differentiated realities: the finite spirit is given to itself in order to become itself in the uncertainty of its own existence, and is thus in debt of itself, while the absolute spirit is the gift of itself to itself in that ever-new beginning of a bottomless gift which does not need anything but itself to exist and whose infinite nature

7. *EdEES*, 75; *EE*, 185–87; *FE*, 111–13; *EdE*, 38; "Philosophie et spiritualité," 1385–86.
8. *EE*, 183.

is that pure act which never runs the risk of losing itself. Bruaire's *ontodology* does not absorb the finite into the infinite, but it avoids this fallacy at the price of failing to offer the univocal concept of gift that he intends to offer.

Bruaire's methodological emphasis on the speculative mediation of the concept now faces another difficulty, namely, integrating the Christian intimation of the need of a third moment in the absolute movement of self-donation without imploding the necessity proper to the logic of the concept. In fact, if one remains within this speculative structure, it does not seem possible to overcome the representational or dialectical movement of donation, for which the pendulous donating movement of affirmation and reddition seems to suffice. It appears, then, that left to itself, the "speculative effort" is unable to bring forth a third "moment" in its logic, a moment which would finally prove the reality of the concept of absolute spirit (gift). The only attempt we have seen is Hegel's system, but, as we shall see, Bruaire finds its hermeneutical key inadequate.

For Bruaire, the only plausible answer at hand is that he is able to speak about the "confirmation" of the gift because of the intimations of Christian revelation—as it was with the other two pivotal elements of his metaphysics: first, that the absolute is *spirit;* second, that absolute spirit is to be understood in *positive* terms (in contrast to the philosophy of Hegel and Schelling). At this last stage of his reflection, Bruaire acknowledges the need to welcome yet another decisive contribution of revealed religion: the *confirmation* of the Spirit, which requires that there be in the absolute Spirit "the spirit which is nothing but spirit," what Christian Tradition calls the Holy Spirit.[9] Hence, it is not possible to think adequately of God as absolute spirit if "the spirit is not also spirit in its own difference." That is to say, in order for God to be God, he has to be both absolute spirit and Holy Spirit.[10] Despite certain difficulties in forging the link between positivity (freedom) and conceptual necessity when explaining the meaning of "substantial conversion" and the relation between being-gift and being-in-debt, Bruaire seemed able to combine these two sources: the conceptual

9. *EE,* 185. The expression, "spirit which is nothing but spirit," also reminds Bruaire's reader that, in a sense and by means of the *circumincessio* of the divine persons, the Father and the Son are also spirit. "Philosophie et spiritualité," 1385.

10. *EdEES,* 74.

onto-logic of the spirit and Christian intimations. Now that Bruaire wants to bring his speculative effort to its conclusion and to think the *absolute* gratuity of the spirit, it seems that he can no longer rely on this alliance between Christian intimations and ontodology's speculative necessity.

In facing this issue, Bruaire proposes a transcendence, rather than a disavowal, of the conceptual logic. He explains that the necessity of the concept has to "practice silence" and allow the ultimate deduction of the gratuitousness of gift to "*transgress* deductive necessity." Precisely because one must retain both *absolute* gratuity and the "exclusive *singularity* of the overabundant act"—which is the infinite spirit—necessity must give way to gratuity. Indeed, the conceptual necessity of the deduction of the meaning of the concept of gift unveiled the loving interchange between the Father and the Son. Yet, at the apex of its reflection, deduction gives way to pure gratuitousness and becomes "*trans-deductive.*" It is thanks to the difference between the Holy Spirit and the spirit that one discovers the possibility in Christian revelation of affirming absolute gratuity as the truth of the donating necessity required by the concept of gift.[11]

While Bruaire argues that the "necessity" of the concept of gift has as its ultimate root absolute gratuity, he believes that this "transgression" of a seemingly revealed insight into the metaphysical world does not invalidate his philosophical method because absolute gratuity leaves no room for any arbitrariness. Absolute gratuity, in fact, "presupposes the necessity whose actual truth absolute gratuity conclusively posits, the superabundance that *presupposes the paternal generosity which absolute gratuity confirms.*" In this sense, the being that is nothing but being makes the logic of freedom to *be;* it (the Holy Spirit) gives it its fulfilled Presence.[12]

The necessity proper to absolute gratuity, then, is that of being unable to be anything but itself: inexhaustible positivity. The double act of donation (the begetting of the Son and the confirmation of the Holy Spirit, which confirms the original donation) requires, on the one hand, an utter gratuity at its deepest root and, on the other hand, a necessary movement of donation flowing from that unspeakable love. For its part, this "necessity" leads back again to the threshold of absolute gratuity.

Bruaire believes that the circular threefold syllogism is able to convey

11. *EE*, 185. Bruaire's emphasis.
12. *EE*, 185.

adequately, on the one hand, the seemingly contradictory conjunction of the "lack of arbitrariness" proper to absolute gratuity with the necessity proper to the concept, and, on the other hand, the simultaneity of all these moments. Bruaire does not see a contradiction between the necessity of the "concept" and the logic of gift because the latter reveals itself to be the truth, origin, and fulfillment of the former.

The Spirit within Absolute Spirit

Confirmation is that act by which gift is reaffirmed, that is to say, that act in which gift is proved to be the truth of absolute spirit. Remaining within the logic of gift, re-affirmation does not mean to "say again" but rather to "give again." Hence, in a sense, gift is redoubled. Obviously, this "giving again" is not simply a quantitative action. Since the donation of the Father (the begetting of the Son) gives everything, the confirmation of the Spirit does not consist in disclosing something the Father secretly keeps for himself. Without the Father becoming the Son, the Father is *all* in the Son. In this sense, the Spirit is not a surplus of energy, so to speak, which the Father has *not given*. That the gift (begetting) is confirmed means that God's infinite power is "more than itself," that is, absolute spirit, because it is also the Holy Spirit, is able to "frustrate or elude" *(déjoue)* the return of the offer of the gift which is the Son's reddition.[13] Bruaire describes begetting as the *absolute*'s donation of all of itself to itself and confirmation as the "ruse of love" which is the redoubling of the gift: the Spirit "re-posits, regenerates the Fruit of the generation." This re-positing of the gift prevents the logic of gift from finishing at an ontological impasse wherein the gift given has simply been returned.[14]

If this "confirming again" is a reaffirmation of the gift that cannot be understood in quantitative terms, and if, as the logic of gift demands, the Father has given everything of himself to the Son, then the act of confirmation does not introduce anything new into the movement of absolute gift. The Spirit does not add *anything*. Since the whole Gift is given and returned, there is nothing lacking which the Spirit can provide. The Spirit, like the other divine persons, is also God, and so he cannot add anything that the others did not have. The spirit which is nothing but spirit, by con-

---

13. *EE*, 183.

14. Bruaire hints at that moment of Jesus's life when the Holy Spirit descends upon Him and re-poses over Him. See Jn 1:32–34; Mt 3:16.

firming the gift, gives that "being which is nothing but being." The confirmation *makes the gift be.* And thus, in this super-effusive generosity that gives being to the personal Expression of God, the Spirit gives *everything.*[15] It is in this sense that the Holy Spirit "is not the divine essence which the Word expresses." Because of the difference between absolute spirit and the Holy Spirit, absolute spirit (absolute gift) *can be.* The first thing that the confirmation of the gift signifies, then, is that Spirit *is* absolute spirit "because of the *re-doubling* that confirms his gift." The Spirit in the spirit adds nothing to absolute spirit; he simply *makes it be* because he is the act of being of absolute spirit. Gratuitously, the Spirit gives absolute spirit its being (existence); he gives to the event of the donation its ultimate positivity.[16]

To say that the confirmation of the gift does not add anything to the donation of the gift, that it makes gift be *without return,* implies that the spirit which is nothing but spirit *presupposes* the paternal initiative of begetting the Son. In order for the gift to be *confirmed,* the gift must be presupposed. If this were not the case, the Holy Spirit would be the source of the begetting of the gift, which would leave us back at the beginning of our inquiry. Therefore, confirmation implies that the spirit is *different* from the Father and the Son; this difference is what makes the redoubling of the gift possible. The Father could not give himself to the Son if the Spirit were not always-already present; in the same way, the Spirit could not confirm the gift if the gift were not already given.[17]

15. *EdEES,* 74.

16. *EE,* 185. The following text from Pope John Paul II's Encyclical *Dominum et vivificantem* is close to Bruaire's overall intention: "In his intimate life, God 'is love' [1 Jn 4:8, 16], the essential love shared by the three divine Persons: personal love is the Holy Spirit as the Spirit of the Father and the Son. Therefore he 'searches even the depths of God,' [1 Cor 2:10] as uncreated Love-Gift. It can be said that in the Holy Spirit the intimate life of the Triune God becomes totally gift, an exchange of mutual love between the divine Persons, and that *through the Holy Spirit God exists in the mode of gift.* It is the Holy Spirit who is the personal expression of this self-giving, of this being-love [Aquinas, *ST* I, qq. 37–38]. He is Person-Love. He is Person-Gift. Here we have an inexhaustible treasure of the reality, and an inexpressible deepening of the concept of person in God, which *only divine Revelation makes known* to us. At the same time, the Holy Spirit, being consubstantial with the Father and the Son in divinity, is love and uncreated gift from which derives as from its source *[fons vivus]* all giving of gifts vis-à-vis creatures [created gift]: the gift of existence to all things through creation; the gift of grace to human beings through the whole economy of salvation. As the Apostle Paul writes: 'God's love has been poured into our hearts through the Holy Spirit which has been given to us' [Rom 5:5]" (n. 10). Emphasis added.

17. See also Thomas G. Weinandy, O.F.M. Cap., *The Father's Spirit of Sonship: Reconceiving the Trinity* (Edinburgh: T&T Clark, 1995).

The confirmation of the gift, by making it be, transforms absolute gift into a gift *without return*. The Spirit makes the gift be and, since he is the affirmation of love's superabundance, he does not receive the gift in return. Absolute gratuitousness is reached, so to speak, with the Spirit; that is, the bottomless love of absolute spirit which gives itself to itself completely, without either keeping something for himself or expecting to get anything in return, cannot be seen until the gift is confirmed. In this sense, it would be misleading to look for a gratuitous donation "just" in the act of begetting and reddition. That the confirmation of the Spirit brings the absolute act of donation to its truth prevents us from doing so. Of course, this means simply that absolute love reaches its limitless fruitfulness only with the Holy Spirit and not that the begetting of the Father is not an act of pure love, or that it is limited in any sense.[18]

Besides this act of confirmation in which the Spirit within the spirit does not give anything because all of the gift has already been given, is it possible to say anything about the Holy Spirit himself? Bruaire explains that the Spirit in his difference does not possess an essence "of his own" because his essence is the divine essence. The being of the Spirit within the spirit, then, coincides completely with his operation. That is to say: he is what he presupposes inasmuch as "he poses and re-poses" what he presupposes. Yet, since his operation presupposes the begetting of the Son, the action of the Holy Spirit can adequately be called *"pure memory,"* that is to say, the *presence* of the gift of himself to himself. For this reason, the procession of the Holy Spirit *ab utroque* is, on the one hand, "identically from the Father *through* the Son," because the other two persons are the presupposition of the Holy Spirit, the loving exchange from which the Spirit comes, and, on the other hand, "from the Father *for* the Son," because the Holy Spirit, love's "ruse," confirms the gift and makes it *be* without *return*. If absolute spirit can be understood in terms of gift, and the processions of the Son and the Spirit can be represented in this fashion, then the Son, the expression of the gift, is the "great defeated of Love."[19]

---

18. This becoming true cannot be understood in terms of the Hegelian sublation that both denies what comes before and subsumes it on a higher level. In this sense, confirmation is never an *Aufhebung* but rather a *Bewährung:* i.e., establishing as true (albeit not in the sense of "proof").

19. *EE,* 187. Theologically speaking, it could be said that, in his attempt to present the

Bruaire, like Hegel, talks about the "kenosis" of the Holy Spirit. Yet, the Spirit's withdrawal into himself is not a negation of the negation or an "eternal Calvary." The "silence" of the Holy Spirit does not reveal utter negativity but rather the sheer "ontogenic force of Absolute love."[20] The confirmation of the Spirit, because it posits difference within the absolute spirit, is the truth of Hegel's negative movement; it makes the "negation of the negation" be *other* in God.[21] This positive conception of abnegation is another major difference between Hegel's and Bruaire's ontology. For the former, there is ultimately nothing which is not revealed. For Bruaire, by contrast, there is always a "secret," an unfathomable mystery at the very heart of the absolute spirit that human reason is never able to exhaust.

In fact, although spirit can be described as "pure memory," Bruaire is aware that, unlike the source (the Father) and the reddition of the gift (the Son), the Spirit within the spirit has no name in the divine Trinity. This is because it is the Spirit who makes the gift be without return and who does not claim any "recompense." The Spirit is "silence in his infinite discretion. . . . The pure Spirit, who makes absolute gift be *(donne d'être)*, who defies and overcomes the reddition [of the gift], who gives back without anything being given back to him, is completely oblivious to himself, lacking any private glory," not even a personal name. If the Holy Spirit were to

---

procession of the third person in the Trinity within the framework of the ontology of gift, Bruaire seems to combine the Latin and the Greek understandings of the spiration of the third Person. The Spirit in God is both the fully achieved mutual relationship between the Father and the Son—in this sense, Bruaire represents the Latin understanding of the procession of the Holy Spirit—and the ultimate opening of God in his manifestation of his own bottomless love—in this sense, Bruaire represents the Greek view. Hence, according to the first perspective, the confirmation of the gift is the ratification of its absolute gratuity, and, with respect to the second viewpoint, the Holy Spirit regenerates the Fruit of the begetting and reaches outside absolute spirit to confirm the gift which is other than God, the finite spirit. Needless to say, there is a predominance of the Latin scheme over the Greek in Bruaire, because he thinks of the divine processions in terms of God's essence (gift) and not in terms of the divine persons. See Hans Urs von Balthasar, "The Unknown Lying Beyond the Word," in *Creator Spiritus,* vol. 3 of *Explorations in Theology,* trans. Brian McNeil, C.R.V. (San Francisco: Ignatius Press, 1993), 107. See also id., *Der Geist der Wahrheit,* vol. 3 of *Theologik,* 189–200; Leo Scheffczyk, "The Meaning of the 'Filioque,'" *Communio* 13 (1986): 124–38.

20. *EE,* 187.

21. In this sense, it seems that for Bruaire, Hegel offers no satisfactory explanation of the third divine person. See Heribert Mühlen, *Der Heilige Geist als Person: In der Trinität bei der Inkarnation, und im Gnadenbund. Ich, du, wir* (Münster: Aschendorf, 1980).

look to his own glory, and not to that of the Father, there would be no real donation, only emanation.[22]

The confirmation of the gift, then, makes it possible for the absolute gift to be; it presents absolute gift as an actual and eternally existing *event* of love. It clarifies that the absolute's gift of itself to itself is not a vague ideal movement. Gift is not a fictitious entity; rather, the being which is nothing but spirit renders the infinite identical act "effective" and real, giving "factual truth" to absolute spirit. Hence, the Holy Spirit undergirds the fact that *donation* is real and not ideal. For this reason, the "being which is nothing but spirit is that being which is nothing but being, but a being which he himself is not."[23]

Three Persons and the One Personal God

Following the Trinitarian intimations of Christian revelation, Bruaire, as we have seen, calls the source Father, the reddition Son, and the confirmation of the gift Holy Spirit. Bruaire's analysis tries to illustrate in what sense the absolute spirit is not a faceless movement of a self-determining substance but a person-gift. It is crucial to perceive that the requirement contained in the concept of gift, "to be given to *itself*," in order for the gift to be real gift, is true for both the human being and the absolute spirit. In this sense, if creation is the positing of the person because the human being-of-spirit is given to itself in order to become itself, donation and confirmation of the gift are the positing of other absolute "selves" within the unity of the absolute gift. The inner-

---

22. *EE,* 184. It is true that, by means of *circumincession,* the other two persons are also, in a certain sense, spirit, and that they thus also look for the glory of the other. Nevertheless, what is proper to the person of the Spirit as opposed to the other two in this respect is this discreet silence which reveals God's unfathomable richness. Balthasar expresses the gratuitous transparency of God in these terms: "He [the Holy Spirit] does not wish to be glorified but 'to glorify me,' by 'taking what is mine and revealing it to you' (Jn 16:14), in the same way that the Son neither wishes nor is able to glorify himself but glorifies only the Father (Jn 5:41; 7:18). But the Father likewise seeks not his own glory but ultimately the glory of the Son (Eph 1:10–12; Phil 2:9–11). Although it is indeed true (philosophically) that God does everything for the sake of his own glory, it is nevertheless the case (theologically) that the selfless transparency of the Spirit of love holds sway over the whole Trinity and only in this way discloses the ultimate meaning of the creation" (Balthasar, "The Unknown Lying Beyond the Word," 111).

23. *EE,* 187.

Trinitarian movement of donation is not the translocation of the same identical divine substance from one place to the other but the processions which constitute God's unique personhood. If these constitutive "moments" of the spiritual rhythm of the absolute were not three different "persons" of the same divine nature, then the "gift of itself to itself," contrary to what Bruaire claims, would fall under the same category of ineffective donation as Schelling's absolute.

Indeterminacy and anthropomorphization seem to be, according to Bruaire, the two main obstacles that prevent most contemporary philosophers from describing God as person.[24] Bruaire forcefully rejects the indeterminate understanding of God on the by now familiar basis of the identification between absolute spirit and freedom. Obviously, this rejection of indeterminacy as a condition for affirming absolute spirit as person shifts the emphasis from the rationality of spiritual beings to *freedom*. Still, Bruaire continues, it seems that to say that absolute spirit is freedom (and hence gift) is not enough to ground the claim that absolute spirit is also some*one*, that is, that it is a person, because "person"—as the original meaning of the concept ("mask" and "relationship") indicates—may seem to refer only to the "individual" and the "particular."[25] If person did, in fact, mean particularity, then to affirm that absolute spirit is a person

24. In addition to the texts already cited, I would like to mention: M. Nédoncelle, "Prosopon et persona dans l'antiquité classique," *Revue des sciences religieuses* 22 (1948): 277–99; René Braun, *Deus Christianorum: Recherches sur le vocabulaire doctrinal de Tertullian* (Paris: PUF, 1962); Carl Andresen, "Zur Entstehung und Geschichte des trinitarischen Personbegriffs," *Zeitschrift für Neutestamentliche Wissenschaft* 52 (1961): 1–39; Cornelia J. de Vogel, "The Concept of Personality in Greek and Christian Thought," *Studies in Philosophy and the History of Philosophy* (Washington, D.C.: Catholic University of America Press, 1963), 2: 20–60.

25. As an example of one of the earliest uses of "person" as *prosopon*, see Homer, *Odyssey*, 19, 361. See also Aristotle, *Historia Animalium*, 1.8.491b9-15, for his understanding of the "human" face. For an interesting combination of the Latin and Greek senses of person with regard to the meaning of face, see Schmitz, "The Geography of the Human Person," 31. See also G. K. Prestige, *God in Patristic Thought* (London: S.P.C.K., 1981). The development of the concept of person as relation requires always bearing in mind its theological origin. Tertullian is the first to use the notion of person to express who God is: *una substantia, tres personae*. See Tertullian, *Adversus Praxeam*, 18, 2, and 27, 11. It was one of the greatest merits of St. Augustine, and, with him, of late patristic theology, to have explained that God's dialogical nature should be understood in terms of relationship. Augustine adopts this term in order to show the compatibility of one substance with the trinity of persons. See Augustine, *De Trinitate* V, 5, 6; id., *De Civitate Dei* XI, 10, 1; Ratzinger, "Concerning the Notion of Person in Theology"; Balthasar, "On the Concept of the Person"; Massimo Camisasca, *Persona e Famiglia: Riflessioni* (Milan: Jaca Book, 1998), 11–31.

would mean that God depends on his relationship with creation and that, by virtue of this necessary relation, he is bound to reveal himself in history. If this anthropomorphic reading were true, then God would no longer be the absolute but just another being among many. Still, what that interpretation fails to see is that it is only because absolute spirit is personal that finite spirit is also personal. It is because the human being is *given* to be *spirit* that human beings are *analogically* called persons.[26]

What needs to be seen, says Bruaire, is that the determination proper to the absolute spirit itself, that is, the gift of itself to itself, is the posing of another within the absolute spirit. In fact, if there is no "other" within the absolute spirit, there ultimately is no absolute other at all. The gift of itself to itself is the gift of a one which, by means of its inner ontological relations, is also three. Donation indicates, then, subsisting relations in God which make him be three persons in one person. Thus, the ontodological elucidation of the absolute spirit concludes with a God who is personal in himself by means of a donating reciprocity which nonetheless does not divide the unity because what makes God be one is also what makes him be three. The absolute is one person and, *for this very same reason,* says Bruaire, is three.[27]

To support his position, Bruaire discusses Aquinas's notion of person as presented in the *Summa Theologiae,* a work which he considers to be one of the most significant models of Catholic theology. It is this conception of person that forms the foundation of the adequate understanding of donation in God in terms of relation and hence of God's personhood. For Bruaire, there are two obstacles that Aquinas must overcome if he is to adopt successfully Boethius's definition of *rationalis naturae individua substantia* without giving unnecessary weight to "individuality," an emphasis which could lead to an unacceptable tritheism.[28] The first is the Aristote-

---

26. *EE,* 162.

27. *EE,* 163. It is impossible to separate the two elements: God is a personal spirit *and* three persons. "The tri-personal God is given [in divine revelation] as a necessary truth of the God-Person, and not as a belated and replaceable, random and juxtaposed commentary" (*EE,* 160). Regarding the Spirit within the Spirit, Bruaire says: "More than anyone else, the Christian is suspected of archaic delirium. Not only must he deny that 'spirit' is nothing, he has to confess it as the essential; not only must he say that the absolute is spirit, he must hold that God is not himself except by receiving the personal Spirit in the fullness of his life" (*EdEES,* 70). See also *EE,* 167–68.

28. Bruaire is in agreement with some authors who consider that Boethius's under-

lian understanding of substance; the second is the category of relation.[29]

Bruaire explains that *substantia* can mean either *ousia* or *hypostasis.* In the first case, it also means quiddity. According to the second connotation, *suppositum,* taken in its transitive sense, substance means the propositional subject, which, as such, is opposed to accident.[30] The first connotation, *ousia,* is easily misread as "nature." The second, *hypostasis,* lends itself to being interpreted in terms of the *individual.* The problem here, says Bruaire, is the failure to demonstrate the identity in God of essence and hypostasis. To overcome these possible ambiguities, says Bruaire, Aquinas interprets *rationalis naturae* in terms of *dominium sui actus.*[31] That is to say, rational nature is the capacity to be the master of one's own acts; or, more specifically, it is self-possession. This description of rational nature, says Bruaire, brings Aquinas very close to the contemporary understanding of *subject,* which, instead of using the term "rational nature" speaks of "singular freedom." This meaning of self-possession, or mastery of one's own acts, makes the concept of person the supreme term for naming both a human being and, by way of eminence, God himself.[32]

In addition to modifying the concept of substance so as to make it apt

---

standing of person has made more difficult the theological and philosophical reflection on person. J. Ratzinger expresses his disagreement with Boethius's definition in these terms: "Boethius's concept of person, which prevailed in Western philosophy, must be criticized as entirely insufficient. Remaining on the level of the Greek mind, Boethius defined 'person' as *naturae rationalis individua substantia,* as the individual substance of a rational nature. One sees that the concept of person stands entirely on the level of substance. This cannot clarify anything about Christology" (Ratzinger, "Concerning the Notion of Person in Theology," 448). Balthasar expresses his perplexity as follows: "Does not this definition, dominant through the Middle Ages, make it extremely difficult, on the one hand, to apply the term to God? (St. Thomas, who essentially takes it over, will have all sorts of difficulties in applying it to the triune God.) On the other hand, does not it level once again the difference between *persona* and individual?" (Balthasar, "On the Concept of Person," 22).

29. *ST,* I, qq. 27–43. See also *SCG,* CXII, 2.

30. *EE,* 164. *Hypostasis* has a twofold origin: γφίστημι which means to lay underneath, and the passive voice of the verb, which means to support or sustain.

31. "Further still, in a more special and perfect way, the particular and the individual are found in the rational substances which have dominion over their own actions; and which are not only made to act, like others; but which can act of themselves; for actions belong to singulars. Therefore also the individuals of rational nature have a special name even among other substances; and this name is *person*" (*ST* I, q. 29, a. 2).

32. According to Bruaire, Thomas Aquinas's understanding of person is concordant with that of Richard of Saint Victor: *divinae naturae incommunicabilis existentia.* See Richard of Saint Victor, *De Trinitate* IV, 28, and IV, 12. This statement, however, does not seem to correspond to Aquinas's own interpretation. See *ST* I, q. 29, a. 3, ad. 4.

for God himself, it is vital, Bruaire says, to revisit the category of *relation*. An adequate treatment of this concept requires a clarification of the distinction between nature and person. In fact, person in God—and this is one of Aquinas's most ingenious intuitions—stands for subsisting relation.[33] Aquinas needed to modify Aristotle's category of relation in order to use it in the definition of the divine person. In fact, for Aristotle, relation is an accidental predication; that is to say, it is that by means of which a substance is oriented toward the other in a certain way. Obviously, if divine personhood were interpreted in this way, the divine persons would be accidents of the divine substance. Relation, for Aquinas, is not a category inhering in a substance. Instead, in God, it means a substantial relative opposition *(esse ad)*;[34] that is to say, the subsistence proper to the divine persons is to be understood, not in opposition to the divine essence, but between the divine persons themselves.[35] Accordingly, Aquinas says, the divine persons are subsisting relations really distinct from one another.[36] By the same token, this real subsisting relation does not represent a division between the divine persons and the divine essence. The concept of relation expresses reference to the opposite (person)—something which the concept of essence is unable to do—while at the same time indicating that, mysteriously, the relations between the hypostases are really identical with the divine essence.[37]

The issue becomes even more complex when one tries to decide whether this concept of person is directly applicable to the essence and indirectly

33. Although St. Augustine was the first to describe the divine persons as relation, he was also reluctant to use the term "person" for fear of tritheism. Augustine, *De Trinitate,* VII, 4, 7-6, 12. Aquinas's contribution is to have made it possible for the concept of person to be understood in terms of relation. See *ST* I, q. 29, a. 4.

34. *ST* I, q. 29, a. 4.

35. *ST* I, q. 30, aa. 1–2.

36. To the two divine processions correspond four relations, but only three of these constitute subsisting relations really distinct among themselves (that is to say, really opposed and incommunicable): paternity, filiation, and passive spiration. See Aquinas, *ST* I, q. 30, a. 2.

37. *ST* I, q. 28, a. 1. Balthasar indicates in his "On the Concept of Person" that with Boethius's and Augustine's understanding of "person," we have person as "being-in-itself." With Richard of Saint Victor, along with person as "being-in-itself," person as "being-from" is made explicit. With Aquinas, when person is conceived in terms of relation, its meaning of "being-for-the-other" will take its place with those two meanings. In this regard, the being-gift of the human spirit, as understood by Bruaire, can be considered as an attempt to formulate the ontological ground for this concept of person.

to the divine persons, or vice versa. From the outset, Bruaire corrects and rejects the theological misconception that Aquinas adopts the concept of person for the divine persons but not for the divine essence. On the contrary, for Aquinas, the divine *esse* is not an impersonal being.[38] Bruaire believes that Thomas sides with those who claim that the concept of person is to be applied to the divine persons *in recto* and only *in obliquo* to the divine essence.[39] The main reason behind this decision, says Bruaire, is that Thomas privileges a monotheistic affirmation of God in terms of a universal singularity. God is one, and this uniqueness makes him to be the only singular being to be everything, that is, absolute spirit.[40] Now, this universal singularity, claims Bruaire, requires the abstraction of every particularity, of every "*proprietas* expressly reserved to the three persons." In fact, Aquinas explains that it is possible to perceive God as one person if one abstracts from the Godhead the three divine persons, as one can find in some religions (Judaism, Islam) and philosophies.[41] Still, one must rec-

38. In this sense, I think that Bruaire would be in agreement with Malet's classical presentation of Aquinas's Trinitarian theology. (See A. Malet, *Personne et amour dans la théologie trinitaire de Saint Thomas d'Aquin* [Paris: J. Vrin, 1956], 71–105.) Malet cites some of the main representatives of this understanding of Aquinas, both among Orthodox theologians and Thomists themselves: Sergei Bulgakov, *Le paraclet,* trans. Constantin Andronikov (Paris: Aubier, 1946); Vladimir Lossky, *Essai sur la théologie mystique de l'Eglise d'Orient* (Paris: Aubier, 1944); Hyacinthe F. Dondaine, *La Trinité* (Paris, 1946); and M. Bergeron, "Le concept latin de personne," *Études d'histoire littéraire et doctrinale du XIIIème siècle* (Paris, 1932). For a remarkable presentation of the issue of personalism versus essentialism in the thought of Thomas Aquinas, see Gilles Emery, "Essentialisme ou personnalisme dans le traité de Dieu chez saint Thomas d'Aquin?" *Revue thomiste* 98 (1998): 5–38. Matthew Levering's English translation of this article appears in *The Thomist* 64 (2000): 521–63. To have a better sense of the importance of Aquinas's treatise on the Triune God, it is important not to neglect the soteriological value of Aquinas's treatise on the Trinity. In fact, as Aquinas says, had God not revealed himself to be Triune, then one would not have a correct understanding of the meaning of creation and would not be able to "think rightly concerning the salvation of the human race, accomplished by the Incarnate Son, and by the gift of the Holy Spirit" (*ST* I, q. 32, a. 1, ad 3). See also *ST* I, q. 43.

39. *EE,* 166. See *ST* I, q. 29, a. 4.

40. It is important to remember that, proceeding inversely with respect to Peter Lombard's *Sentences,* Aquinas places the questions regarding the divine persons after those which deal with God's essence. Nevertheless, this order does not establish the "classical division" of the treatise of God into two parts, *De Deo Uno* and *De Deo Trino.* This nomenclature cannot be found in Peter Lombard or Aquinas. In fact, Aquinas studies God under two different aspects: "*ea quae pertinent ad essentiam divinam*" and "*ea quae pertinent ad distinctionem personarum.*" The above-mentioned division appears only with the later theology of the manuals.

41. *ST* III, q. 3, a. 3, ad 1; also see ad 2.

ognize that, for Aquinas, this knowledge of God as one person, although accessible to human reason without the aid of revelation, is less complete than the knowledge offered by faith. It is only faith, and not human reason, that can give an understanding of the Godhead as Triune. Moreover, to affirm that the knowledge of God as one person is less complete than the knowledge of him as Triune also means that, as Aquinas forcefully and repeatedly states, "nothing of the Godhead remains if the persons are removed from the divine essence."[42] In order for God to be a unique someone, that is to say, a *one* which cannot be counted among many, Bruaire contends that "it is necessary that God be universal in and by himself [and] singular in and by himself, by means of the internal concretion of the universal particularity of himself."[43] Bruaire thinks, however, that there is no need to choose between these two positions. In fact, they must be harmonized because "God is personal by means of the triplicity of persons; God is tri-personal because he is one person." In this regard, what Christianity adds to monotheism is the affirmation that the truth of the One God is his being one nature and three persons.[44]

The Kingdom of the Father

Bruaire, as we have seen, has great admiration for Aquinas's understanding of person, and it is thanks to Aquinas that he sees donation as subsisting relations of opposition. Yet he thinks that Hegel proposes a speculative system that, once its hermeneutical principle has been modified, can offer an elucidation of the relation between the one essence and the three hypostases and of the relation between the persons that better respects the nature of a God understood in terms of donation.[45] This speculative structure, which leads Bruaire to approach the issue at hand from the point of view of "the concept" and "the spirit," prompts him to emphasize

---

42. *In I Sent.*, d. 26, q. 1, a. 2, quoted in Emery "The Essence and the Persons," 550.

43. *EE*, 167.

44. Although one could say that, in a certain sense, Aquinas would agree with Bruaire's affirmation that "God is personal by means of the triplicity of persons," he would not state as Bruaire does, that "God is three persons because he is one person." This second part of Bruaire's polemical statement, read independently of the first, seems not to safeguard adequately the distinction between natural and revealed knowledge—a distinction which Aquinas carefully respected.

45. What I now present completes my previous presentation of Bruaire's reading of

the circularity between the philosophical reading of God as person and the theological understanding of God as Triune in such a way that sometimes it seems to offer an excessively rationalistic approach to the Trinitarian mystery as revealed in Jesus Christ. Having examined Bruaire's theological reading of Hegel to a certain extent, we now need to look more intently at Bruaire's account of Hegel's conception of the Trinitarian movement and to examine the negative principle that governs it.

The Syllogism of the Trinity

As is well known, Hegel's explanation of the divine persons follows what could appear to be two disconnected types of language. He proposes a peculiar understanding of the person in terms of love—where love is of such a nature that the person is himself inasmuch as he denies himself and finds himself in the other.[46] Nevertheless, since the bond of love, which distinguishes the persons in God in order to unite them, does not suffice in itself to penetrate the meaning of the concept of the divine Trinity, Hegel moves from the representational level (the persons understood in terms of love) to the syllogistic form. The latter is *necessary* to give precision to the human articulation of the personal life of the living absolute. In fact, the syllogistic form shows how the divine person can be thought as singular (subject, inalienable freedom) and universal (eternal identity with itself) in itself because it is determined (particular). If particularity were missing, then the so-called "divine person" (both absolute spirit as *one* person and the *three* divine persons) would be only an abstract universality in which identity (universality) would be unable to subsist along with difference.

To understand Bruaire's account, it is necessary to see that, although faithful to Hegel's intention, he stresses the priority of the logic of essence over that of the concept. Undoubtedly, the former does not stand by itself; that is, the logic of essence leads to that of the concept. Nonetheless, Bruaire characterizes the *logic of essence* as the natural place for the doc-

---

Hegel's syllogistic theory as the structuring principle of the latter's speculative thought. As we know, Bruaire used it to articulate the logic of human existence, to demonstrate God's existence, and to explain Hegel's concepts of religion, Trinity, and the Incarnate Word (respectively: *AD*, 95–168; *LR*, 54–61, 93–112, 121–31). Among the most important authors who have meditated upon Hegel's syllogistic theory, I must mention: Chapelle, *Hegel et la religion*, vol. 3, 84–111; Léonard, *La foi chez Hegel*, 349–58, 367–77; Brito, *La Christologie de Hegel*, 502–22.

46. See Chapelle, *Hegel et la religion*, vol. 2, 62.

trine of the Trinity because he wants to highlight the way in which, according to Hegel, absolute spirit creates itself. Bruaire underscores the importance of the syllogism in order to explain accurately the immanent and economic Trinity.[47] The complete threefold circle of reflection shows that God is both pure *act* and *subject.* Inasmuch as he is *act,* God is perceived as a living reality eternally determined and determining itself. Inasmuch as he is *subject,* God is one person and three persons. This, then, is the principle that guides Bruaire's reading of Hegel's Trinitarian philosophy: "the doctrine of the Trinity conjugates a twofold analysis: one according to the circular reflection of the essence [act], and the other according to the principle of the personal relations [subject]."[48] To study the first point, the logic of essence, Bruaire refers to Hegel's *Lectures on the Philosophy of Religion.* To approach the second issue, the personal nature of absolute spirit, he turns to the syllogisms of philosophy which appear in the last section of the *Encyclopedia* (§§ 567–77).

Bruaire names each syllogism of the Trinity after its *first* element and not from the middle term—which determines the nature of the syllogism.

---

47. Since Bruaire contends that everything is to be found in the first syllogism, the truth of this hypothesis needs to be proven there, and thus there is no need to present the other two syllogisms of revealed religion. Although we shall indicate some possible deficiencies in Bruaire's elucidation, even his critics agree with the inspiration that moves Bruaire in his speculative design. Omission of these two issues is not critical since this study is limited to Bruaire's understanding of the Trinity as a self-donating movement, which, to a certain extent, reflects Hegel's syllogism of the Trinity. It needs to be said, however, that whereas Hegel's demand for externality draws him to the elaboration of a philosophy of nature, Bruaire is exempted from this move by his concept of fullness. In this sense, Bruaire's reading of Hegel indicates his departure from the German philosopher at the same time as it illuminates Hegel's thought itself. Chapelle argues against the first two changes as follows: "Cette perspective est sans doute celle de Hegel, même si on constate dans les textes de Bruaire certains glissements de vocabulaire et certains raccourcis. En quel sens par exemple la circularité de la vie divine se définit-elle comme réflexion de l'Essence? Comment celle-ci détermine-t-elle le lieu naturel de la théologie trinitaire? Celle-ci peut-elle se penser spéculativement sinon par la Partition du Concept 'qui distingue pour unir,' et la compénétration de ses moments? Si la *Phénoménologie* (pp. 532–535) et l'*Encyclopédie* (§567) parlent du Dieu-Trinité comme de l'Essence divine, la logique de l'Essence détermine-t-elle pour autant la vie trinitaire plutôt que la logique du Concept? Ou est-ce seulement que ces textes ne conçoivent le Dieu vivant et éternel que selon son essence universelle, c'est-à-dire *en tant que* Concept *(Begriff)* pur, abstraction faite *(Urteil)* de l'immédiateté, de l'être particulier et de la parousie idéale, historique et conclusive *(Schluss),* de l'unique Esprit?" (Chapelle, *Hegel et la religion,* 107–9 n. 324).

48. *LR,* 86–87.

Hence, the first syllogism is that of the Father (A-B-E), the second, that of the Son (B-E-A), and the third that of the Holy Spirit (E-A-B).[49]

According to the *Lectures on the Philosophy of Religion,* the syllogism of the Father (F-S-HS) represents God before the creation of the world and hence without historical revelation.[50] This syllogism represents the first moment of the Trinity, where the source, the Father, who is the universal being-in-himself, particularizes himself in the Son, being-for-other. The Son is the perfect expression of the Father, who would remain exterior were he not interiorized by the Holy Spirit, the singular which is absolute spirit's return-to-itself. In the syllogism of the Father, the Son mediates the relation between the Father and the Holy Spirit. Thanks to the Holy Spirit, who interiorizes the Word by bringing him back to the Father, the Father "becomes" a singular absolute subject. It is in this sense that the Father can also be considered spirit—not in the sense that he is the Holy Spirit within absolute spirit, but in the sense that, thanks to the reconciliatory love of the Holy Spirit, the Father becomes a singular absolute subject.[51]

---

49. As a reminder, (E) stands for "Einzelheit," (B) for "Besonderheit," and (A) for "Allgemeinheit." It should be noted that the nomenclature adopted by Bruaire cannot be found in Hegel. Bruaire talks about the syllogism of the Trinity when Hegel refers to the absolute concept. At the same time, the French philosopher speaks of "syllogisms" where Hegel speaks of "kingdoms" of the Father, Son, and Spirit. Chapelle also points out that to "transform" the concept of religion into the syllogism of religion is abusive. In fact, Hegel speaks only of the "concept" of religion and not of the "syllogism of religion." Chapelle believes that his interpretation is more faithful to Hegel's intention than Bruaire's, because, although the "syllogism of religion" is indeed present in the "concept" of religion (from this point of view Bruaire's reading is legitimate), the syllogism of religion is nonetheless only "*virtually* present" in this concept. See Chapelle, *Hegel et la religion,* vol. 3, 104 n. 114. Chapelle, like Brito, refers to the reading of Léonard because of its clarity and its faithfulness to the letter of Hegel's text. See Léonard, *La foi chez Hegel,* 349–58, 367–77.

50. Obviously "F" stands for Father, "S" stands for Son, and "HS" for Holy Spirit. In the *Enzyclopädie,* the terms used, as we know, are Logic (L), Nature (N), Spirit (S), and in the *WL,* they are Universal (A), Particular (B), and Singular (E). Therefore, the synonymity between the terms is as follows: F = A = L; S = B = N; HS = E = S. Despite the fact that Bruaire continually relates the syllogisms of the Absolute Idea to those of the *Logic,* the form of the latter is not exactly the same as that of the former. The middle term in both cases remains the same, but the other two are systematically inverted. Thus, in the *Logic,* the forms of the three syllogisms are respectively: E-B-A, A-B-E, and B-A-E. Bruaire is aware of this change, yet the only justification he offers for making it is that the logical exposition needs to invert the terms, in order to transcribe into our language the divine ontological order (*LR,* 104). Bruaire does not give any more importance to this issue, because for him it is the middle term that determines the syllogistic figure.

51. *LR,* 95.

It is because the first syllogism of the Trinity represents God before the creation of the world that it can adequately characterize the *Science of Logic*. Nevertheless, Bruaire contends that the syllogism of the Father is *also* the complete structure of the Trinity, because the other two are included there. Bruaire suggests turning to the three last syllogisms of the *Encyclopedia* to understand this delicate point. The first, which represents the whole movement of the *Encyclopedia,* is Logic-Nature-Spirit. It might very well seem that the absolute idea comes only at the end of the process when the absolute idea is supposedly complete and autonomous. In this sense, the first two elements (i.e., Logic and Nature) would be only transitional stages. Nevertheless, as Bruaire reminds the reader, Hegel views Nature not only as a transitional moment; it is also the Idea itself, in which the other two terms are included.[52] For Hegel, the Idea needs to be present in the other two moments, because each of them is a whole which, as such, requires the presence of the other two within itself. Moreover, each divine person is a universal singularity because of the relation that each one has with the other two. In the hypothetical case of a divine person who did not require the necessary bond with the other two, the other two would not exist either. For this reason, we need to recognize "the same division between the Spirit or its Idea in and for itself *and* for us."[53] That is to say, the appearance of the syllogisms as three successive moments derives from the fact that our knowledge of the divine essence requires this type of progression. This gnoseological development must not, however, obscure our awareness that the absolute idea would not be complete if it did not include the other two syllogisms. As I mentioned above, the Spirit is not only the result of the process; it is also its indispensable presupposition.

Bruaire draws two important conclusions from this analysis. The first is that the syllogism of the Trinity represents the whole absolute Idea, conceived as a living tri-personal reality that exists according to a rhythmic movement of exteriorization and interiorization. The second is that, in this threefold syllogism, Bruaire also reads the concept of confirmation as decisive for the logical system. In fact, "the Idea thinks itself, [and is] the truth which knows itself *confirmed* (§236), in both its concrete content and its effective reality."[54] The reader might be puzzled by Bruaire's reading

52. *Enzyklopädie* §577.   53. *LR*, 97.

54. I would like to underscore that Bruaire translates *"bewährt ist"* with the verb *to con-*

of this passage. As the full citation shows, Hegel is explaining what philosophy is; in his view, as is well known, philosophy comes after, and supersedes *(aufheben)*, revealed religion. Bruaire responds to this objection by stating that, for Hegel, philosophy's task is to know the absolute truth, which is nothing but the Triune God. This is why, Bruaire writes, "philosophy is not a superior stage with respect to Christian religious knowledge; it is its confirmation *(bewähren)*, its achievement, in an intimate union with the Triune God."[55]

The second syllogism is the syllogism of spiritual reflection or the syllogism of the Son.[56] If the syllogism of the Father illustrated how the person of the Father is formed, the second, perhaps on a somewhat gnostic note, illuminates how the person of the Son is constituted. Whereas the direction of the first syllogism is from the Father to the Son, in the second it is from the Son to the Holy Spirit: S-HS-F. In the first it was the Son who brought together the Father and the Holy Spirit. It is now the turn of the Holy Spirit to unite the Father and the Son. The Son, says Bruaire, would remain an "atheistic and dead nature" if the act of spiritual personalization did not give him the consciousness and the universality proper to the concept. "The Son proceeds from the Father and becomes God by means of the Holy Spirit which unites him to the Logic (i.e., the Father)."[57] Although the kingdom of the Son, which this syllogism represents, also refers to the economic Trinity (the Incarnation and the history of salvation), what matters, says Bruaire, is to seize the necessity of this moment within the syllogism of the Trinity, based on the fact that the historical deeds of Christ are nothing but the historical transcription of the necessity of the Son (Nature). The Son, then, in order to be a divine, free person, must receive his own identity and abandon himself to the Father by means of the action of the Holy Spirit. Hence, this second syllogism reveals the mediation of the Spirit, thanks to which the Son is eternally constituted as *person*.

The third syllogism, the syllogism of the Holy Spirit (HS-F-S), closes

---

firm. The decisiveness of this terminological choice will become clear shortly. The German original reads as follows: "Dieser Begriff der Philosophie ist die sich denkende Idee, die wissende Wahrheit (§236), das Logische mit der Bedeutung, dass es die im konkreten Inhalte als in seiner Wirklichkeit bewährte Allgemeinheit ist" (*E*, §574).

55. *LR*, 100. 56. *Enzyklopädie* §575.
57. *LR*, 101.

the circle of the divine Trinity. If the syllogism of the Father rendered the relationship between the Father and the Holy Spirit by means of the Son necessary, and the syllogism of the Son rendered necessary the relation between the Son and the Father by means of the Holy Spirit, the mediation of the Father makes necessary the relation between the Son and the Holy Spirit. This third syllogism, which also represents the idea of philosophy, would not create any difficulty if the middle term were not defined as self-knowing reason *(die sich wissende Vernunft)*.[58] This makes the situation a little bit more delicate because, as reason which knows itself, the middle term is not only the Father or the Idea but the Father with the Holy Spirit. Hence, the Spirit would be both major and middle term.

Let us follow Bruaire in the explanation of this complex moment of the Hegelian logic. The Idea (the Father) divides itself into Nature (Son) and Spirit (Holy Spirit), because God "gives himself" a Nature on which he confers absolute freedom. The begotten Son, in order to be the particular determination of the Father, is separated from him and, in a certain sense, becomes "independent." This first partition is possible because the Son gives the Holy Spirit to the Father and so makes him a divine person. Nevertheless, this first moment of the syllogism of the Trinity (F-S-HS) is possible because, in the second syllogism, the Holy Spirit "relates and conforms" the Son to the Father. The Son does not remain "alone," so to speak, once he gives the Holy Spirit to the Father, because it is the Holy Spirit who makes it possible for the Son to be conformed to the Father (S-HS-F). It is in this way that the Son becomes a divine person. Now, this second syllogism is possible, that is, the Son is conformed to the Father, because the singularity that characterizes the Holy Spirit is "attuned" to the particularity of the Son by means of the universality of the Father. The Holy Spirit can therefore give the Son to the Father, because the Father unites the Holy Spirit to the Son and in this way makes him become the third divine person (HS-F-S). Hence, the syllogism of the Spirit requires the other two, *and* at the same time, makes them possible.[59] The obvious difficulty here lies in the fact that this explanation seems, at first, to involve a vicious circle: the Father requires the person of the Spirit in order to be a person (first syllogism), but the Spirit cannot accomplish this task

58. *Enzyklopädie* §577.
59. *LR*, 106.

within the Trinity until the Father makes him become a personal Spirit *in the spirit* (third syllogism).

Bruaire corrects this possible confusion by repeating that the syllogistic movement is *circular* and not linear. Therefore, no time can be said to elapse between the three syllogisms. In this sense, in the movement from absolute spirit, the complete spirit, to the spirit in God (HS) there is no chronological sequence. What is posited in the third syllogism is presupposed in the first. "God, universal and personal spirit, Spirit-Idea, eternally determines himself, divides himself in order to be differentiated, and constitutes in and by himself Father and Son, thanks to whom he discloses himself as third person." In the same movement, God separates himself from himself and finds himself to be one *and* three. "God is a concrete, universal singularity provided with a Nature, only inasmuch as the Spirit is the third person." The shifting of the Spirit to the opposite extreme of the Son (HS-F-S) is contemporaneous with the act by which the Spirit, universalizing and divinizing the Son, constitutes the Father as person (second syllogism) to whom the Son communicates spiritual singularity (first syllogism). It is in this sense that the Idea is reason which knows itself. In other terms, it can be said that for the Spirit to be the major term and part of the middle term is not a contradiction because the third syllogism, which makes the other two possible, represents "one act with two functions." It is the same act in which the Father, as middle term, is simultaneously the simple and impersonal logical idea and the first person of the Trinity. In the first place, absolute spirit deposes its universality in the begetting of the other, the Son. At the same time, this universality is conferred upon this other and made a divine person by the Spirit. The Father is such (i.e., the person of the Father) because of the mediation (relation) of the Son, which is made possible by the discreet loving work of the Holy Spirit, whom the Father makes a divine person. It is in these terms that Bruaire illustrates Hegel's perception of the Spirit as the discreet final victory of Love. The syllogistic approach to the mystery of the Trinity confers upon the Holy Spirit the last place according to the order of exposition but the first in the ontological order.[60]

This ontological precedence of the spirit over the logical Idea confers upon the third syllogism a particularly important value. It illustrates the

---

60. *LR*, 109.

fact not only that the Holy Spirit is made a person thanks to the mediation of the Father (HS-F-S) but also that, since the middle term of the syllogism is the Spirit inasmuch as it constitutes the logical Idea, it is also necessary to affirm, Bruaire says, that the Father is posited by the Spirit. For this reason, there are two ways of representing the third syllogism. The first corresponds to the form of the other two: HS-F-S. The second is the developed form of the syllogism which brings to light the mediations of the syllogisms of the Father and of the Son. According to this second form, the middle term is no longer the simple and impersonal logical Idea but the Father in and by the Spirit, the Idea-Spirit or "reason which knows itself":

Holy Spirit—Son—Idea-Spirit—Holy Spirit—Son.[61]

Bruaire concludes his brilliant analysis of Hegel's Idea of the Trinity by reminding the reader that the same distinction made in the syllogism of the Son (the distinction between the Trinity *in itself* and *with respect to our knowledge*) needs to be kept in mind at the end of the third syllogism. In fact, the second syllogism represented both the begetting of the Son and his incarnation within human history. The third syllogism represents the Holy Spirit both as person and as the fulfillment of the Son's redemptive work, thanks to which the separation between the finite and the infinite is overcome.

Hegel and Spirit's Absolute Negativity

Some indication has already been given regarding the principle which, according to Hegel, prompts the absolute spirit's self-genesis: very much the same as for Schelling, for Hegel too, absolute spirit's inner force is sheer negativity, the total abnegation of itself. This issue needs to be carefully examined because, while preserving the Hegelian syllogistic structure, it is in contradiction to its negative principle that Bruaire constructs the Trinitarian movement of affirmation, reddition, and confirmation. The analysis presented in the preceding pages represents, so to speak, the basic "formal" structure that this inner principle of absolute negativity originates.[62]

Bruaire explains that Hegel conceives the ontogenesis of the spirit ac-

61. *LR,* 109.

62. For a more elaborate presentation of Hegel's conception of negativity and the Trinity, see Piero Coda, *Il negativo e la Trinità: Ipotesi su Hegel* (Rome: Città Nuova Editrice, 1987).

cording to the negation of the negation; "from nothingness to nothingness."[63] In this sense, to affirm that absolute spirit determines itself in its expression is to say, following Spinoza's axiom, that *it denies itself.* The expression of the Father is particular because it involves a partition, a division from the Father. At the same time that he is posited, the Son opposes himself to indeterminate being. This first negation, however, is not the Word in the Trinitarian movement. The same potency that denies indeterminacy and sets particularity in opposition to universality denies particularity and "makes of the Particularity of the Word that of the universal One."[64] There is a first negation which is at the same time denied by the Spirit. This second negation Hegel calls the *Gegenstoss des Geistes,* the counter-thrust of the spirit. Here, the reflection of the spirit is a double negativity, a denial of the first negation, of alterity, of exteriority. The self-determination of the spirit is able to come full circle because it is guided by the abnegating omnipotence of the spirit. "The Spirit is the Negative, both in God, in his manifestations, and in the social and individual adventures of the human being."[65]

According to Bruaire's reading of Hegel, it is precisely this negative movement, and not his relation to the finite, that constitutes God as personal in himself. The infinite, as negation of particularity in God, cannot be distinguished from the absolute freedom that liberates itself from indetermination by means of the negation of itself. The negation of the negation is what prevents the partition (universal-particular) from generating two independent realities; on the contrary, it gives the absolute a sublimated personal unity. Because of this reflection into itself, the absolute becomes a person, that is, a concrete spiritual singularity, which is divine because "it is self-constituted by the all-powerful negativity that frees it from the original lack."[66] In this sense, the divine person cannot be understood in Hegel as the outpouring of generosity but rather as extreme self-renunciation and self-effacement before the other.

The absolute's "negative abnegation," as Bruaire describes it, explains not only the divine persons but also the existence of a person-*spirit* within the absolute *spirit.* Bearing in mind the procession of the Holy Spirit explained previously, we may now simply affirm that the spirit is both at

---

63. *LR,* 24.   64. *EE,* 172.
65. *PM,* 272; *EE,* 173.   66. *EE,* 173.

the beginning (ontologically speaking) and at the end of the threefold syllogism, because the spirit's work of "partition and reflection, of division
and converting reflection, of the negation of the negation," introduces
the difference in the absolute spirit by which the spirit also becomes, in
its absolute discretion, a divine person. In this way, God is absolute spirit
"unitarily" and divine spirit, "singularly"; he is God because "he is spirit,
unitarily and at the beginning; and by means of his all-powerful negativity, he is singularly and in difference from himself." The "secret force" of
Hegel's system is, then, the infinite absolute negativity of the Spirit. It is a
negativity at first in the form of vacuity (i.e., the logic of being) that has
the promise of fulfillment, which can be realized only through the "infinite
frustration" of the negation of the negation. In this sense, the life of the
Trinity is indeed a "drama" in which from the *Tabor* of the Son springs
forth the *eternal Calvary* of the negative abnegation of the Spirit.[67]

Hegel's ontology of spirit thus conceives absolute spirit as this absolute
negativity which makes it itself by means of division, abnegation, and restitution. The only other plausible alternative left for the ontology of spirit, Bruaire contends, is to perceive absolute spirit in exactly the opposite
terms. On this reading, its "secret force" would not be an "all-powerfully
negative abnegation" but rather sheer positivity, pure gift. Consequently,
in place of the first negation, there would be effusion, donation, positive
begetting of the gift, and, instead of the negation of the negation which
closes the Trinitarian circle of reflection in Hegel, there would be a confirmation of the donation.

Bruaire, of course, follows his own interpretation of the ontology of
spirit. However, because he regards Hegel's syllogistic system as an adequate way of presenting the Trinitarian mystery, he does not altogether
abandon it. For him, it is as though Hegel sees the Trinitarian movement
rightly but interprets it incorrectly. Thus, Bruaire believes it will suffice
to replace Hegel's *negative* moving principle with one of utter *positivity*. Despite Hegel's influence on Bruaire, the decision to adopt a positive
rather than a negative principle can be traced back to the very beginning
of Bruaire's philosophical reflection.[68] In a certain sense, it is a tacit, and

---

67. *EE*, 175. See *PM*, 299.

68. For this reason, the link between alterity and wonder as the beginning of Bruaire's
philosophy was mentioned above along with the judgment that Bruaire's anthropology is
"governed" by an implicit concept of gift.

perhaps not thoroughly considered choice that later on reveals itself as the governing principle of *every* philosophical reflection.[69] Hegel's philosophy received from Christian revelation the conception of the absolute as spirit, but, as I have pointed out, the philosopher neglected the unfathomable depth that constitutes absolute spirit.[70] Since this all-powerful negativity is a first principle, indeed the beating heart of the absolute, Bruaire does not argue against it. He simply indicates certain consequences, perceived by Hegel himself, which show the inadequacy of Hegel's negative principle and which, once read in light of the ontology of gift, are the positive outcome of Bruaire's *ontodology:* the divine logic absorbs the human logic within itself, thereby ultimately eliminating (and not just negating) the finite, and it thus becomes unable to account for difference, for the nonabsolute other; man's impossibility of coming back to himself results in both the transformation of man's relation with the human other into mutual abnegation and the denial of the existence of a salvation for the human being that involves his participation;[71] human language is "burdened by contingency, by the particularity of human languages"; the sacramentality of Nature is annihilated and thus, "is no longer able effectively to signify the Spirit"; moral obligation cannot be grounded in ontology; and, last but not least, since the human being is not seen as being-in-debt, thinks he can live without the joyful discovery that he becomes a subject when he reciprocates the love which, *de facto,* originates him.[72]

These negative consequences, as Bruaire repeats on different occasions, derive from Hegel's identification of theology and philosophy, of absolute

69. The opening remarks of Balthasar's Trilogy are very much to the point here: "Beginning is a problem not only for the thinking person, the philosopher, a problem that remains with him and determines all his subsequent steps; the beginning is also a primal decision which includes all later ones for the person whose life is based on response to that decision. God's truth is, indeed, great enough to allow an infinity of approaches and entryways. And it is also free enough subsequently to expand the horizons of one who has chosen too narrow a starting point and to help him to his feet" (Hans Urs von Balthasar, *Seeing the Form,* vol. 1 of *The Glory of the Lord: A Theological Aesthetics,* trans. Erasmo Leiva-Merikakis [San Francisco: Ignatius Press, 1982], 17).

70. This is why, for Bruaire, the abnegation of the spirit is what makes Hegel's Trinitarian philosophy so original and, at the same time, so fragile (*EE,* 173).

71. "God alone will save the human being in his Good Friday" (*EE,* 178). This consequence reveals how deeply influenced Hegel's philosophy was by his own Lutheranism—of which he thought himself to be the most significant intellectual exponent (ibid.). See *PM,* 272.

72. *EE,* 179.

religion and the logic of the absolute. If human language is able to transcribe the divine logic, then there is no real "negative" consequence which
cannot be accepted. Bruaire, as we have tried to show, makes it abundantly
clear that Hegel's speculative system stands or falls with the validity of the
identification between the logic of the absolute and revealed religion. Hegel
defends this identity as the most important consequence of God's revelation. In fact, says Bruaire, Hegel, diverging significantly from Christian
theology, holds that "God reveals himself completely and that his mystery
is dissolved in this absolute revelation. Revelation is no longer the word
that God addresses to the human being, but it is language conformed to
the divine Word in which absolute spirit eternally expresses itself."[73] It can
thus be said that, in a sense, the identification of revelation and the logic
of the absolute (the means by which human language is able to re-present
the divine word), the principle of sheer negativity, and the dissolution of
the logic of human existence form an inseparable unity. That is to say, it
is impossible to claim that philosophy and theology are identical without
embracing a concept of God as utter negativity, because the identification
of these two sciences—at least as Hegel explains it—is ultimately the negation, not of the infinite, but of the finite, a negation not of theology, but
of philosophy. The absorption of theology into philosophy is, ultimately,
the denial of philosophy, because, as it seems to me, to grant to human
language a capacity to express the divine logos is not to trust the power
of human reason but to identify it with the divine logic and thus to deny
finite reason. It seems, then, that it is the excessive rationalism of Hegel's
philosophy that ultimately explains how this philosophy can consider as
benign the drastic consequences for the human being unleashed by the
principle of sheer negativity.

If this is true, then Hegel's rationalistic excesses reveal in the end that an
absolute that does not have the capacity positively to posit the finite as different from itself, and to preserve it as such, presupposes an anthropology
that rejects the freedom of the human being. As Bruaire would say, Hegel's
anthropology does not admit that the finite spirit is given to itself in order
to become itself. Bruaire always claims that it is one's idea of the absolute
that determines and governs one's philosophical system. We may also say

73. *LR*, 181.

that one's idea of the absolute determines the way in which one conceives of the human being. Hegel's idea of absolute spirit, as Bruaire explains it, seems to be unable to account for human freedom; or, expressed more radically, it seems actually to reject finite freedom itself—prompted perhaps by an unspoken sense of scandal at the actual existence of a fragile, limited freedom. The human subject's self-certainty, carried to the extreme proposed by Hegel, implies then a negation of the self.

Bruaire, then, proposes his own philosophy as a positive spiritual ontology and a negative anthropology—as opposed to Hegel's negative spiritual ontology and positive anthropology.[74] He claims that only the recognition and acceptance of man's ontological infirmity give both human and divine freedom their real value. This is why Bruaire contends that whereas Hegel's system is *in a sense* able to "transcribe faithfully and integrally" the doctrine of the Trinity, its hermeneutical key, utter negativity, is seriously deficient.[75] Bruaire thinks that to give an account of God's personhood, and thus of God as gift, it is possible to adopt Hegel's syllogistic Trinitarian *form* while correcting it with a principle of sheer *positivity.* This is the only way, he contends, to overcome the impasse of Hegel's spiritual ontology without losing its contribution.[76]

74. *PM,* 281–82.

75. *LR,* 182–83.

76. *D,* 107. Chapelle reacts to Bruaire's assertion with these words: "Cette question semble pourtant posée et résolue par Hegel au niveau de la Logique de l'Idée absolue et des moments de la méthode spéculative. Celle-ci n'est rien que l'accès contrarié et contrastant de l'Esprit à sa propre présence idéale (*Logic,* II, pp. 495–98; *Enzyklopädie* §242). Ainsi la négation de la négation, c'est-à-dire l'autodétermination du terme différencié, n'est proprement rien d'autre que la négativité par laquelle l'Absolu se confirme en se distinguant de sa différence. Car c'est tout un pour la négativité spéculative de se nier comme objet déterminé, comme autre, et de se nier en tant que sujet à même de se déterminer. Mais cette unité de la négativité absolue et de la négation de la négation en est la contradiction, c'est-à-dire 'le simple point de la relation négative à soi,' dès lors 'la source la plus intime de toute activité, du mouvement de soi par soi, de la vie et de l'Esprit' (*Logic,* II, p. 496b). Cette idée de l'identité et de la distinction est-elle 'équivoque' comme le suggère Bruaire selon lequel 'il manque à l'achèvement du système une clef d'interprétation dont l'absence marque peut-être la limite de notre discours?' Pour Hegel en tout cas, tout est dit puisque rien n'est plus caché de l'absolu de la contradiction" (Chapelle, *Logique et religion,* 102–3 n. 294).

Trinity and Person

In light of Aquinas's contribution, Bruaire understands "person" in terms of relation, and, differing from him here, he understands that "relation," conceived in terms of ontological freedom, designates donation, which constitutes otherness within the unity. The personal character of the Triune God is not described by Bruaire according to the classical presentation of subsisting relations of opposition, nor does he take up the psychological model of the Trinity to offer an account of how the hypostases of the Son and the Spirit proceed from the Father. God's personhood is characterized according to the "roles" that the persons play within the movement of donation as portrayed by the circular movement of Hegel's threefold syllogism, shaped this time by the principle of sheer positivity.

Considering the absolute from the point of view of its essence, absolute gift, one must affirm that, in order for God to be *personal* in his *unity*, the particularization (S) of universality (F) needs to be confirmed by the Spirit—a fact which, as we now know, requires a difference between the spirit and the Holy Spirit. Indeed, absolute spirit as infinite positive act consists of the spiritual movement of donation and reddition, of reflection and expansion. It is this movement of donation—conceived in terms of gratuity, of an excess of love, and not of partition, judgment, or negation of the determination—which, according to Bruaire, makes absolute spirit be personal in its unity and so know itself. Hence, we could say that because God is gift he is one, because he is gift his unity is threefold, and because the communion of the persons is always absolute the threefoldness sends us back to the one gift.

To address the issue of the personal character of the three hypostases better, Bruaire revisits and modifies the expositive order of the Trinitarian movement presented by Hegel. The change of sequence of the syllogistic movement, it seems to me, is prompted by the need to put the syllogism at the service of the principle of sheer positivity, and thus it is an attempt to escape from Hegel's rationalistic excesses. Bruaire, then, indicates first that the beginning is the original act of donation: F-S. At the same time, the donation is double, a "hair-triggered gift," because the Father not only gives the gift, he also confirms it. Therefore, the unity of God is absolute positivity, and donation has "the effective positivity of the absolute freedom in act" because the Holy Spirit is presupposed (and not posited). The Holy Spirit is that ruse of love of the Father which the Father "keeps in reserve" and which confirms the gift in its absolute gratuity. To affirm the conceptual necessity that requires gift to be absolute, as the donation of the Father to the Son is absolute, one must keep in mind the eternal unity of the re-donation of the gift, the Holy Spirit. This is why Bruaire's first syllogism is Hegel's third: HS-F-S. In this syllogism, the Father is the mediating principle, the one which gives the syllogism its meaning and holds the two extremes together. It is from him that the affirmation of the gift (S) proceeds, and it is he who enables its re-affirmation (redoubling). The act of confirmation "reveals the reflective expression which he is not and which he re-posits, reestablishes."[77] The act of confirmation is "absolutely *singular*"; it is an act in which, in his total discretion (abnegation), the Holy Spirit reveals the superabundance of the absolute gift.

Once the gratuity of the absolute gift is secured through the Holy Spirit, who, mysteriously always present from the very beginning, makes the gift "be" without return, it is possible to discern the role of the Son in the Trinitarian procession. If the necessity of the concept of absolute gift called for the confirmation of the gift, what also needs to be kept in view is that he who is presupposed, the Holy Spirit, can confirm only that which is the presupposition of his very existence: the original donation. It is in this sense that the relation between the previous syllogism and this one is also necessary. Hence, precisely because the Spirit presupposes the donating act of the Father to the Son, and because nothing of what is confirmed is returned, the Son becomes the mediation between the Father and the Holy Spirit. What this syllogism clarifies is that the Holy Spirit is another, who is different from the Father. The "re-affirmed Son *proves* the Spirit in his difference" because the Son is the eternal present, which is "fulfilled by means of the infinite discretion of the Spirit."[78] It is in this sense that the Holy Spirit proceeds from the Father *and* the Son: F-S-HS (Hegel's first syllogism).

Finally, once the respective mediations of the Father and the Son have been delineated, it is possible to understand the mediation of the Holy Spirit, which does not consist in confirming the original donation. Since

77. *EE*, 191.
78. *EE*, 192–93.

confirmation is the "ruse of love," the Father is the principle and so the middle term, the ultimate source of both donating acts. The role of the Holy Spirit is a fundamental one, since he is the one who "confirms by distinguishing the generating act from the begotten." Therefore, the spirit within the spirit keeps the persons of the Father and the Son united in their difference and makes the gift infinitely fruitful. It is in this way that the Father and the Son are constituted as persons: S-HS-F (Hegel's second syllogism). Without making the middle term simultaneously the Father and the Holy Spirit as Hegel did, Bruaire also uses the developed form of Hegel's third syllogism to make explicit the fundamental role of the Father and the unity of the three persons:

Holy Spirit—Son—Father—Holy Spirit—Son

The first part of this developed form is Holy Spirit—*Son*—Father (which is the first syllogism with the opposite terms inverted). The second part of this version of the third syllogism is Father—*Holy Spirit*—Son (which is the second syllogism with the opposite terms inverted). The "developed" third syllogism is the most important one, insofar as it is the most synthetic expression of the relation of the three persons in the one personal God. This threefoldness is "by means of and for the personal unity of the One which is Unique, the beginning and end of itself, which proves itself to be the absolute gift of itself to itself."[79]

We could then say that Bruaire states that the Father—act of giving, of expressing himself—is person because he is his relation with the Son, a relation which is confirmed by the Holy Spirit. In this sense, the Holy Spirit, by returning the gift, also "contributes" to the Father's being a person. The Son is the uttered Word (Logos), which, being pure gift, "returns" the gift given; he is person because the Holy Spirit mediates, that is, unites and distinguishes, the source (Father) and its perfect expression (Son). The Holy Spirit, the ruse of love, makes the Triune Godhead exist as absolute gift. The Holy Spirit is a person because he proceeds from the Father "through" the Son and "for" the Son so that the gift of the Father may be confirmed and thus, may be real.[80]

79. *EE*, 192–93.
80. For an interesting and analogous reflection on the person of the Holy Spirit that takes Hegel's contribution into account, see John Milbank, "The Second Difference," 183–90.

What the speculative mediation of the concept tries to convey through the threefold syllogistic reflection is something that faith has always considered impossible: the expression at once of both the unity of God and the triplicity of persons. The human mind cannot conceive by itself the simultaneity of the necessity for the absolute spirit to be one and also for there to be a threefold difference within the absolute. Bruaire's Trinitarian ontology welcomes the intimations of Christianity and elaborates an onto-logic of absolute gift in which the absolute is the Triune God. As awkward as it may sound to postmodern ears, for Bruaire, it is God's infinite love that gives logic its necessity. If we are to take both God's essence and creation *ex nihilo* seriously, logic cannot be seen as something that stands eternally before and alongside God judging him, or as something that, somehow, contains him. On the contrary, "logic" has its roots in ontology; it is onto-logic. The coextensiveness of being's nature with logic is what could justify the above-mentioned "necessity" of the speculative mediation of the concept. One could claim that this understanding of logic does not seem to diverge significantly from Hegel's. Nevertheless, one cannot disregard the primary difference that separates them: Hegel subsumes divine logic into human logic and thus, as explained earlier, his ontology of the spirit cannot but be "negative." This negativity is what makes Hegel's speculative movement begin with reason and strive toward speculative knowledge through dialectics. Bruaire's trans-deductive onto-logic claims to escape Hegel's rationalistic absolute system because his explanation of the conceptual necessity, which contemplates simultaneously the donation and the confirmation of the gift, is ultimately grounded by Christian revelation. This is why, according to Bruaire, the revisited threefold syllogism, which was prompted by his understanding of the encounter between theology and philosophy, can cogently illustrate that absolute gift reveals itself as the bottomless exchange of love among the three divine persons, a unity which is sheer and eternal fullness, pure gift.[81]

If logic and thus onto-logic needs to be conceived beginning from the God-gift, then it seems to me that the speculative form of thought needs to

81. Affirmation, reddition, and confirmation, for Bruaire, are not three different manifestations of the one divine essence to the human consciousness, but three different persons. The one divine mystery is the gift of the Father to the Son and the gift of the Spirit—who is the Father's ruse of love.

be shaped even more radically than it is in Bruaire by its ontological truth. If God is absolute positivity, then clearly there is no room for a Hegelian dialectics that finds one of its main pillars in the principle of contradiction (negative determination). As we have seen, Bruaire does not explain the movement of donation in these terms; that is, there is no dialectical relation between the Father and the Son which is then sublated into a higher unity by the mediation of the Holy Spirit. If the relation between the Father and the Son is not understood in those dialectic terms, then it seems that one should not adopt, as Bruaire does, the syllogistic structure to convey the inner-Trinitarian processions and the personality of the Godhead. It is true that Bruaire's new syllogistic order is prompted by the principle of gratuity, that there is a real distinction between the persons, that the Holy Spirit is the memory of the secret of God himself which is never fully manifested, and that there is no identification between human and divine logic. Yet, his syllogistic explanation many times appears to pursue an account of the Trinitarian processions which is not shaped by a "positive" perception of the mystery and which hurries too quickly toward a crystal-clear presentation of the spirit within the spirit. With this, I do not mean to say that rooting logic in (ontological) love should entail either rejecting man's capacity to know, or reducing theology's contribution to philosophy to a revelatory source of inspiration for human thought—as Bruaire claims is the case with Blondel. Nevertheless, one should not forget that the revelation of the Triune mystery in Jesus Christ does not make this mystery "com-prehensible." The Triune mystery illuminates human inquiry precisely because it is, and remains, a mystery. The revelation of God in Jesus Christ allows the human being to participate in the always surprising and inexhaustible *ever-greatness* of the Triune mystery. The onto-logic "necessity" of absolute love cannot be then a "conceptual," all-clarifying necessity explained through the developed syllogistic form. Rather, the "necessity" of absolute love that the human being is given to contemplate is the radiant mystery of the Triune God, which remains ever-greater than man who contemplates it. It is this "positive" understanding of the mystery—as opposed to the interpretation that would like to circumscribe the mystery to the incomprehensible—that needs to shape man's speculative endeavors in its three aspects: "positivity" (charity), "understanding" (since God created man to participate in the Word), and "mystery" (ever-greaterness).

Since absolute personal gift is unfathomable, the human being will never finish being surprised by it. In this sense, I think that the coalescence of wonder and the speculative mediation of the concept indicated by Bruaire calls for further reflection. It is precisely the fact that human reason ceaselessly pursues the knowledge of the absolute within divine charity that should prevent philosophical reflection from following the mesmerizing draw of an all-clarifying reason and should allow the methodology of philosophy to be shaped by the unifying positivity that, far from eliminating difference, gratuitously posits and confirms otherness.

Confirmation of Finite Spirit

The confirmation of the spirit affects every being-of-spirit that is given. There is thus also a sense in which the Holy Spirit confirms the created finite spirit that is given to itself in order to become itself. When Bruaire speaks about creation, he refers mainly to the creative act, that moment in which the finite spirit is posited in existence. Nevertheless, while it is true that the human spirit is given to itself and cannot be taken back, being-gift is not endowed with an absolutely independent subsistence. Although given to itself in order to become itself, finite spirit is ontologically unable to remain in existence unless it is sustained in it. What is needed, however, writes Bruaire, is not a continuous reiteration of the creative act but a *further donation;* that is to say, the human spirit needs something other than itself in order to be: "it needs to be confirmed in its existence."[82] In the same way that the Holy Spirit re-posits, confirms, the gift which is the Son, the spirit which is nothing but spirit re-posits, re-gives that gift which is given to itself in order to become itself. The confirmation of the human spirit, its conservation in existence, has, according to Bruaire, both an ontological and an existential level.

Bruaire says that the confirmation of the finite being by the spirit which is nothing but spirit reveals the truth of the ontological difference. If both the human spirit and created realities subsist in their ephemeral existence, it is because the spirit "actualizes the gift" in a sustained existence. The very existence of these things, then, attests to the "presence of that which is

82. Milbank, "The Second Difference," 188; Bruaire, "La prière du chrétien," *Communio* 10 (1985): 5 (hereafter *PdC*). Also see *EdE*, 38.

present"; it reveals the essence of every being: that being which is nothing but being is the spirit which is nothing but spirit. The ontological difference finds its ultimate truth "in the difference of the spirit which is nothing but spirit, which is nothing but being, and which alone confirms the being of everything that is."[83] For Bruaire, then, the ontological difference does not need to be conceived as opposing the absolute and the finite—insofar, obviously, as these terms are understood after the manner of Heidegger for whom the supreme being *(étant)* always remains within the limits of onto-theology and is never altogether different from the finite (i.e., it is never truly infinite). The difference is between *entia* and being, but it needs to be rooted *in* the infinite. It is now possible to see that Bruaire's conception of creation and begetting is governed by this understanding of the ontological difference. In fact, begetting is "identity in the absolute difference"— the identity of the gift in the difference between the divine persons—and creation is the "difference in the identity of being given"—finite beings are the *other*, that which the infinite *is not*, but they are also given and preserved in existence by the spirit.

The fact that Bruaire proposes an understanding of the "ontological difference" from the point of view of the Trinitarian difference unveils an answer to the philosophical question *par excellence:* "what is being?" If confirmation is the effectiveness of being as such, then "either being is only an abstraction from whatever is, or being is the act which confirms in effective presence the existence of each being, to whose essence, however, it does not add anything: *the being which is only being is the being which is nothing but spirit.*"[84] Paying close attention to the suggestion put forth by Christianity, Bruaire invites us to "search for what makes the presence of that which is present, the light of what is illuminated, the being of all that is, of God himself. But it is impossible to begin to answer, at least so it seems to us, without asking ourselves for the effect of being, renewing all that is, regenerating all that comes and which is proper to the spirit which is nothing but spirit."[85] Hence, Bruaire contends that it is not possible to begin to answer the question "what is being as such" unless one takes into serious consideration Christian revelation, which suggests that the Spirit

---

83. *EE*, 190.
84. Bruaire, "Philosophie et spiritualité," 1386; *EdE*, 38. Bruaire's emphasis.
85. *EdEES*, 75.

confirms itself (absolute spirit) and its *other* (finite spirit). Every single being, by the simple fact that it is there, attests to the presence of the spirit
which makes that being be present. Obviously, Bruaire is not saying that
the simple observation of the created being leads to a direct intuition of
the presence of the absolute being. If this were the case, the long process
from human spirit to absolute spirit by means of the speculative effort of
the concept would be pointless. Bruaire's answer, supported by the foregoing analysis, states that being as such is absolute spirit, which is nothing but the unrestricted gift of itself to itself. He is not simply identifying
being, gift, and the Holy Spirit. This would be a reductive reading of the
Trinitarian movement and of the circumincession of the three persons. It
is rather the whole of the spirit, understood in *ontodological* terms, that
answers the eternal question, "what is being *qua* being?" Henceforth, in
dialogue with other major philosophical answers to this question, namely,
being as substance (Aristotle), as *ipsum esse* (Aquinas), or as absolute spirit
(Hegel), Bruaire's *ontodology* ultimately aims to illustrate that God, as absolute spirit and hence being itself, is gift: that gift of himself to himself
which is also the confirmation of himself and the gift to the other than
himself.

Since being is spirit, and hence free, the conservation of the human
spirit necessarily entails the limited participation of human freedom. The
drama of the human being consists in that mysterious and wonder-full
combination of eternity and ontological precariousness. The first aspect
comes from the fact that the human spirit is completely given to itself.
This has a double root: on the one hand, finite spirit is not the origin of
itself and therefore does not have the capacity to preserve itself in existence; on the other hand, the gift that brings the human spirit into existence makes this spirit in-carnate and finite. The human spirit knows no
other existence than that of a spirit-in-flesh and thus knows that its body
is essential for it to be and to become itself. The combination of eternity
with the ontogenic incapacity to confirm itself prompts finite spirit's *desire* to be eternally confirmed in being. Desire is not blind necessity, but a
spiritual dimension of the human being (along with freedom and reason),
the echo of the being-gift whose most complete expression is the language
freely addressed to him who is man's origin. God creates the human spirit
in such a way that the fulfillment of the latter's conversion to the origin

cannot but take the form of a dialogue. This dialogue is the adequate response to the language which God speaks *to* man (revelation) and whose fundamental presupposition is the language *in* God. This dialogue with God, or prayer, is then before all else a *response* to the creative initiative of the absolute spirit.

In one of the many editorials he wrote for *Communio,* Bruaire offered an explanation of the meaning of Christian prayer, saying that God's revelation in Jesus Christ eliminates the anonymity which otherwise characterizes the "unknown origin" of the human being, and hence in Christ, the human being learns not only that the origin is Father but also how to address him. For this reason, the prayer of the human being, the adequate expression of his desire, cannot but follow that of Christ. The imitation of Christ reveals that human speech to God is twofold. On the one hand, it consists in the joyous acceptance of having being given. Prayer, then, is the loving recognition of who one is before it is a request for what is lacking. Yet, as one learns in Christ, there is no true acceptance of the gift which is not, at the same time, a handing of oneself over to the source. In the same way that the Son is himself only in his absolute referentiality (reddition) to the Father, so the human spirit fulfills the "logic of gift" only when, in prayer, he gives himself freely and completely to the one who creates him and continuously renews his existence. Prayer, then, is not just "a motion of the soul," or a repetition of more or less meaningful sentences. It requires the whole of one's being. This is why "it is the most difficult gift of oneself, the most precious, and even for the saints themselves, the most uncommon."[86]

Christian revelation teaches that, as the Son is confirmed because he gives himself in return to the Father, any human being "is renewed if he offers himself to the author of being. This happens by means of a secret ruse of the paternal love, in which the Holy Spirit manifests himself as he who gives without receiving."[87] The human spirit, which is indeed freely given to itself, cannot but be confirmed gratuitously. The divine confirmation is not guaranteed to the human spirit—as it is for the infinite spirit (thanks to the previously explained coalescence of necessity and gratuity); it is given to finite spirit. The finite spirit needs the offer of an "additional

86. *PdC*, 5.
87. *PdC*, 5.

increase" *(surcroît)* of gift, a re-doubling of the gift that is its very essence, in order to remain in existence. This need is both what prompts the verbalization of desire as entreaty for the renewing power of the spirit and what gives hope for a definitive, eternal confirmation, which will also renew its corporeal being.[88] Man's "request for abidance" and for a "new heaven and new earth," no longer marked by the law of obliteration proper to finite phenomena, awaits an eternal fulfillment of history which is the definitive and ever-new confirmation of the gift, the gratuitously given persistence of the gift which the finite spirit is.

88. *EdE,* 38.

Conclusion

It is not at all easy to free human awareness from the captivating idea that the human being can account for his own existence without coming to terms with the question of his own origin. The anthropological turn of modernity, for the sake of pursuing more pressing matters or more deceivingly fundamental issues, presumed that severing the question of God from the inquiry into the human being's own identity would give wings to the quest for knowledge. Instead, as postmodernity witnesses, this too-often rated "successful" revolution has yielded a radical dissolution of any unifying principle and thus, of man himself. As Bruaire's work shows, it is only when anthropological reflection does not prevent man's questioning from facing the mysterious origin of the human being that it becomes capable of accepting the relation between positivity and being. This unsettling discovery reveals, on the one hand, that the ultimate shepherd of being is another, different from man, and, on the other, that this mysterious source of man's own being is neither a shadowy threat to his own autonomy nor an intractable engineer who has determined everything before it comes to pass.

Bruaire's reflection poignantly illustrates that in retrieving the truth of its own questioning, anthropology expresses itself in an ontology of gift that is dominated by the surprising discovery that the finite being is given to itself in order to become itself. At first, Bruaire's anthropology, going hand in hand with a reflection on the nature of the absolute as self-determinate, self-determining absolute and infinite freedom, perceives the human being as a self-determining, limited, and finite freedom that, not being the origin of itself, desires, through language, absolute knowledge, that is to say, to be in communion with the pure ideality of absolute spirit. This negative anthropology, however, requires a metaphysical renewal consisting in the elaboration of a positive ontology that is able to transform the inquiry into the origin. In fact, it is because this other, through its indelible presence in the human being, shows itself as that incontestable infinite positivity that makes the human being be what he is, in total freedom, that the question of the nature of the absolute becomes, in the end, the verification of the circumincession of being and gift.

Since the systematic elimination of spirit from thinking about being has resulted both in the dismissal of spirit's being and in the forgetfulness of being, Bruaire's ontodology contends that the retrieval of "spirit," in its twofold meaning of νοῦς and πνεῦμα, is decisive for a restoration of the notion of being to philosophical reflection. Being, for Bruaire, is being-of-spirit. The concept of spirit, however, cannot be dissociated from freedom, where freedom is conceived not so much as freedom of choice but, more radically, as a transcendental, as the twofold rhythm of reflection and expression proper to spirit's self-determination. Freedom, in this sense, is coextensive with spirit and so also with being. In this light, Bruaire compellingly shows that spirit is freedom that conforms itself to itself through the donation to itself that is characterized as the loving movement of expansion and contraction which makes the spirit one, makes the spirit be. According to Bruaire, then, the most adequate name of the ternary spirit-being-freedom is *gift*, because "gift" expresses the ultimate positivity that is the very nature of the free being of spirit. Gift is being in its spiritual way of being. Bruaire's fruitful elucidation of gift, which is neither yet another attempt to rename being with a more suitable term nor a *démodé* rejection of metaphysics, encompasses both finite and infinite spirit. In fact, it is only possible to conceive of finite being-of-spirit in terms of "gift" because absolute spirit, God, can be shown to be not only determinate spirit but more radically, gift. Otherwise, the discourse on gift would inevitably deteriorate into a vague circumlocution to avoid dealing with more fundamental matters. The intimations of Christian revelation suggest that the Triune absolute spirit, that is, the loving movement of donation, reddition, and confirmation of the gift, is the unique, ever-surprising ground from which an unexpected finite other can blossom. Spirit's gift, then, is both the gift of himself, which God is, and the gift of what absolute spirit is not: finite being.

Bruaire's *ontodology* cannot be conceived outside its unique relationship with Christian theology, or, more precisely, with a Catholic understanding of Christian revelation. The very concept of gift, the importance of freedom and spirit, the emphasis on positivity over negativity, the confirmation of the gift, and the understanding of God as Triune, are some of the basic pillars of Bruaire's philosophy. The construction of his philosophical system, however, is not *a priori* truncated by the fact that Bruaire adopts categories derived from Christian revelation. On the contrary, as we saw, his distinctive way of conceiving the relationship between philosophy and theology is beneficial for both disciplines. Nevertheless, the particular relation between theology and philosophy envisioned by Bruaire does seem to require that his philosophy, contrary to his view, be qualified as a "theological philosophy," rather than as philosophy *tout court*. Bruaire's reflection is, it seems to me, a compelling attempt to pursue the inquiry into the nature of absolute truth within Christian revelation without making philosophy subservient to theology.

As we saw, Bruaire's philosophy is also carried out in a close dialogue with the Hegelian system. Nevertheless, reading the movement of gift in terms of "donation, reddition, and confirmation," instead of the Hegelian concepts of "negation, negation of the negation, and affirmation," represents a radical modification of Hegel's thought that indicates a keen perception of the distinction between the Hegelian speculative structure and its governing negative principle. In this sense, as this book has shown, Bruaire, who, although a remarkable Hegel scholar, was never a Hegelian, proposes a cogent and compelling metaphysics which puts all the right elements in place for an adequate presentation of "gift" and "being" in terms of donation. However, as I indicated, Bruaire fails to allow the reality of absolute gratuity to guide his philosophical reflection sufficiently to liberate the concept of gift from a too constrictive speculative mediation of the concept. If one is willing to accept the understanding of being-gift in terms of utter fullness, it stands to reason that the finite conceptual net is too fragile to snare such a mystery. Admittedly, Bruaire indicates, on the one hand, that although "there is no spirit without its manifestation," there is equally "no spirit without its secret" and, on the other hand, that the concept of gift falls short of saying the *haecceitas* of the human person. He also acknowledges the revealed origin of the threefoldness of gift. Still, as the analysis of gift has shown, affirming the utter positivity of gift—which calls for the distinction between begetting and creating, and between the three divine hypostases in the one personal God—breaks open the univocity of the concept of gift and calls for the adoption of a concept better able to reflect the differences between finite and eternal gift. With this, I do not wish to suggest that "gift" is inadequate. I wish instead to underscore that to reconcile the absolute with the alterity of created being through the concept of gift seems to require an analogical concept of gift, provided that one maintain the absolute exchange of love between the Father and the Son is "identity in absolute difference" and that "creation means difference in the identity of being-given." Without demeaning reason's capacity to know, the transgressive root of the concept of gift requires the integration of a positive perception of the ever-greater mystery into the speculative system. Thus, it does not suffice to equate absolute gratuity's lack of arbitrariness with conceptual necessity, a necessity that considers the threefold syllogism as its most complete expression.

Regardless of the difficulties found in his work, Bruaire's ontodology, through the coming together of freedom, spirit, and being in the concept of gift, represents a very compelling argument for understanding being as love—not "love" as an adjunct to being, or as a denial of ontology, but as the very form of being. For Bruaire's philosophy, there is no difference between representing being as gift and being as love. The advantage of elucidating a metaphysics of charity through the concept of gift is that one is able to see that the nature of love is the affirmation of another. In this sense, being-gift indicates that otherness is an absolute good and not a degradation from a first principle, whose absolute perfection was inexplicably unable to keep itself to itself. Thinking of gift ontologically will be an aid in seeing that the "otherness" that the absolute affirms does not preexist it, determine it, or come to existence necessarily, as warmth and light proceed simultaneously from a fire which remains irremediably unaware of both itself and its own offspring. That the absolute spirit affirms otherness means that it posits another who is given to himself; that is to say, absolute love, since it is pure gift, is the positing of another person in itself. From the very beginning, absolute charity wants another to be: the Father the Son, the Son the Father, and both the Holy Spirit, who, in turn, is the confirmation of the gift. Absolute love's eternal decision not to be a solitary One is the rejection of positing a speechless other. Love, and this is the second characteristic that the concept of gift unfolds, wants to be reciprocated gratuitously. This is why the Son, in absolute freedom, both receives himself from the Father who begets him and also reciprocates the gift, and it is why the Holy Spirit is both the "ruse of love" that confirms the gift and also the one who eternalizes divine love's unconsumable fruitfulness. As the absolute proves, by revealing himself in history, the eternal decision of wanting another to be is of such a superabundant nature that it freely posits another finite self, which, as with the divine absolute itself, is not a speechless other. The finite being-of-spirit, created in the Word, is made a truly free participant from the very beginning in the dialogue of self-giving love that the absolute is. The human person, then, is given to himself that he may discover the mysterious origin from which he proceeds with the hope of being eternally confirmed in being.

Bibliography

Works by Claude Bruaire[1]

Bruaire, Claude. Logique et religion chrétienne dans la philosophie de Hegel. Paris: Seuil, 1964.

———. L'affirmation de Dieu: Essai sur la logique de l'existence. Paris: Seuil, 1964.

———. Philosophie du corps. Paris: Seuil, 1968.

———. Schelling ou la quête du secret de l'être. Paris: Seghers, 1970.

———. La raison politique. Paris: Fayard, 1974.

———. Le droit de Dieu. Paris: Aubier, 1974.

———. Une éthique pour la médecine. Paris: Fayard, 1978.

———. Pour la métaphysique. Paris: Fayard, 1980.

———. L'être et l'esprit. Paris: PUF, 1983.

———. La dialectique. Paris: PUF, 1985.

———. La force de l'esprit: Entretiens avec Emmanuel Hirsch (France-Culture). Paris: Desclée de Brouwer, 1986.

———, ed. La confession de la foi chrétienne. Paris: Fayard, 1977.

———, ed. La morale, sagesse et salut. Paris: Fayard, 1981.

(II) Articles

Bruaire, Claude. "Idéalisme et philosophie du langage." Hegel-Jahrbuch (1964): 16–26.

———. "Connaître Dieu." In Dieu aujourd'hui, 157–65. Semaine des intellectuels catholiques "Recherches et débats," vol. 52. Paris: Desclée de Brouwer, 1965.

———. "Ferdinand Ulrich: Homo Abyssus. Das Wagnis der Seinsfrage." Zeitschrift für philosophische Forschung 19, no. 1 (January–March 1965): 171–75.

———. "Logique et non-sens de l'histoire chez Hegel." Hegel Studien 4 (1965): 161–68.

---

1. The bibliography of Claude Bruaire presented here is an updated version of the one published by Raphaël Gély, "Bibliographie de Claude Bruaire," in Revue philosophique 1 (1990): 89–93.

———. "Réflexions sur le congrès de Salzbourg (Congrès international de la Hegel-Gesellschaft tenu à Salzbourg du 6 au 12 septembre 1964)." *Archives de Philosophie* 20 (1965): 62–63.

———. "Démythisation et conscience malheureuse (Colloque Castelli)." *Archivio di filosofia* 2–3 (1966): 383–93.

———. "Négation et dépassement de l'humanisme." In *Homo homini homo: Festschrift für Joseph Drexel zum 70. Geburtstag*, 271–83. Munich: C. H. Beck'sche Verlagsbuchhandlung, 1966.

———. "Abstraction juridique et revendication légitime." *Hegel-Jahrbuch* (1967): 76–83.

———. "Certitude, énigme ou mythe du sujet." *Revue philosophique de Louvain* 65 (1967): 226–38.

———. "Formalisme et matérialisme." *Revue philosophique de Louvain* 65 (1967): 53–65.

———. "Peut-on invoquer une certitude philosophique de l'existence de Dieu?" In *Le doute et la foi*, 65–88. Semaine des intellectuels catholiques "Recherches et débats," vol. 61. Paris: Desclée de Brouwer, 1967.

———. "Sens de la peine et non-sens du corps." In *Le mythe de la peine*, edited by Enrico Castelli, 323–39. Colloque Castelli. Paris: Aubier, 1967.

———. "Absolu." In *Encyclopaedia Universalis*, vol. 1, 36–39. Paris: Encyclopaedia Universalis, 1968.

———. "Un Dieu homme?" In *Qui est Jésus-Christ?* 185–86. Semaine des intellectuels catholiques "Recherches et débats," vol. 62. Paris: Desclée de Brouwer, 1968.

———. "L'enjeu métaphysique de la crise de l'humanisme." *Revue internationale de philosophie* 22, nos. 85–86 (1968): 276–83.

———. "Leibniz. L'articulation de la logique et de la théologie." In *Leibniz (1646–1716): Aspects de l'homme et de l'oeuvre. Journées Leibniz organisées au centre international de synthèse 28–29–30 mai 1966*, 227–35. Paris: Aubier-Montaigne, 1968.

———. "Liberté du philosophe et révélation." In *L'herméneutique de la liberté religieuse*, edited by Enrico Castelli, 297–305. Colloque Castelli. Paris: Aubier, 1968.

———. "Profession de foi." In *Qui est Jésus-Christ?* 246. Semaine des intellectuels catholiques "Recherches et débats," vol. 62. Paris: Desclée de Brouwer, 1968.

———. "Réflexions d'un philosophe sur l'avenir de la religion." *Bulletin saint Jean-Baptiste* 8 (February–March 1968): 234–41.

———. "L'invention dans le langage religieux." In *L'analyse du langage théologique*, edited by Enrico Castelli, 305–12. Colloque Castelli. Paris: Aubier, 1969.

———. "La mort . . . et puis après?" In *Problèmes actuels du catholicisme*, 170–74. Semaine des intellectuels catholiques "Recherches et débats," vol. 64. Paris: Desclée de Brouwer, 1969.

———. "Vérité et liberté." In *Chercher la vérité*, 236–42. Semaine des intellectuels catholiques "Recherches et débats," vol. 66. Paris: Desclée de Brouwer, 1969.

———. "Athéisme et Philosophie." In *Des chrétiennes interrogent l'athéisme*, edited by Jean-Francois Six, vol. 2, 9–22. Paris: Desclée de Brouwer, 1970.

———. "L'enjeu politique d'une réflexion sur l'éternité." *Revue philosophique de Louvain* 68 (1970): 473–82.

———. "Etat hégélien et société sans classes." In *Hegel et Marx: La politique et le réel. Travaux du Centre de Recherche et de Documentation sur Hegel et sur Marx,* edited by Jacques D'Hondt, 9–13. Poitiers: Faculté des Lettres et Sciences Humaines, 1970.

———. "Hegel et l'athéisme contemporain." *Revue internationale de philosophie* 24, no. 91 (1970): 72–80.

———. "Politique et métaphysique." *Science et Esprit* 22 (May–September 1970): 139–47.

———. "Le problème de Dieu dans l'explication de l'erreur." In *L'infallibilité. Son aspect philosophique et théologique,* edited by Enrico Castelli, 73–90. Colloque Castelli. Paris: Aubier, 1970.

———. "Le problème éthique de la culture." *Axes* 10 (January 1970): 11–17.

———. "Justice et eschatologie." In *Herméneutique et eschatologie,* edited by Enrico Castelli, 247–54. Colloque Castelli. Paris: Aubier, 1971.

———. "Leibniz et la critique hégélienne." In *Akten des internationalen Leibniz-Kongresses Hannover, 14.–19. November 1966,* vol. 5, 116–23. Wiesbaden: Franz Steiner Verlag, 1971.

———. "Qu'est-ce qu'affirmer Dieu?" *Resurrection* 36 (1971): 123–29.

———. "L'homme, miroir de Dieu." *Revue internationale de philosophie* 26, no. 101 (1972): 345–54.

———. "Pour un christianisme inventif." In *Fidelité et ouverture,* edited by Gérard Soulages, 147–49. Colloque des intellectuels chrétiens de Strasbourg. Paris: Mame, 1972.

———. "Schelling: Une philosophie en devenir." *Revue des sciences philosophiques et théologiques* 56 (1972): 617–20.

———. "Témoignage et raison." In *Le témoignage,* edited by Enrico Castelli, 141–49. Colloque Castelli. Paris: Aubier, 1972.

———. "Au procès de Dieu." *Revue de théologie et philosophie* 23 (1973): 289–95.

———. "Critique du soupçon: Idéologie et philosophie." In *Démythisation et idéologie,* edited by Enrico Castelli, 165–72. Colloque Castelli. Paris: Aubier, 1973.

———. "Les ordres de justice." *Les Études philosophiques* 2 (April–June 1973): 141–44.

———. "La dialectique et l'Esprit absolu." *Hegel-Jahrbuch* (1974): 51–56.

———. "Une lecture du *Journal métaphysique* (Entretiens de Dijon de mars 1973)." *Revue de métaphysique et de morale* 79 (1974): 254–361.

———. "Le sacré et l'apparence." In *Le sacré: Études et recherches,* edited by Enrico Castelli, 113–20. Colloque Castelli. Paris: Aubier, 1974.

———. "Le nouveau défi du paganisme." *Communio* 1, no. 1 (1975): 28–33.

———. "La servitude et le temps mutilé." In *Temporalité et aliénation,* edited by Enrico Castelli, 67–72. Colloque Castelli. Paris: Aubier, 1975.

———. "Dieu sait souffrir (compte rendu de F. Varillon, *La souffrance de Dieu*)." *Communio* 1, no. 7 (1976): 93.

———. "Politique et miséricorde." *Communio* 1, no. 6 (1976): 18–22.

———. "Pour une ontologie de l'esprit." In *Savoir, faire, espérer: Les limites de la raison,* vol. 1, 63–70. Brussels: Facultés Universitaires Saint-Louis, 1976.

———. "Sécularisation et demande d'esprit." In *Herméneutique de la sécularisation,* edited by Enrico Castelli. Colloque Castelli. Paris: Aubier, 1976.

———. "Le divin et Dieu." In *Filosofia e desenvolvimento.* Atas da III semana internacional de filosofia realizada na cidade de Salvador, BA, de 17 a 23 de Julho de 1976, vol. 2, 20–23. Salvador, Brazil: Sociedade Brasileira de filósofos católicos, 1977.

———. "Le droit du concept chez Blondel et Bergson." In *Journées d'étude des 9 et 10 novembre 1974: Blondel, Bergson, Maritain, Loisy,* 31–38. Louvain: Peeters, 1977.

———. "L'épreuve de la rationalité philosophique." *Les Études philosophiques* 2 (April–June 1977): 131–36.

———. "L'épreuve philosophique nécessaire." In *La confession de la foi chrétienne,* edited by Claude Bruaire, 83–90. Paris: Fayard, 1977.

———. "Hegel et le problème de la théologie. L'absolu dans l'histoire?" In *Hegel et la théologie contemporaine: L'absolu dans l'histoire?* 94–98. Neuchâtel: Delachaux & Niestle, 1977.

———. "Philosophie du développement et développement de la philosophie." In *Filosofia e desenvolvimento.* Atas da III semana internacional de filosofia realizada na cidade de Salvador, BA, de 17 a 23 de Julho de 1976, vol. 1, 47–61. Salvador, Brazil: Sociedade Brasileira de filósofos católicos, 1977.

———. "La tentation communautaire." *Communio* 2, no. 2 (1977): 2–6.

———. "Conversion et communion dans la foi aujourd'hui," 1–12. Cahiers "Lumen Gentium." Paris: Association Sacerdotale "Lumen Gentium," 1978.

———. "A ética e as ciências médicas." *Presença Filosofica* 4, no. 1 (1978): 51–55.

———. "L'interiorité et la pensée contemporaine." In *Recherches et expériences spirituelles.* Paris: Notre-Dame de Paris, 1978.

———. "La justice et le droit." *Communio* 3, no. 2 (1978): 2–4.

———. "La philosophie du droit et le problème de la morale." In *Hegels Philosophie des Rechts. Die Theorie der Rechtsformen und ihre Logik,* edited by Henrich Dieter and Rolf-Peter Horstmann, 94–102. Stuttgart: Klett-Cotta, 1978.

———. "Sciences humaines et anthropologie philosophique." *Les Études philosophiques* 2 (April–June 1978): 151–55.

———. "Le Dieu de l'histoire." *Communio* 4, no. 6 (1979): 5–7.

———. "Le don de Dieu." *Communio* 4, no. 5 (1979): 2–3.

———. "La foi chrétienne et la science aujourd'hui." In *Revue des travaux de l'Académie des Sciences morales et politiques,* 567–93. Paris: Académie des Sciences morales et politiques, 1979.

———. "Hegel." In *Encyclopaedia Universalis,* 276–79. Paris, 1979.

———. "L'odyssée psychologique de la liberté." In *Hegels philosophische Psychologie,* edited by Dieter Henrich, 183–89. Bonn: Bouvier Verlag Herbert Grundmann, 1979.

———. "Satan, actif et vaincu." *Communio* 4, no. 3 (1979): 2–3.

———. "Transmettre la foi à l'intelligence." *Communio* 4, no. 4 (1979): 2–3.

———. "Crucifié pour nous." *Communio* 5, no. 1 (1980): 2–3.

———. "En attendant la résurrection des corps." *Communio* 5, no. 3 (1980): 2–3.

———. "L'esprit du corps." *Communio* 5, no. 6 (1980): 2–3.

———. "Etica social y ontología del espíritu." *Anuario Filosófico* 13, no. 1 (1980): 65–72.

———. "L'opium des fausses religions." *Communio* 5, no. 4 (1980): 2–3.

———. "Préface." In *Yves Labbé, Le sens et le mal. Théodicée du Samedi Saint*, 7–9. Paris: Beauchesne, 1980.

———. "Violence à l'esprit." *Communio* 5, no. 2 (1980): 2–3.

———. "De l'invention comme fidélité." *Communio* 6, no. 5 (1981): 2–7.

———. "Hegel et Kierkegaard." *Obliques* (1981): 167–75.

———. "Sacrifice et privilège." *Communio* 6, no. 4 (1981): 29.

———. "Création et inspiration." *Communio* 7, no. 6 (1982): 2–3.

———. "L'esprit n'est pas l'ennemi de la chair." *Communio* 7, no. 2 (1982): 2–3.

———. "Pouvons-nous y croire?" *Communio* 7, no. 1 (1982): 2.

———. "Logique de l'alliance." *Géopolitique* 2 (1983): 32–35.

———. *L'historie et le divin. Autour de l'oeuvre du Cardinal de Lubac.* Paris: Notre-Dame de Paris, 1983.

———. "Le pluralisme des consciences et la liberté de l'infini." *Communio* 8, no. 2 (1983): 2–4.

———. "Problème de la métaphysique et conversion." *Archivio di filosofia* 51, nos. 1–3 (1983): 121–26.

———. "Rembourser l'avortement? Non!" *Communio* 8, no. 1 (1983): 92–95.

———. "Réminiscence du concept et mémoire de la révélation." In *Pour une philosophie chrétienne*, 137–53. Namur: Lethielleux, 1983.

———. "La médiation de l'habitude." *Les Études philosophiques* 4 (October–December 1984): 467–79.

———. "Philosophie et spiritualité." In *Dictionnaire de spiritualité, ascétique et mystique, doctrine et histoire*, 1377–85. Paris: Beauchesne, 1984.

———. "Sedet ad dexteram Patris." *Communio* 9, no. 1 (1984): 5–9.

———. "Il reviendra dans la gloire." *Communio* 10, no. 1 (1985): 4–6.

———. "La prière du chrétien." *Communio* 10, no. 4 (1985): 4–6.

———. "A quoi bon la politique?" *L'enjeu-France* 2 (1986): 56–57.

———. "Dialectique de l'action et preuve ontologique." *Revue philosophique de la France et de l'étranger* 4 (1986): 425–33.

———. "L'être de l'esprit et l'Esprit-Saint." *Communio* 11, no. 1 (1986): 70–75.

———. "Gabriel Marcel-Gaston Fessard. Correspondance (1934–1971)." *Archives de Philosophie* 49, no. 3 (1986): 497–98.

———. "Maurice Blondel (1861–1949)." *Revue philosophique* 4 (1986): 421–33.

———. "Réflexions d'un philosophe." In *Des motifs d'espérer? La procréation artificielle*, edited by Emmanuel Hirsch, 71–82. Paris: Cerf, 1986.

———. "L'être de l'esprit." In *L'univers philosophique*, edited by André Jacob, 34–38. Paris: PUF, 1987.

———. "Idéologie et spiritualité." *Giornale di Metafisica*, n.s., 9 (1987): 227–36.

Secondary Sources

Abitando la Trinità: Per un rinnovamento dell'ontologia. Edited by Piero Coda and L'ubomír Zák. Rome: Città Nuova, 1998.

Adam, Michel. "Claude Bruaire, L'être et l'esprit." *Revue philosophique* 2 (1984): 247–51.

Andresen, Carl. "Zur Entstehung und Geschichte des trinitarischen Personbegriffs." *Zeitschrift für Neutestamentliche Wissenschaft* 52 (1961): 1–39.

Anselm. *S. Anselmi Cantuariensis archiepiscopi opera omnia.* 6 vols. Stuttgart: F. Frommann, 1984.

Aquinas, St. Thomas. *Scriptum Super Libros Sententiarum: Magistri Petri Lombardi Episcopi Parisiensis,* Vols. 1 and 2. Paris: P. Lethielleux, 1929.

———. *Quaestiones Disputatae De Potentia Dei.* In *Opera Omnia.* Editio Leonina, 1882 ss. Turin: Marietti, 1931.

———. *Scriptum Super Sententiis: Magistri Petri Lombardi,* Vol. III. Paris: P. Lethielleux, 1933.

———. *Scriptum Super Sententiis: Magistri Petri Lombardi,* Vol. IV. Paris: P. Lethielleux, 1947.

———. *De Ente et Essentia.* Turin: Marietti, 1948.

———. *In Duodecim Libros Metaphysicorum Aristotelis Expositio.* Edited by M. R. Cathala. Turin: Marietti, 1950.

———. *Summa Contra Gentiles.* In *Opera Omnia.* Editio Leonina, 1882 ss. Turin: Marietti, 1961.

———. *Summa Theologiae.* In *Opera Omnia.* Editio Leonina, 1882 ss. Turin: Marietti, 1962–1963.

———. *Quaestiones Disputatae De Veritate.* In *Opera Omnia.* Editio Leonina, 1882 ss. Turin: Marietti, 1964.

———. *Super Dionysium: De divinis nominibus.* In *Opera Omnia.* Turin: Marietti, 1972.

Aristotle. *Metaphysica.* Edited and translated by William D. Ross. *The Works of Aristotle,* vol. 8. Oxford: The Clarendon Press, 1928.

———. *Analytica Posteriora.* Translated by G. R. G. Mure. *The Works of Aristotle,* vol. 1. William D. Ross, gen. ed. London: Oxford University Press, 1955.

———. *Analytica Priora.* Translated by A. J. Jenkinson. *The Works of Aristotle,* vol. 1. William D. Ross, gen. ed. London: Oxford University Press, 1955.

———. *Categoriae and De Interpretatione.* Translated by E. M. Edghill. *The Works of Aristotle,* vol. 1. William D. Ross, gen. ed. London: Oxford University Press, 1955.

———. *Topica and the Sophisticis Elenchis.* Translated by W. A. Pickard. *The Works of Aristotle,* vol. 1. William D. Ross, gen. ed. London: Oxford University Press, 1955.

Aubenque, Pierre. *Le problème de l'être chez Aristotle: Essai sur la problématique aristotélicienne.* Paris: PUF, 1962.

Augustinus, Aurelius S. *De Civitate Dei Libri XXII.* Corpus Christianorum. Series Latina, vol. 47. Edited by B. Dombart and A. Kalb. Turnhout: Typographi Brepols, 1955.

————. *De Vera Religione.* Corpus Christianorum. Series Latina, vol. 32. Edited by K. D. Daur, 169–260. Turnhout: Typographi Brepols, 1962.

————. *De Trinitate Libri XV.* Corpus Christianorum. Series Latina, vol. 50. Edited by W. J. Mountain and F. Gloire. Turnhout: Typographi Brepols, 1968.

————. *Confessionum.* Corpus Christianorum. Series Latina, vol. 27. Edited by Lucas Verheijen. Turnhout: Typographi Brepols, 1981.

Ayer, Alfred J. *Language, Truth, and Logic.* New York: Dover Publications, 1952.

Berry, Christopher J. *Hume, Hegel, and Human Nature.* The Hague: Martinus Nijhoff, 1982.

Bertuletti, Angelo. "Il concetto di esperienza nel dibattito fondamentale della teologia contemporanea." *Teologia* 5 (1980): 283–341.

————. "La problematizzazione e la rifondazione della metafisica nell'idealismo specualtivo e il dibattito teologico contemporaneo." *La Scuola Cattolica* 1 (1990): 68–89.

————. "L'assolutezza della verità e l'evidenza della fede." *Teologia* 6 (1991): 31–52.

————. " L'Europa e il cristianesimo. Fede e modernità." In *Il caso Europa,* edited by Giuseppe Colombo, 59–65. Milan: Glossa, 1991.

Birault, Henri. "Existence et vérité d'après Heidegger." *Revue de métaphysique et de morale* 35, no. 1 (1951): 139–91.

Blondel, Maurice. *La philosophie et l'esprit chrétienne.* Paris: PUF, 1944–46.

————. *L'action* (1893). Paris: Quadrige/PUF, 1993.

Bobil, Joseph. "Aquinas on *Communication,* the Foundation of Friendship and *Caritas.*" *Modern Schoolman* 64 (November 1986): 1–18.

Bonaventure. *Breviloquium.* Paris: Éditions Franciscaines, 1967–68.

————. *Collationes in Hexaemeron.* Vol. 5 of *The Works of Bonaventure.* Translated by José de Vinck. New York: St. Anthony Guild Press, 1970.

————. *Journey of the Mind to God.* Translated by Philotheus Boehner. Edited by Stephen F. Brown. Indianapolis: Hackett Publishing Company, 1993.

Borne, Étienne. *Le problème du mal.* Paris: PUF, 1958.

Boss, Marc. "Jacques Derrida et l'événement du don." *Revue de théologie et de philosophie* 128 (1996): 113–26.

Bourg, Dominique. *L'être et Dieu: Travaux du C.E.R.I.T.* Edited by Henri Vergote. Paris: Cerf, 1986.

Bourgeois, Bernard. *Éternité et historicité de l'Esprit selon Hegel.* Paris: J. Vrin, 1991.

Boutang, Pierre. *Ontologie du secret.* Paris: Quadrige/PUF, 1988.

Brague, Rémi. "Comme quoi le bon Dieu ne se donne pas sans confession." In *La confession de la foi chrétienne,* edited by Claude Bruaire, 305–16. Paris: Communio/Fayard, 1977.

Bréhier, Emile. "La notion de la philosophie chrétienne." *Bulletin de la société française de philosophie* 31 (1931): 37–39.

————. "Y-a-t-il une philosophie chrétienne?" *Revue de métaphysique et de morale* 38, no. 2 (1931): 133–62.

Brito, Emilio. *Hegel et la tâche actuelle de la christologie.* Paris: Lethielleux, 1979.

————. *La christologie de Hegel: Verbum Crucis.* Paris: Beauchesne, 1983.

————. *La création selon Schelling.* Leuven: Leuven University Press and Peeters, 1987.

Brun, Jean. "La pensée de Hegel selon Claude Bruaire." *Les Études philosophiques* 3 (1988): 309–13.

Brunner, August. *Dreifaltigkeit. Personale Zugänge zum Geheimnis.* Einsiedeln: Johannes Verlag, 1976.

Brunvoll, Arve. *"Gott ist Mensch" Die Luther-Rezeption Ludwig Feuerbachs und die Entwicklung seiner Religionskritik.* Frankfurt: Peter Lang, 1996.

Buckley, Michael. *At the Origin of Modern Atheism.* New Haven: Yale University Press, 1990.

Bufo, Giuseppe. "Claude Bruaire: La Raison Politique." *Revue philosophique* 4 (1976): 451–53.

Bulgakov, Sergei. *Le Paraclet.* Translated by Constantin Andronikov. Paris: Aubier, 1946.

Bussanich, John. "Plotinus's Metaphysics of the One." In *The Cambridge Companion to Plotinus,* edited by Lloyd P. Gerson, 38–65. Cambridge: Cambridge University Press, 1996.

Cabada Castro, Manuel. *Sein und Gott bei Gustav Siewerth.* Düsseldorf: Patmos, 1971.

———. "Del 'indeterminado' griego al 'verdadero infinito' hegeliano. Reflexiones sobre la relación finitud-infinitud." *Pensamiento* 28 (1972): 321–45.

———. *El humanismo premarxista de Ludwig Feuerbach.* Madrid: BAC, 1975.

Camisasca, Massimo. *Persona e famiglia: Riflessioni.* Milan: Jaca Book, 1998.

Cantone, Carlo. "Dio, l'Essere' e il 'volto.'" *Rivista internazionale di filosofia* 31 (1988): 151–69.

Capánaga, Victorino. "Interpretación agustiniana del amor. Eros y Agape." *Augustinus* 18 (1973): 213–78.

Caputo, John D. "Meister Eckhart and the Later Heidegger: The Mystical Element in Heidegger's Thought. Part One." *Journal of the History of Philosophy* 12 (1974): 479–94.

———. "Meister Eckhart and the Later Heidegger: The Mystical Element in Heidegger's Thought. Part Two." *Journal of the History of Philosophy* 13 (1975): 61–80.

———. "Heidegger's 'Dif-ference' and the Distinction Between *Esse* and *Ens* in St. Thomas." *International Philosophical Quarterly* 20 (1980): 161–81.

———. "Apostles of the Impossible: On God and the Gift in Derrida and Marion." In *God, the Gift, and Postmodernism,* edited by John D. Caputo and Michael J. Scanlon, 185–222. Bloomington: Indiana University Press, 1999.

Carnap, Rudolf. *The Logical Structure of the World: Pseudoproblems in Philosophy.* Translated by Rolf A. George. Berkeley: University of California Press, 1967.

Chapelle, Albert. *Hegel et la religion.* 3 vols. Paris: Éditions Universitaires, 1964–67.

———. "L'itinéraire philosophique de Claude Bruaire: De Hegel à la métaphysique." *Revue philosophique* 1 (1990): 5–12.

———. "Présence de Hegel en France: G. Fessard et Cl. Bruaire." *Revue philosophique* 1 (1990): 13–26.

Chenu, Marie-Dominique. *Nature, Man, and Society in the Twelfth Century.* Translated by Jerome Taylor and Lester K. Little. Toronto: University of Toronto Press, 1997.

Chrétien, Jean-Louis. "Le Bien donne ce qu'il n'a pas." *Archives de philosophie* 43 (1980): 263–77.

Clarke, Norris W. "Person, Being, and St. Thomas." *Communio* 19 (Winter 1992): 601–18.

———. *Person and Being.* Milwaukee: Marquette University Press, 1993.

———. "Response to David Schindler's Comments." *Communio* 20 (Fall 1993): 593–98.

Coda, Piero. *Il negativo e la Trinità: Impotesi su Hegel.* Rome: Città Nuova, 1987.

Colette, Jacques. "Bulletin de philosophie contemporaine." *Revue des sciences philosophiques et théologiques* 49 (1965): 705–19.

———. "La manifestation phénoménologique de l'absolu." *Revue des sciences philosophiques et théologiques* 80 (1996): 23–34.

Colombo, Giuseppe. "La ragione teologica." In *L'evidenza e la fede,* edited by Giuseppe Colombo, 7–20. Milan, 1988.

Courtine, Jean-François. *Suárez et le système métaphysique.* Paris: PUF, 1990.

Cugno, Alain. "Le désir de Dieu dans *L'affirmation de Dieu* de Claude Bruaire." *Revue philosophique* 1 (1990): 27–33.

———. "Bible et philosophies contemporaines du corps." In *La Bible en philosophie: Approches contemporaines,* edited by Dominique Bourg and Antoine Lion, 145–62. Paris: Cerf, 1993.

Daigler, Matthew A. "Heidegger and von Balthasar: A Lover's Quarrel Over Beauty and Divinity." *American Catholic Philosophical Quarterly* 69, no. 2 (1995): 375–94.

De Lubac, Henri. *Sur les chemins de Dieu.* Paris: Aubier, 1956.

———. "Ludwig Feuerbach, Protagonist of Atheist Humanism." In *Theologians Today,* edited by Martin Redfern, 63–88. London and New York: Sheed and Ward, 1972.

———. "On Christian Philosophy." *Communio* 19 (Winter 1992): 478–506.

———. *The Drama of Atheist Humanism.* Translated by Edith M. Riley and Anne E. Nash. San Francisco: Ignatius Press, 1995.

Della Mirandola, Pico. *On the Dignity of Man.* Translated by Charles G. Wallis. Indianapolis: Hackett Publishing Company, 1998.

Derrida, Jacques. *La voix et le phénomène: Introduction au probleme du signe dans la phénoménologie de Husserl.* Paris: Quadrige/PUF, 1967.

———. *Marges de la philosophie.* Paris: Les Éditions de Minuit, 1972.

———. *La question de l'esprit.* Paris: Galilée, 1987.

———. *La fausse monnaie.* Vol. 1 of *Donner le Temps.* Paris: Galilée, 1991.

———. "Donner la mort." In *L'éthique du don. Jacques Derrida et la pensée du don,* edited by Jean-Michel Rabaté and Michael Wetzel, 11–108. Paris: Métailié-Transition, 1992.

Descartes, René. *Méditations métaphysiques.* Paris: Garnier-Flammarion, 1992.

Doz, André. "Les sens du mot 'absolu' chez Hegel." *Revue des sciences philosophiques et théologiques* 80 (1996): 5–11.

Dubarle, Dominique. "Absolu et histoire dans la philosophie de Hegel." In *Hegel et la théologie contemporaine: L'absolu dans l'histoire,* 99–123. Neuchâtel: Delachaux & Niestle, 1977.

———. *Dieu avec l'être: De Parménide à Saint Thomas. Essai d'ontologie théologale.* Paris: Beauchesne, 1986.

Elders, Leo J. *The Metaphysics of Being of St. Thomas Aquinas in a Historical Perspective.* Leiden-New York: E. J. Brill, 1993.

Emery, Gilles. *La Trinité créatrice: Trinité et création dans les commentaires aux Sentences de Thomas d'Aquin.* Paris: J. Vrin, 1995.

———. "Essentialisme ou personnalisme dans le traité de Dieu chez saint Thomas d'Aquin?" *Revue Thomiste* 98 (1998): 5–38.

Engels, Frederick. "Ludwig Feuerbach and the End of Classical German Philosophy." In *Marx and Frederick Engels: Selected Works in Two Volumes,* 324–64. London: Lawrence and Wishart, 1950.

Fabro, Cornelio. *Tra Kierkegaard e Marx: Per una definizione dell'esistenza.* Florence: Valecchi Editori, 1952.

———. *L'assoluto nell'esistenzialismo.* Catania: Guido Miano Editore, 1954.

———. *Partecipazione e causalità secondo S. Tommaso d'Aquino.* Turin: Società Editrice Internazionale, 1958.

———. "Dall'essere di Aristotele allo *esse* di Tommaso." In *Mélanges offerts à Étienne Gilson de l'Académie française,* 227–47. Toronto: Pontifical Institute of Mediaeval Studies, 1959.

———. *Introduzione all'ateismo moderno.* Rome: Editrice Studium, 1964.

Fackenheim, Emil L. *The Religious Dimension in Hegel's Thought.* Bloomington: Indiana University Press, 1967.

Fessard, Gaston. *La dialectique des "Exercices spirituels" de Saint Ignace de Loyola.* 3 vols. Paris: Aubier, 1956–84.

Feuerbach, Ludwig. *The Essence of Christianity.* Translated by George Eliot. New York: Harper & Row, 1957.

———. *The Essence of Faith According to Luther.* Translated by Melvin Cherno. New York: Harper & Row, 1967.

———. *Lectures on the Essence of Religion.* Translated by Ralph Manheim. New York: Harper & Row, 1967.

———. *Vorlesungen über das Wesen der Religion.* Gesammelte Werke, vol. 6. Berlin: Akademie Verlag, 1967.

———. *Das Wesen des Christentums.* Gesammelte Werke, vol. 5. Berlin: Akademie Verlag, 1973.

Fichte, Johann G. *Schriften zur Wissenschaftslehre.* Vol. 1 of *Werke.* Edited by Wilhelm G. Jacobs. Frankfurt: Deutscher Klassiker Verlag, 1997.

Filoni, Fernando. "Claude Bruaire. La ricerca ontologica e l'affermazione di Dio." *Aquinas* 28, no. 3 (September–December 1985): 301–69.

Findlay, John N. *Hegel: A Re-examination.* New York: Oxford University Press, 1958.

Forte, Bruno. *Trinità come storia.* Cinisello Balsamo, Milan: Edizione Paoline, 1985.

Frogé, E.-C. "Le droit tient-il l'éthique en l'état?" *Les Études philosophiques* 3 (1988): 358–64.

Gadamer, Hans G. *Philosophical Hermeneutics.* Translated by David E. Linge. Berkeley: University of California Press, 1977.

Galindo Rodrigo, José Antonio. "El amor cristiano en su perspectiva de gratuidad según San Agustín." *Augustinus* 42 (1997): 297–319.

García Baró, Miguel. "La filosofía primera de Edmund Husserl en torno a 1900." *Diánoia* (1986): 41–69.

———. *Vida y mundo. La práctica de la fenomenología.* Madrid: Trotta, 1999.

Gatti, Maria L. *Plotino e la metafisica della contemplazione.* Milan: Vita e Pensiero, 1996.

Gély, Raphaël. "Bibliographie de Claude Bruaire." *Revue philosophique* 1 (1990): 89–93.

Gilbert, Paul. "Pour une métaphysique réflexive." *Gregorianum* 69, no. 1 (1988): 77–116.

———. "L'acte d'être: un don." *Science et Esprit* 41, no. 3 (1989): 265–86.

———. "Substance et présence. Derrida et Marion, critiques de Husserl." *Gregorianum* 75, no. 1 (1994): 95–133.

Gilson, Étienne. *L'être et l'essence.* Paris: J. Vrin, 1948.

———. *Jean Duns Scot: Introduction à ses positions fondamentales.* Paris: J. Vrin, 1952.

———. "God and Philosophy." In *A Gilson Reader,* edited by Anton C. Pegis, 170–211. New York: Doubleday/Image, 1957.

———. "What is Christian Philosophy?" In *A Gilson Reader,* edited by Anton C. Pegis, 38–73. New York: Doubleday/Image, 1957.

Giussani, Luigi. *Il senso di Dio e l'uomo moderno: La "questione umana" e la novità del cristianesimo.* Milan: BUR, 1994.

God, The Gift, and Postmodernism. Edited by John D. Caputo and Michael J. Scanlon. Bloomington: Indiana University Press, 1999.

Godbout, Jacques. *L'esprit du don.* Paris: La decouverte, 1992.

Godelier, Maurice. *L'énigme du don.* Paris: Fayard, 1996.

Grenier, Hubert. "La pensée politique de Claude Bruaire." *Les Études philosophiques* 3 (1988): 339–45.

Greshake, Gisbert. *Der dreieine Gott.* Freiburg: Herder, 1997.

Grimaldi, Nicolas. "L'être et l'esprit." *Revue de métaphysique et de morale* 89, no. 3 (1984): 427–30.

Grodin, Jean. "Réflexions sur la différence ontologique." *Les Études philosophiques* 3 (1984): 337–47.

Guibal, Francis. "Cultural Significations and Ethical Sense: On Emmanuel Levinas." *Graduate Faculty Philosophical Journal* 20–21, nos. 1–2 (1998): 189–218.

Guthrie, William K. C. *Aristotle: An Encounter.* Vol. 6 of *A History of Greek Philosophy.* Cambridge: Cambridge University Press, 1981.

Harris, Henry S. *Hegel: Phenomenology and System.* Indianapolis: Hackett Publishing Company, 1995.

Hegel, Georg W. F. *Die Philosophie Platons.* Stuttgart: Verlag Freies Geistesleben, 1962.

———. *Science of Logic.* Translated by A. V. Miller. New York: Humanities Press, 1969.

———. *Logic.* Translated by William Wallace. 2nd ed. Oxford: Clarendon Press, 1974.

———. *Phenomenology of Spirit.* Translated by A. V. Miller. Oxford: Oxford University Press, 1977.

———. *Lectures on the Philosophy of Religion.* Translated by R. F. Brown, P. C. Hodgson, and J. M. Steward. Edited by Peter Hodgson. 3 vols. Berkeley: University of California Press, 1984–85.

———. *Vorlesungen über die Geschichte der Philosophie.* Edited by Walter Jaeschke. 4 vols. Hamburg: Felix Meiner Verlag, 1984–87.

———. *Vorlesungen über die Philosophie der Religion.* Vols. 16–17 of *Werke.* Frankfurt am Main: Suhrkamp, 1995–96.

———. *Hauptwerke.* 6 vols. Hamburg: Felix Meiner Verlag, 1999.

Heidegger, Martin. *Über den Humanismus.* Frankfurt: M. V. Klostermann, 1949.

———. *An Introduction to Metaphysics.* Translated by Ralph Manheim. New Haven: Yale University Press, 1975.

———. *Being and Time.* Translated by Joan Stambaugh. New York: State University of New York Press, 1996.

———. *Identität und Differenz.* Stuttgart: Neske, 1999.

Hemmerle, Klaus. *Thesen zu einer trinitarischen Ontologie.* Einsieldeln: Johannes Verlag, 1976.

Henry, Michel. *Voir l'invisible: Sur Kandinsky.* Paris: F. Bourin, 1988.

———. *L'essence de la manifestation.* Paris: PUF, 1990.

———. *C'est moi la vérité.* Paris: Seuil, 1996.

Hirsch, Emmanuel. "Éthique et médicine dans la pensée de Claude Bruaire." *Les Études philosophiques* 3 (1988): 347–57.

Hösle, Vittorio. *Hegels Systems: Der Idealismus der Subjektivität und das Problem der Intersubjektivität.* Hamburg: Felix Meiner Verlag, 1988.

Hume, David. *An Enquiry Concerning Human Understanding.* Oxford: Clarendon Press, 2000.

Husserl, Edmund. *Ideen zu einer reinen Phänomenologie und phänomenologische Philosophie.* Vol. 5 of *Gesammelte Schriften.* Hamburg: Felix Meiner Verlag, 1992.

Hyppolite, Jean. *Genèse et structure de la "Phénoménologie de l'esprit" de Hegel.* Paris: Aubier, 1946.

———. *Logique et existence. Essai sur la logique de Hegel.* Paris: PUF, 1953.

———. *Logic and Existence.* Translated by Leonard Lawlor and Amit Sen. New York: State University of New York Press, 1997.

Incardona, Nunzio. "L'ontodologie di Claude Bruaire." *Giornale di Metafisica,* n.s., 6 (1984): 397–409.

Janicaud, Dominique. *Le tournant théologique de la phénoménologie française.* Paris: L'Éclat, 1991.

John Paul II. *Veritatis Splendor.* Rome, 1978.

———. *Dominum et Vivificantem.* Rome, 1986.

———. *Fides et Ratio.* Rome, 1998.

Kainz, Howard P. *Paradox, Dialectic and System: A Contemporary Reconstruction of the Hegelian Problematic.* University Park: Pennsylvania State University Press, 1988.

———. *G. W. F. Hegel: The Philosophical System.* New York: Twayne Publishers, 1996.

Kant, Immanuel. *Kritik der reinen Vernunft.* Leipzig: F. Meiner, 1922.
———. *Critique of Pure Reason.* Translated by Norman K. Smith. New York: St. Martin's Press, 1965.
Kaplan, Francis. "Philosophie du corps, par Claude Bruaire." *Revue de métaphysique et de morale* 74, no. 1 (1969): 118–22.
———. "Le problème de la mort dans la philosophie de Claude Bruaire." *Les Études philosophiques* 3 (1988): 329–38.
———. "Le Dieu de Claude Bruaire." *Revue philosophique* 1 (1990): 34–45.
Kemp, Peter. "L'Éthique au lendemain des victoires des athéismes. Réflexions sur la philosophie de Jacques Derrida." *Revue de théologie et de philosophie* 111 (1979): 105–21.
Kimmerle, Hans. "Différence et contradiction." *Tijlschrift voor Filosofie* 43 (1981): 510–37.
Kojève, Alexandre. *Introduction à la lecture de Hegel.* Paris: Gallimard, 1947.
Kosky, Jeffrey L. "The Disqualification of Intentionality: The Gift in Derrida, Levinas, and Michel Henry." *Philosophy Today* 41 (1997): 186–97.
Kühn, Rolf. "Les présupposés métaphysiques de la 'lisibilité' de l'être. Examen critique de 'la lecture dé-créative' chez Simone Weil." *Archives de philosophie* 54 (1991): 43–64.
———. *Französische Reflexions und Geistesphilosophie.* Frankfurt: Anton Hain, 1993.
———. "Bedürfen und Vorstellungsdestruktion." *Gregorianum* 76, no. 2 (1995): 323–42.
Kyungu Ilunga, Pascal. "La liberté comme sens du politique. Reflexion critique sur la pensée politique de Claude Bruaire." Ph.D. diss., Pontificia Università Gregoriana, 1996.
Lafont, Ghislain. *Peut-on connaître Dieu en Jésus Christ?* Paris: Cerf, 1969.
———. "Mystique de la Croix et question de l'être. A propos d'un livre récent de Jean-Luc Marion." *Revue théologique de Louvain* 10 (1979): 259–304.
———. "Écouter Heidegger en théologien." *Revue des sciences philosophiques et théologiques* 67 (1983): 371–98.
———. *Dieu, le temps, et l'être.* Paris: Cerf, 1986.
Lamb, David. *Hegel—From Foundation to System.* The Hague: Martinus Nijhoff, 1980.
Lamb, Matthew L. "Divine Transcendence and Eternity." In *Continuity and Plurality in Catholic Theology,* edited by Anthony J. Cernera, 77–106. Fairfield, Conn.: Sacred Heart University Press, 1998.
———. "Eternity and Time." In *Gladly to Learn and Gladly to Teach: Essays on Religion and Political Philosophy in Honor of Ernest L. Fortin,* edited by Michael Foley and David Kries, 195–214. Lanham, Md.: Lexington Books, 2002.
Le Guillou, Marie-Joseph. *Le mystère du Père.* Paris: Fayard, 1973.
Le Lannou, Jean Michel. "La conversion à la substantialité." *Revue philosophique* 1 (1990): 59–69.
Leduc-Fayette, Denise. "Claude Bruaire, 1932–1986." *Revue philosophique* 1 (1987): 5–19.
———. "Désir et destin." *Les Études philosophiques* 3 (1988): 289–300.
———. "Du retour à l'origine." *Revue philosophique* 1 (1990): 47–57.

Leibniz, Gottfried W. *Discourses on Metaphysics: Correspondence with Arnauld and Monadology.* Translated by George R. Montgomery. 2nd ed. Chicago: Open Court Publishing House, 1962.

Leroux, Gilles. *Plotin. Traité sur la liberté et la volonté de l'Un (Enneáde VI, 8).* Paris: J. Vrin, 1990.

Lessing, Gotthold E. *Lessing's Theological Writings.* Edited by Henry Chadwick. Stanford, Calif.: Stanford University Press, 1997.

Léonard, André. *La foi chez Hegel.* Paris: Desclée de Brouwer, 1970.

———. "La structure du système hégélien." *Revue philosophique de Louvain* 69, no. 4 (1971): 495–524.

———. "Comment lire Hegel?" *Revue philosophique de Louvain* 70, no. 8 (1972): 573–86.

———. *Commentaire littéral de la logique de Hegel.* Paris-Louvain: J. Vrin, 1974.

———. *Pensées des hommes et foi en Jésus-Christ. Pour un discernement intellectuel chrétien.* Paris: P. Lethielleux, 1980.

Locke, John. *An Essay Concerning Human Understanding.* Amherst, N.Y.: Prometheus Books, 1995.

Lonergan, Bernard. *Verbum: Word and Idea in Aquinas.* Edited by Frederick Crowe and Robert M. Doran. Toronto: Toronto University Press, 1997.

Lossky, Vladimir. *Essai sur la théologie mystique de l'Église d'Orient.* Paris: Aubier, 1944.

López Triana, Antonio. "*El ser y el espíritu* o la ontología como donación." *Revista Española de Teología* 61, no. 2 (2001): 149–71.

Malet, A. *Personne et amour dans la théologie trinitaire de Saint Thomas d'Aquin.* Paris: J. Vrin, 1956.

Marcel, Gabriel. *Journal métaphysique.* Paris: Gallimard, 1927.

———. *Position et approches concrètes du mystère ontologique.* Paris: Desclée de Brouwer, 1933.

———. *Essai de philosophie concrète.* Paris: Gallimard, 1940.

———. "Schelling, fut-il un précurseur de la philosophie de l'existence?" *Revue de métaphysique et de morale* 63, no. 1 (1957): 72–78.

———. *Coleridge et Schelling.* Paris: Aubier, 1971.

———. "Esquisse d'une phénoménologie de l'avoir." In *Être et avoir,* 111–25. Paris: Éditions Universitaires, 1991.

———. *Être et avoir.* Paris: Éditions Universitaires, 1991.

———. *Le mystère de l'être.* Paris: Association Présence de Gabriel Marcel, 1997.

Marengo, Gilfredo. *Trinità e creazione.* Rome: Città Nuova, 1990.

Marinelli, Francesco. *Personalismo trinitario nella storia della salvezza. Rapporti tra la SS.ma Trinitá e le opere ad extra nello Scriptum super Sententiis di San Tommaso.* Rome: Libreria editrice PUL, 1969.

Marion, Jean-Luc. *L'idole et la distance: Cinque études.* Paris: Grasset, 1977.

———. *Dieu sans l'être.* Paris: Quadrige/PUF, 1982.

———. *Réduction et donation: Recherches sur Hegel, Heidegger et la phénoménologie.* Paris: PUF, 1989.

———. "L'argument relève-t-il de l'ontologie?" *Archivio di filosofia* 58, nos. 1–3 (1990): 43–69.

———. *Étant donné: Essai d'une phénoménologie de la donation.* Paris: PUF, 1998.
———. "A Note Concerning the Ontological Indifference." *Graduate Faculty Philosophical Journal* 20–21, no. 1–2 (1998): 25–40.
———. "L'événement, le phénomène et le révélé." *Transversalites* (1999): 4–25.
———. *De surcroît.* Paris: PUF, 2001.
Maritain, Jacques. *De la philosophie chrétienne.* Paris: Desclée de Brouwer, 1933.
Marquet, Jean-François. "Le philosophe devant le mystère de la Trinitè." *Les Études philosophiques* 3 (1988): 323–27.
———. "Corps et subjectivité chez Claude Bruaire." *Revue philosophique* 1 (1990): 71–78.
———. "Singularité et absolu dans la philosophie de Hegel." *Revue des sciences philosophiques et théologiques* 80 (1995): 45–57.
Martis, John. "Thomistic *Esse*—Idol or Icon? Jean-Luc Marion's God Without Being." *Pacifica* 9 (February 1996): 55–68.
Marx, Karl. "Theses on Feuerbach." In *Karl Marx and Frederick Engels: Selected Works in Two Volumes,* 365–67. London: Lawrence and Wishart, 1950.
Mattheeuws, Alain. *Les "dons" du mariage: Recherche de théologie morale et sacramentelle.* Brussels: Culture et vérité, 1996.
Maurer, Armand. *The Philosophy of William of Ockham in the Light of Its Principles.* Toronto: Pontifical Institute of Mediaeval Studies, 1999.
Mauss, Marcel. "Essai sur le don." In *Sociologie et anthropologie,* 145–279. Paris: Quadrige/PUF, 1999.
McCarthy, Donald. "Marcel's Absolute Thou." *Philosophy Today* 10 (1966): 175–81.
McCord Adams, Marilyn. *William Ockham.* 2 vols. Notre Dame, Ind.: University of Notre Dame Press, 1987.
Melchiorre, Virgilio. *La differenza e l'origine.* Milan: Vita e Pensiero, 1987.
Melina, Livio. *Sharing in Christ's Virtues: For a Renewal of Moral Theology in Light of Veritatis Splendor.* Translated by William E. May. Washington, D.C.: Catholic University of America Press, 2001.
Michalson, Gordon E. "Theology, Historical Knowledge, and the Contingency-Necessity Distinction." *International Journal for Philosophy of Religion* 14 (1983): 87–98.
———. "Faith and History: The Shape of the Problem." *Modern Theology* 1, no. 4 (1985): 277–90.
Milbank, John. "Can a Gift Be Given? Prolegomena to a Future Trinitarian Metaphysics." *Modern Theology* 11, no. 1 (1995): 119–61.
———. *The Word Made Strange: Theology, Language, Culture.* Cambridge, Mass.: Blackwell Publishers, 1997.
Mill, John S. *Utilitarianism.* Oxford: Oxford University Press, 1998.
———. *On Liberty.* Orchard Park, N.Y.: Broadview Press, 1999.
Millán Puelles, Antonio. *Léxico filosófico.* Madrid: Rialp, 1984.
Murat, Jean. "Éthique et chirurgie." *Les Études philosophiques* 3 (1988): 365–70.
Müller, Max. *Existenzphilosophie im geistigen Leben der Gegenwart.* Heidelberg: F. H. Kerle, 1949.
Nédoncelle, Maurice. "Prosopon et persona dans l'antiquité classique." *Revue des sciences religieuses* 22 (1948): 277–99.

———. *Existe-t-il une philosophie chrétienne?* Paris: Fayard, 1956.

Olivier, Paul. "Claude Bruaire: L'être et l'esprit." *Revue des sciences religieuses* 77 (1989): 603–8.

Owens, Joseph. *The Doctrine of Being in the Aristotelian Metaphysics.* Toronto: Pontifical Institute of Mediaeval Studies, 1978.

O'Regan, Cyril. *The Heterodox Hegel.* New York: State University of New York Press, 1994.

O'Rourke, Fran. "The Gift of Being: Heidegger and Aquinas." In *At the Heart of the Real: Philosophical Essays in Honor of Dr. Desmond Connell, Archbishop of Dublin,* edited by Fran O'Rourke, 309–38. Blackrock: Irish Academic, 1992.

O'Shea, Kevin F. "Divinization: A Study in Theological Analogy." *The Thomist* 29, no. 1 (1965): 1–45.

Palacios, Juan Miguel. *El idealismo transcendental: Teoría de la verdad.* Madrid: Gredos, 1979.

Pannenberg, Wolfhart. *Christianity in a Secularized World.* New York: Crossroad, 1989.

Pelloux, Luigi. *L'assoluto nella dottrina di Plotino.* Milan: Vita e Pensiero, 1994.

Pieper, Joseph. *"Divine Madness": Plato's Case Against Secular Humanism.* Translated by Lothar Kraut. San Francisco: Ignatius Press, 1995.

Plato. *The Dialogues of Plato.* Translated by Reginald E. Allen. 4 vols. New Haven: Yale University Press, 1984.

———. *The Republic of Plato.* Translated by Allan Bloom. New York: Basic Books, 1991.

Plotinus. *The Enneads.* Translated by Stephen MacKenna. New York: Larson Publications, 1992.

Pompa, Leon. *Human Nature and Historical Knowledge: Hume, Hegel, and Vico.* Cambridge: Cambridge University Press, 1990.

Pope Leo XIII. "Aeterni Patris. On the Restoration of Christian Philosophy." In *The Church Speaks to the Modern World: The Social Teaching of Leo XIII,* edited by Étienne Gilson, 29–54. New York: Doubleday/Image, 1954.

Prades López, Javier. *Deus specialiter est in sanctis per gratiam. El misterio de la inhabitación de la Trinidad en los escritos de Santo Tomás.* Rome: PUG, 1993.

———. "De la Trinidad económica a la Trinidad inmanente. A propósito de un principio de renovación de la teología trinitaria." *Revista española de teología* 58, no. 3 (1998): 285–344.

Prestige, George K. *God in Patristic Thought.* London: S.P.C.K., 1981.

Protevi, John. *"Given Time* and the Gift of Life." *Man and World* 30 (1997): 65–82.

Pseudo-Dionysius. *The Complete Works.* Translated by Colm Luibheid. New York: Paulist Press, 1987.

Rahner, Karl. *Hearers of the Word.* Translated by Michael Richards. New York: Herder and Herder, 1969.

———. *Foundations of Christian Faith: An Introduction to the Idea of Christianity.* Translated by William V. Dych. New York: Crossroad, 1982.

Ratzinger, Joseph. "Concerning the Notion of Person in Theology." *Communio* 17 (Fall 1990): 439–53.

Ravaisson, Félix. *De l'habitude: Métaphysique et morale.* Paris: Quadrige/PUF, 1999.

Reale, Giovanni. "I fondamenti della metafisica di Plotino e la struttura della processione." In *Graceful Reason: Essays in Ancient and Medieval Philosophy Presented to Joseph Owens, CSSR,* edited by Lloyd P. Gerson, 153–75. Toronto: Pontifical Institute of Mediaeval Studies, 1983.

Renaud, Michel. "La *Philosophie du corps* selon M. Claude Bruaire." *Revue philosophique de Louvain* 67, no. 1 (1969): 104–42.

Ricoeur, Paul. *Philosophie de la volonté.* 2 vols. Paris: Aubier, 1960.

———. *The Conflict of Interpretations.* Edited by Don Ihde. Evanston, Ill.: Northwestern University Press, 1974.

———. *Temps et récit.* Paris: Nabert, 1983.

———. *Le mal. Un défi à la philosophie et à la théologie.* Paris: Labor et Fides, 1996.

Rist, John M. *Plotinus: The Road to Reality.* Cambridge: Cambridge University Press, 1967.

Rosenkranz, Karl. *Georg Wilhelm Friedrich Hegels Leben.* Darmstadt: Wissenschaftliche Buchgesellschaft, 1971.

Ross, William D. *Aristotle's Metaphysics.* Oxford: Clarendon Press, 1924.

Rotenstreich, Nathan. *From Substance to Subject: Studies in Hegel.* The Hague: Martinus Nijhoff, 1974.

Rousselot, Pierre. "Amour spirituel et synthèse aperceptive." *Revue de philosophie* 16 (March 1910): 225–40.

———. "L'être et l'esprit." *Revue de philosophie* 16 (June 1910): 561–74.

———. "Métaphysique thomiste et critique de la connaissance." *Revue néoscholastique de philosophie* 17 (November 1910): 476–509.

Rovighi, Vanni. *Elementi di filosofia.* 3 vols. Brescia: La Scuola, 1962.

Rovira i Belloso, Josep M. "La reflexión sobre el misterio de Dios en la teología del siglo XX. La tesis teológica del ser como don del amor, bajo la forma de un boletín biobibliográfico." *Revista española de teología* 50, nos. 2–3 (1990): 319–40.

Sales, Michele. *Gaston Fessard (1897–1978). Genèse d'une pensée.* Paris: Culture et vérité, 1997.

Sartre, Paul. *Being and Nothingness: An Essay on Phenomenological Ontology.* Translated by Hazel E. Barnes. New York: Philosophical Library, 1956.

Scheffczyk, Leo. *Création et providence.* Translated by P. Prévot. Paris: Cerf, 1967.

———. "The Meaning of the 'Filioque.'" *Communio* 13 (Spring 1986): 124–38.

Schelling, Friedrich W. J. *Sämtliche Werke.* Edited by K. F. A. Schelling. 14 vols. Stuttgart and Augsburg: Cotta, 1856–61.

———. *On Human Freedom.* Translated by James Gutmann. Chicago: Open Court, 1936.

———. *The Ages of the World.* Translated by Jason M. Wirth. New York: State University of New York Press, 2000.

Schiffers, Norbert. "Bruaire, Claude: Die Aufgabe, Gott zu Denken." *Theologische Revue* 3 (1975): 220–21.

Schindler, David L. "Norris Clarke on Person, Being and St. Thomas." *Communio* 20 (Fall 1993): 580–92.

———. *Heart of the World, Center of the Church: Communio Ecclesiology, Liberalism, and Liberation.* Grand Rapids, Mich.: Eerdmans, 1996.

Schlick, Moritz. *General Theory of Knowledge.* Translated by Albert E. Blumberg. New York: Springer-Verlag, 1974.

Schmitz, Kenneth L. "Hegel's Philosophy of Religion: Typology and Strategy."
Review of Metaphysics 23 (1970): 717–36.

———. "Hegel's Attempt to Forge a Logic for Spirit." *Dialogue* 10, no. 4 (1971):
653–72.

———. "Hegel's Assessment of Spinoza." In *The Philosophy of Baruch Spinoza,*
edited by Richard Kennington, 229–43. Studies in Philosophy and the History
of Philosophy, vol. 7. Washington, D.C.: Catholic University of America Press,
1980.

———. *The Gift: Creation.* Milwaukee: Marquette University, 1982.

———. "Hegel on Kant: Being-in-Itself and the Thing-in-Itself." In *The
Philosophy of Immanuel Kant,* edited by Richard Kennington, 229–51. Studies
in Philosophy and the History of Philosophy, vol. 12. Washington, D.C.:
Catholic University of America Press, 1985.

———. "The Geography of the Human Person." *Communio* 13 (Spring 1986):
27–48.

———. "Metaphysics: Radical, Comprehensive, Determinate Discourse." *Review
of Metaphysics* 39 (June 1986): 675–94.

———. "Notes and Comments. Concrete Presence." *Communio* 14 (Fall 1987):
300–15.

———. "Substance Is Not Enough. Hegel's Slogan: From Substance to Subject."
In *The Metaphysics of Substance: Proceedings of the American Catholic
Philosophical Association,* edited by Daniel O. Dahlstrom, 52–68. Washington,
D.C.: Catholic University of America Press, 1987.

———. *What Has Clio to Do with Athena? Etienne Gilson: Historian and
Philosopher.* The Etienne Gilson Series, vol. 10. Toronto: Pontifical Institute of
Mediaeval Studies, 1987.

———. "From Anarchy to Principles: Deconstruction and the Resources of
Christian Philosophy." *Communio* 16 (Spring 1989): 69–88.

———. "Postmodern or Modern-Plus?" *Communio* 17 (Summer 1990): 152–66.

———. "Selves and Persons: A Difference in Loves?" *Communio* 18 (Summer
1991): 183–206.

———. "Natural Religion, Morality and Lessing's Ditch." In *Religions and the
Virtue of Religion,* edited by Thérèse-Ann Druart and Mark Rasevic, 57–73.
Washington, D.C.: Catholic University of America Press, 1992.

———. "Theological Clearances: Foreground to a Rational Recovery of God." In
Prospects for Natural Theology, edited by Eugene Thomas Long, 28–48. Studies
in Philosophy and the History of Philosophy, vol. 25. Washington, D.C.: The
Catholic University of America Press, 1992.

———. "The God of Love." *The Thomist* 53, no. 3 (1993): 495–508.

———. "The First Principle of Personal Becoming." *Review of Metaphysics* 47
(June 1994): 757–74.

———. "On a Resistant Strain Within the Hegelian Dialectic." *Owl of Minerva* 25,
no. 2 (Spring 1994): 147–54.

———. "Created Receptivity and the Philosophy of the Concrete." *The Thomist*
61, no. 3 (1997): 339–71.

———. "The Transfiguration of Gnosis in Late Enlightenment German
Thought." *Communio* 24 (Winter 1997): 691–712.

———. "The Idealism of the German Romantics." In *The Emergence of German Idealism,* edited by Michael Baur and Daniel O. Dahlstrom, 176–97. Studies in Philosophy and the History of Philosophy, vol. 34. Washington, D.C.: Catholic University of America Press, 1999.

———. "Postmodernism and the Catholic Tradition." *American Catholic Philosophical Quarterly* 73 (1999): 233–52.

Scola, Angelo, Gilfredo Marengo, and Javier Prades López. *La persona umana: Antropologia teologica.* Milan: Jaca Book, 2000.

Scotus, John Duns. *Quaestiones Subtilissimae super Libros Metaphysicorum Aristotelis.* Vol. 7 of *Opera Omnia.* Wadding. Paris: Vivès, 1891–95.

———. *Reportata Parisiensia.* Vol. 11 of *Opera Omina.* Wadding. Paris: Vivès, 1891–95.

———. *Commentaria Oxoniensia. Ad IV Libros Magistri sententiarium.* 2 vols. Quaracchi: Collegium S. Bonaventurae, 1912–14.

———. *Philosophical Writings: A Selection.* Translated by Allan Wolter. Indianapolis: Hackett Publishing Company, 1987.

Sequeri, Pierangelo. *Sensibili allo Spirito.* Milan: Glossa, 2001.

Serenthà, Mario. "La teologia trinitaria oggi." *La Scuola Cattolica* 118 (1990): 90–116.

Shakespeare, William. *The Complete Works.* London and Glasgow: Collins, 1987.

Shanley, Brian J. "Eternity and Duration in Aquinas." *The Thomist* 61, no. 4 (1997): 525–48.

Siewerth, Gustav. *Metaphysik der Kindheit.* Freiburg: Johannes Verlag, 1957.

Simon, René. "Éthique et anthropologie de la mort. Approches bibliographiques." *Revue des sciences religieuses* 67 (1979): 209–42.

Smith, James K. A. "Respect and Donation: A Critique of Marion's Critique of Husserl." *American Catholic Philosophical Quarterly* 71, no. 4 (1998): 523–38.

Soual, Philippe. "Amour et croix chez Hegel." *Revue philosophique* 1 (1998): 71–96.

Spinoza, Baruch. *Tractatus Theologico-Politicus.* Gebhardt Edition (1925). Translated by Samuel Shirley. Leiden-New York: E. J. Brill, 1989.

———. *Ethics.* Edited and translated by G. H. R. Parkinson. Oxford: Oxford University Press, 2000.

Splett, Jörg. "Claude Bruaire: Logique et religion chrétienne dans la philosophie de Hegel." *Hegel Studien* (1965): 369–74.

Suarez, Franciscus. *Disputationes Metaphysicae.* Vols. 25–26 of *Opera Omnia.* Paris: Vivès, 1856–77.

Sweeney, Leo. "Are Plotinus and Albertus Magnus Neoplatonists?" In *Graceful Reason: Essays in Ancient and Medieval Philosophy Presented to Joseph Owens, CSSR,* edited by Lloyd P. Gerson, 177–202. Toronto: Pontifical Institute of Mediaeval Studies, 1983.

Tertullian. *Liber Adversus Praxeam.* Edited by Jacques P. Migne. Patrologiae Latinae, vol. 2. Paris: Migne, 1879.

Tilliette, Xavier. "In Memoriam. Claude Bruaire 1932–1986." *Giornale di Metafisica,* n.s., 9 (1987): 237–48.

———. *L'absolue et la philosophie.* Paris: PUF, 1987.

———. "Schelling e Gabriel Marcel: Un compagno esaltante." *Annuario filosofico* 3 (1987): 243–54.

———. "Le rationalisme chrétienne de Claude Bruaire." *Les Études philosophiques* 3 (1988): 315–22.

———. "La philosophie et l'absolu." *Revue philosophique* 1 (1990).

———. "Quelques défenseurs de l'argument ontologique." *Archivio di filosofia* 58, nos. 1–3 (1990): 405–20.

———. "Dalla teologia alla filosofia." In *Filosofia e teologia nel futuro dell'Europa. Atti del quinto colloquio su filosofia e religione (Macerata, 24–27 Ottobre 1990),* edited by Giovanni Ferretti, 175–83. Macerata: Università di Macerata: Facoltà di lettere e filosofia, 1992.

———. *Schelling: Une philosophie en devenir.* 2 vols. Paris: J. Vrin, 1992.

———. "La théologie philosophique de Claude Bruaire." *Gregorianum* 74, no. 4 (1993): 689–709.

———. "L'absolu du *Frühidealismus.*" *Revue des sciences philosophiques et théologiques* 80 (1996): 13–22.

———. *Schelling.* Paris: Calmann-Lévy, 1999.

Tourpe, Emmanuel. "La liberté comme don. À propos d'un ouvrage récent de M. Bieler." *Laval théologique et philosophique* 54, no. 2 (June 1998): 411–22.

———. *Siewerth "après" Siewerth. Le lien idéal de l'amour dans le thomisme spéculative de Gustave Siewerth et la visée d'un réalisme transcendantal.* Louvain-Paris: Éditions Peeters, 1998.

Toussaint, Renée. "Le don, l'envers positif du *'ex nihilo.'* Le concept de création chez Claude Bruaire." Ph.D. diss., Institut Supérieur de Philosophie, Catholic University of Louvain, 2001.

La Trinità e il pensare. Figure, percorsi, prospettive. Edited by Piero Coda and Andreas Tapken. Rome: Città Nuova, 1997.

Ulrich, Ferdinand. "Logik der Existenz und Offenbarung. Ein Gespräch mit Hegel anhand zweier Bücher von Claude Bruaire." *Zeitschrift für philosophische Forschung* 23 (1969): 249–75.

———. *Der Mensch als Anfang. Zur philosophischen Anthropologie der Kindheit.* Freiburg: Johannes Verlag, 1970.

Vatican Council II: The Conciliar and Post Conciliar Documents. Edited by Austin Flannery. Northport, N.Y.: Costello Publishing Company, 1975.

te Velde, Rudi A. *Participation and Substantiality in Thomas Aquinas.* Leiden-New York: E. J. Brill, 1995.

Verweyen, Hansjürgen. *Ontologische Voraussetzungen des Glaubensaktes. Zur transzendentalen Frage nach der Möglichkeit von Offenbarung.* Patmos: Verlag Düsseldorf, 1969.

Vieillard-Baron, Jean-Louis. "La notion d'esprit dans la philosophie chrétienne de Claude Bruaire." *Les Études philosophiques* 3 (1988): 301–8.

———. "L'art et l'absolu: Schelling, Hegel, Hölderlin." *Revue des sciences philosophiques et théologiques* 80 (1996): 35–44.

Vignaux, Paul. *Nominalisme au XIVème Siècle.* Paris: J. Vrin, 1948.

———. *Philosophie au Moyen-Âge.* Paris: Armand Colin, 1958.

———. *Dieu et l'être: Exégèses d'Exode 3:14 et de Coran 20:11–24.* Paris: Études Augustiniennes, 1978.

Virgoulay, René. "Dieu ou l'être? Relecture de Heidegger en marge de J.-L.

Marion, *Dieu sans l'être.*" *Recherches de science religieuse* 72, no. 2 (1984): 163–98.

von Balthasar, Hans Urs. *Theologik.* 3 vols. Trier: Johannes Verlag, 1947–87.

———. *Herrlichkeit. Eine theologische Ästhetik.* 7 vols. Freiburg: Johannes Verlag, 1961–69.

———. *Theodramatik.* 4 vols. Trier: Johannes Verlag, 1973–83.

———. *The Glory of the Lord: A Theological Aesthetics.* Translated by Oliver Davies. 6 vols. San Francisco: Ignatius Press, 1982–91.

———. "On the Concept of Person." *Communio* 13 (Spring 1986): 18–26.

———. *Epilog.* Trier: Johannes Verlag, 1987.

———. *Theo-Drama. Theological Dramatic Theory.* Translated by Graham Harrison. 5 vols. San Francisco: Ignatius Press, 1988–98.

———. *Mein Werk. Durchblicke.* Freiburg: Johannes Verlag, 1990.

———. *Mysterium Paschale: The Mystery of Easter.* Translated by Aidan Nichols. Grand Rapids, Mich.: Eerdmans, 1993.

———. "The Unknown Lying Beyond the Word." Translated by Brian McNeil. In *Creator Spiritus.* Vol. 3 of *Explorations in Theology.* San Francisco: Ignatius Press, 1993.

———. *Wenn ihr nicht werdet wie dieses Kind.* Freiburg: Johannes Verlag, 1998.

Widmann, Joachim. *Johann Gottlieb Fichte: Einführung in seine Philosophie.* Berlin: Walter de Gruyter, 1982.

Wittgenstein, Ludwig. *Tractatus logico-philosophicus.* Vol. 1 of *Werkausgabe.* Frankfurt: Suhrkamp, 1989.

Wojtyla, Karol. "The Structure of Self-Determination as the Core of the Theory of the Person." In *Tommaso d'Aquino Nel Suo VII Centenario,* 37–44. Naples: Edizioni Domenicane Italiane, 1975–76.

Wolter, Allan, and Frank William. *Duns Scotus, Metaphysician.* West Lafayette: Purdue University Press, 1995.

Yepes, Ricardo. "Persona: intimidad, don y libertad nativa. Hacia una antropología de los transcendentales personales." *Anuario filosófico* 29 (1996): 1077–1105.

Index

Abnegation, 106, 193, 208–10, 211, 215

Absolute, the: concept of, 26–29, 54–55, 97–98, 100–101, 103, 212–13; as gift, viii–ix, 123, 229; God as, 13–14, 20n21, 152, 164, 175, 188, 210; orientation toward, 120n18; principle of, 34–35, 138–52; revelation of, 15, 17, 40, 124; self-determination, 6, 43–44, 57–58, 65–67, 185, 225–26; understanding of, 87, 219–20; unity of, 209. *See also* Being; Fullness; Knowledge, absolute; One, the

Absolute freedom, 59–79, 87, 145, 166n76, 170, 176–78, 209; absolute spirit and, 40, 156–57, 195; donation as, 185; of God, 99, 206, 214–15. *See also* Freedom

Absolute spirit, ix–x, 46n26, 138–96, 199, 201, 207–12, 221; as gift, 7, 79, 228; in Hegel, 57, 201–3; human spirit and, 28, 35, 37, 52, 87–88, 92, 94, 134; movement of, 19n17, 214; ontology of, 117n9, 217; self-determination of, 40–41, 43–45, 226. *See also* Being; Holy Spirit; Spirit

Abstraction, 44

Abstract simultaneity, 181–82

Act, 104–6, 119, 122, 123n23, 133, 136; creative, 79n43, 185, 219; eternal, 7, 39, 145, 147n31; human, 113, 130–31, 171, 176; moral, 20; pure, 4–5, 61–62, 64, 154–59, 166–67, 178, 188–89, 202

Adseity, 119, 121, 123

Aestheticism, 137

Affirmation, 16, 121, 183; in Hegel, 43n16, 45, 227; movement of, 185–86, 188–89, 208; ontological, 28; of others, 180, 228; in Schelling, 71; of spirit, 192, 195. *See also* Reaffirmation; Self-affirmation

Affirmation of God, The (Bruaire), 6n8, 18, 21, 50, 56, 136

Ages of the World (Schelling), 67

Albert the Great, 151n47

Alterity, 50, 110, 146, 166–67, 209, 210n68, 228. *See also* Other, the

Alternation, infinite, 186

Analogia entis, ix, 139

Analogy, ix–x

Anamnesis, 33, 35, 97, 99, 106–7. *See also* Memory

Andresen, Carl, 195n24

Animation, 102, 106

Another. *See* Other, the

Anselm, Saint, 26, 141, 142n5

Anthropology, 4, 35n62, 37–58, 87n13, 225; dualistic, 96; negative, ix, 5–6, 75–76, 174, 180n113, 226; positive, 179, 213; systematic, 59, 65, 88, 112, 137n60; theomorphic, 93–94. *See also* Bruaire, Claude, anthropology of

Anthropomorphism, 40, 76, 179, 195–96; avoidance of, 60, 66, 140, 142, 162, 181

Apparition, 108–9

Arianism, 164n74

Aristotle, 102, 104n53, 105, 123n24, 142–43, 145, 173; categories of, vii–viii, 18n17, 35n62, 94–95, 127n33, 158–59, 174, 196–98, 221; metaphysics of, 87, 91, 114n2, 117–18; philosophy of, 96n33

Art, 90, 170–71

Atheism, 33, 60, 66

Atrophic existence, 137

Augustine, Saint, 89n18, 150, 173–74, 195n25, 198n33, n37

Grace, 191n16

Gratuity, 1–3, 111, 118, 125–32, 147, 161–64, 168, 214–15, 218, 222–23; absolute, 7, 71, 158–59, 167n80, 180, 184–87, 189–90, 192, 227–28

Grenier, Hubert, 55n48

Greshake, Gisbert, 152n48

Ground, 148–49, 159, 162

Guardini, Romano, 92n26, 111n67

Haecceitas, 107, 112, 122, 124, 227

Having, 113, 115–25, 146, 167n80

Hegel, Georg W. F., 89n18, 95, 105, 117n11, 127n33; Bruaire's analysis of, vii–viii, 5–6, 30, 65–66, 99, 119–20, 159, 162n69, 166n76, 209; on creation, 164n75; dialectics of, 107–8, 192n18, 218; logic of, vii, 18n17, 42–50, 57–58; metaphysics of, 39n5, 49; on negation, 123, 208–13; ontology of, 141n5, 153–55, 193, 217–18; philosophy of, 14, 30–31, 53, 96, 130, 173, 188, 205–6, 210–12; on self-determination, 68; on spirit, 72n27, 73, 79, 179, 186n5; syllogism of, 214–16; system of, 36–37, 76–77, 90–91, 200–202, 227; theology of, 23, 38–42; Trinitarian concept of, 185, 201–4, 207

Heidegger, Martin, 3, 33n58, 67, 84n2, 89, 141, 148–52, 162, 220

Hemmerle, Klaus, 152n48

Henry, Michel, 3n4, 3n5

Heraclitus, 173

History, 4, 23, 50–51, 175–79, 196; eternity and, 56, 63, 174n93, 223, 229; God's intervention in, 60; logic and, 47, 58; truth of, 181, 183

Hölderlin, Friedrich, 153

Holy Spirit, 178, 214–16; confirmation of, 162n69, 188–90, 194, 219, 228–29; donation through, viii, 92–94, 172, 185–86, 222; essence of, 7, 191; as eternal future, 181, 183; as love, 203; mediation of, 52, 65, 218; procession of, 70, 73–75, 168–70, 214–16; role of, 42, 56, 160; syllogism of, 46, 201–8. *See also* Trinity

Homer, 195n25

Human being, 18–27, 40n12, 88, 171–73, 209, 213; creation of, 127, 175, 183; donation and, 6, 63n9, 126, 179, 187; essence of, 86, 126, 156; freedom of, 37, 49, 57, 104; God and, 18, 28–29, 35, 43, 97–100, 165; intelligence of, 101–3; knowledge of, 49, 69, 95, 135, 151; nature of, 64, 71, 84, 133, 197–98; origins of, 112, 125, 211, 222, 225–27, 229; reason and, 16, 66n15, 97–98, 131, 193, 200, 212, 221; stages of, 108–10; time and, 182; truth and, 64, 67–68. *See also* Existence, human

Humanism, 137

Human spirit, viii–ix, 79n43, 83–113, 115–21, 131–35, 137–41, 152–55, 162h68, 169–71, 187; absolute spirit and, 150, 158; confirmation of, 194, 219; freedom of, 20, 52; gift of, 161, 163, 175, 179–80, 198n37, 221–22; origin of, 124; otherness of, 72, 150, 164n75

Husserl, Edmund, ix, 107–8

Hypertrophic existence, 137

Hyppolite, Jean, 37n2, 39n6

Hypostases, 146–47, 197–98, 200, 214, 228

Idea, 42n15, 45–46, 91, 96–98, 143–44, 204; absolute, 103, 203n50; of gift, 63–64; of God, 26, 60, 206–8. *See also* Concept

Idealism, 20, 23, 88n14, 97–98, 106; German, 6, 21n21, 72, 76, 91

Identity, 3, 35n62, 156–57, 167, 170, 220; eternal, 201; ontological, 128; rigid, 175; self, 18n17, 121–22

Ideology, 85. *See also* Prejudice

Impulse, 24

Inaccessibility, of Spirit, 150–51

Incardona, Nunzio, 8n11, 89n16, 103n51

Incarnation, 35, 41n12, 63, 164n74, 205, 208

Incompleteness, 20n20

Independence, 15, 17, 87, 104, 126, 179–80

Indeterminacy, 195, 209

Individuality, 195–97

Infinite, the, 46, 48, 63n9, 68, 138, 160, 175–77, 209; finite and, 40n12, 43, 140, 152–53, 177, 187–88, 212. *See also* Spirit, infinite

Infusion, 155

Inseity, 119, 121, 123

Inspiration, 48, 70–71, 76, 102–4, 106, 124–25, 135

Intellect, 98–100, 144, 148, 154. *See also* Mind

Intelligence, 27, 101–4, 143–44, 173

Intelligibility, 95, 97, 142, 147, 151, 156, 172; pure, 28, 42n15, 91

Interiority, 71, 102, 104, 110–12, 116, 120n18, 136, 154, 203–4

Intuition, 59, 96, 97, 142n7, 174, 221

Invocation, 26n38, 29, 32. *See also* Prayer

Ipseity, 119–23, 127, 129, 133–34, 136–37, 172, 174

Ipsum Esse, 143, 221

Jesus Christ, 29n46, 33–34, 42, 46–47, 60, 161n65, 164n74, 201. *See also* Son

John (Bible), 194n22

John Paul II, Pope, 34n60, 191n16

Judgment, 44–45, 95, 214

Justice, 77n39, 78, 174n95

Spirit's Gift was designed and produced in Minion by Kachergis Book Design of Pittsboro, North Carolina. It was printed on 60-pound Natures Natural and bound by Thomson-Shore of Dexter, Michigan.